Gunshots in
Another Room

Gunshots in Another Room:

The Forgotten Life of Dan J. Marlowe

by Charles Kelly

Gunshots in Another Room: The Forgotten Life of Dan J. Marlowe
Asclepian Imprints Ltd.
ISBN 978-0-9858911-0-7
First Edition
All Rights Reserved

Cover design by J.T. Lindroos
Cover photograph used with permission of the Detroit Free Press

Printed in the USA
This book is a work of nonfiction

For Kristina and Erich, Sara and Hugh

Table of Contents

CHAPTER 1:
No Way Back

THE HEADACHES SEEMED TO WELL UP FROM THE GREEN HELL ENVELOPING him, pounding pain emerging from the sticky heat pungent with saw grass, moss, cypress and brackish water. Paperback writer Dan Marlowe, master of the genre of flesh and gun, clutched his head and tried to think. He was 62, of average height, a rotund man who wore his thinning hair swept back. Usually, thinking was his strong suit, and his reputation was solid. He was highly respected in the writing community, had won an Edgar Award from the Mystery Writers of America and was one of that organization's most active and popular members. His thrillers had sold hundreds of thousands of copies internationally.

Typically, he was exuberant, full of energy. But now he was down and stressed. Living on the edge financially, frustrated by a failed book project, his body booze-battered (though he'd given up alcohol), he was trying to frame a new type of story, one that would assure his earning future. When the pain flashed through his head, it short-stopped all that. Now his mind grasped at possible causes: Perhaps this was a childhood malady suddenly returning, or an insect bite, or the onset of malaria. The man who had always been so clever at plots couldn't figure out what was going on in his own head. All he knew was that something was wrong. The wiring of his brain was becoming tangled, bits of thought were slipping away.

It was late May 1977 and Marlowe was researching his latest novel in Big Cypress and Everglades National Park. Florida was familiar territory. For more than 20 years, Marlowe had owned property near Lake Placid in Highlands County. He had a woman friend here, as he did in many places—Connecticut, Kansas City, Los Angeles. He had a knack for luring the opposite sex despite his looks, said a friend. ("He was about as attractive as a frog," the man said. "This was a very complex human being.") Marlowe had used Florida as background in several of the Fawcett Gold Medal paperbacks he'd been churning out for nearly two decades, their covers raw with gunplay, swelling female breasts and plenty of leg.

South Florida, for instance, had provided the setting for much of Marlowe's masterpiece, *The Name of the Game Is Death* (1962), as well as for *Never Live Twice* (1964), in which government operative Jackrabbit Smith recovers from amnesia and solves his own attempted murder.

Violent drama had helped Marlowe earn his keep since his writing career had begun at 43, but now chaos was raging inside his head, crushing him. And he was nearly 1,500 miles from his home of 15 years—the quaint upper-Michigan town of Harbor Beach, with its lighthouse in the harbor and his circle of friends.

When the headaches eased, Marlowe crawled into his 1976 Chrysler Cordoba and set off for Harbor Beach. The trip took him several days, driving part of each day, then stopping to let the pounding in his head subside. He made it back on Friday, June 3. His first stop was at 220 State Street, the office of Marlowe's closest friend in town, insurance-agency owner Gordon Gempel. Marlowe told Gempel he thought he was suffering from an infection caused by an insect bite. Then he headed home, only a few blocks away.

Marlowe rented a three-room apartment for $125 a month on the second floor of the building that housed the *Harbor Beach Times*. It was filled with Marlowe's working tools—tape recorders, small TV sets, a slide projector, two small movie screens, an *Encyclopedia Britannica*—and the products of his art: paperback and hardback books. Marlowe's typewriter—an IBM Selectric—and his filing cabinets and desk occupied much of his bedroom and hallway. The kitchen was tiny. Though nearly 20 years had passed since she died, a photo of his wife, Evelyn, looked out from the mantel of the Italian marble fireplace. He had never remarried.

Marlowe settled in and arranged to see his physician, Charles M. Oakes, the next day. Then he went to his typewriter and banged out a note to one of his girlfriends, Doris Henry, who lived in Quakertown, Pennsylvania.

> About a week ago I began to get really splitting headaches every day. I had been in two swamps, Big Cypress and Everglades National Park, doing research—more on that later—and Oakes when I talked to him tonight (to make sure he could see me in the morning) immediately concluded it's malaria. I don't think so. But whatever the hell it is, I've never had anything like it. I had migraines as a kid, until about fifteen, but this is like multiplied by five or six, for an hour and a half or two hours a day. After that I might still have a headache but compared to the bad period it's like a vacation. It just about puts me down on the floor. My eyes feel like they're bulging and my head burning. When it stops, it takes as much as an hour to get myself back toge-her (sic) again. I can't even think. I can't remember people's names, not that I was ever very good at that. Can you see all the strikeover corrections in this? I think maybe my sight is a little affected, too. Or it could be that glasses (new ones) are at the bottom of it all. I doubt that, though…I'm going to cut this short. When I say I can't think, I'm not exaggerating at all. I feel bushed, mentally and physically…

Marlowe saw Oakes on Saturday. The 76-year-old physician was a fixture in the community, having lived in Harbor Beach since 1933. He had treated Marlowe for nearly two decades. In May 1976, Oakes had sent him to a specialist who found erosive and chronic gastritis, and suggested Marlowe take antacids, maintain a bland diet and avoid booze and aspirin. Marlowe also suffered from diabetes. Now he was in Oakes' office again in great distress: complaining of headaches, pressure behind the eyes and tender sinuses. The physician examined Marlowe, running many tests, but in the end simply prescribed tetracycline, an antibiotic, and Benadryl, an antihistamine, and sent Marlowe home.

Later that day, Marlowe wrote to Col. William Odell, a retired Air Force officer who lived in Colorado and who—usually without acknowledgement—had worked with him writing and researching more than a dozen novels. Despite his physical suffering, Marlowe was anxious about their efforts to launch a book with maverick New York publisher Bernard Geis, whose literary discoveries included Jacqueline Susann, author of *Valley of the Dolls*, and Helen Gurley Brown, author of *Sex and the Single Girl*. Working with literary agent Joseph Elder, Marlowe and Odell hoped to do a breakout novel for Geis, one that would release them from the grind of banging out action-packed thrillers every few months.

They were moving forward with trepidation, however. The fickle publisher had rejected a sex-blackmail novel they were writing especially for him and had requested, in its place, a Stephen King-like occult thriller. Geis had accepted the outline for that thriller, *Julie*, and had already responded with a critique.

Marlowe's note to Odell read, in part:

> I've been at Oakes' office and the hospital all morning and right now I can't even think. Fifteen X-rays and twenty blood tests with the roof off my head, practically. Oakes convinced himself it wasn't malaria. He's opting now for sinus, but hell, I had sinus years ago—had a piece of bone taken out of my nose once for it—and sinus it's not. When I come out of one of the bad stages now it takes me an hour or more just to get back inside my head and be able to start thinking again.
>
> I'll have more to say with the copy of the letter to Bernie [Geis]. Elder says we may not have to do sample chapters this time "because they know you can write." To get the advance, I mean.

That Sunday, he dropped another note to Doris Henry, touching on his visit to the doctor, saying he hoped to get test results Monday. He wrote in a similar vein to James Batson in Lima, Ohio. Batson had befriended Marlowe and Odell and corresponded with them, asking about the creative process and the business of novel writing.

About 8 a.m. Monday, Marlowe got a call from Henry. A few moments into the conversation, she realized she couldn't understand him. She hung up and called the Harbor Beach City Hall, only a couple of blocks from Marlowe's apartment. About the same time, Gempel called Police Chief Jack Stickney, a poker-playing buddy of Marlowe. "I'm worried. Nobody's seen Dan for a day or two," Gempel told Stickney, perhaps mindful of the health problems Marlowe had reported on Friday. "I'll go up and see what's going on," Stickney replied. At 123 N. First St., the police chief knocked on the apartment door, found it unlocked, and called:

"Dan, are you here?"

Getting no reply, he entered. Marlowe was sitting in an over-stuffed chair in the living room, staring into space.

"What's wrong?" Stickney asked.

Marlowe said nothing. His vacant stare was fixed. A stroke, Stickney thought. The police chief called for an ambulance. Marlowe was taken to the emergency room of Harbor Beach Community Hospital, a tiny institution with only 28 beds. The writer was accompanied by Candy Oeschger, Gempel's assistant, who had been called to come to Marlowe's apartment.

The emergency room nurse was Marjorie Iseler. She knew Marlowe well through her husband, Don. In the early 1960s, Marlowe had hired him to type polished manuscripts from rough drafts. In the emergency room, Marjorie observed Marlowe lying on a gurney, acting as if he didn't recognize her. Candy tried to explain to the nurse what was going on.

"She just kind of said he was confused and didn't know where he was," Marjorie Iseler said. "I guess they hadn't heard from him in a couple of days. He acted like he was dazed, but at this time I thought, 'This is crazy. I don't believe you'…He didn't recognize me, or at least he didn't act like he did."

Her suspicion of Marlowe hinted at his contradictory reputation.

On the one hand, people embraced him. He was, after all, an enthusiastic Rotary member, a former City Councilman, and a gregarious type who loved to booze it up with community leaders, play poker all night, and beat the drum for Republican candidates. On the other hand, the locals whispered about his many affairs, wondered why he had befriended bank robber Al Nussbaum, and speculated about Marlowe's research trips across the country and into Mexico. They also noted that he had spent years as a full-time gambler.

They would have been even more unsettled if they had known he wrote pornography under pen names. Or that he had recently ordered an 8-millimeter film from London called *Home Late from School*, an erotic movie depicting naughty schoolgirls being spanked.

What they did know, or suspect, was more than enough to keep the rumors flying. Later, after Marlowe left Harbor Beach, stricken by this mental attack, some would say he'd gone on the run, hunted by mobsters, or that he had somehow been involved with the Central Intelligence Agency. Now, with Marlowe in the hospital, the rumor mill focused on his current project, *Julie*. The story was set in Louisiana, and the local citizens believed Marlowe had been doing research there, and that his strange illness may have been the result of a voodoo curse.

Of course, Marlowe had really been in Florida, exploring swamp settings he could transfer to Louisiana. Even so, his best friend still theorized Marlowe had been overtaken by supernatural forces while on a dark mission.

"One day, he told me he had diabetes and was taking insulin shots," Gordon Gempel said many years later. "He went away and came back, and he no longer had diabetes…I talked to his doctor, who was a friend of mine, and I said, you know, diabetes doesn't disappear. If you went down to the cypress swamp, there's probably a little doll down there with needles stuck in it. And the doctor said, well, that might have been. He was down there to pick up money, I know dang well he was, though we'll never prove that. Money from a bank robbery. You see, this friend of his, Nussbaum, was involved in a bank robbery in which a guard was killed. Dan kept making trips to Leavenworth where he'd stop to see this Nussbaum, ostensibly because he (Nussbaum) wanted to become a writer. Baloney."

Amid this atmosphere of suspicion, Marlowe drifted without memory. The medical community had issued a diagnosis of amnesia. He couldn't recall anything or anyone from his past life—not his male friends, not his girlfriends, not the books he had written. Not the tragic, sudden death of his wife years before. Not his efforts to churn out the ambitious new novel that he had hoped would revive his bank account.

As time went on, it appeared Marlowe's writing life was over, and that, indeed, he would have a tough time recovering his life at all. This would be a bizarre period, with Marlowe-type characters flitting in and out, disturbing psychological questions to deal with, and the ghosts of his past life rising up to lay their claim on him. In the hospital, he made notes on his friends Gordon and Candy, who he had seen almost every day for years, and on local political figure and friend George Scott. They were now strangers to him, and he obviously was trying to figure them out:

> Gordon Gempel – insurance man...heavyset, swarthy skin... or deeply tanned? Very fluent, gestures with hands, dark eyes, forceful man. Candy Oeschger – young girl from his office, slender, brown hair, brown eyes—soft-spoken but crisp...seemed capable. George Scott—stocky...round-faced...white-haired... glasses...walks with slight limp...said I was on the city council with him. Said he had a store...wore business suit.

His friend Batson asked him to critique *The Name of the Game Is Death*, the book admired by so many lovers of the hard-boiled genre (including Stephen King, who would decades later dedicate a book to Marlowe). Batson intended to spark Marlowe's memory of his past successes. Surely, his best writing would strike a chord. For Batson, the outcome was unsettling: Marlowe read the book, remarking it was strange that the author's name was the same as his. He handed over his brief written review, lower-cased:

> analysis of the name of the game is death...highly structured...effective counterpoint to principal story line via flashback scenes...too many details?...every mile of every highway is listed, much of it now out of date...some awkward sentence construction...rewrite could improve...many printer's typos...juggling act with reader's emotional involvement makes inherently downbeat principal character acceptable.

Bottom line: Marlowe believed the stranger with his name had written a good novel. But would Marlowe himself ever be able to write an effective novel again, or to solve the riddle of his own mind? He'd had a strange life up to this point, but things were about to get even odder.

CHAPTER 2:
Solitary Traveler

THE WOMAN IN THE PHOTO IS SWAN-LIKE. SHE HAS A WIDE MOUTH, a long neck, high forehead. Her blue eyes are kind. Reddish-brown hair sweeps to her shoulders. She's in her 20s and won't grow much older. Once, she told Marlowe he wasn't capable of real love, but he will display her photo wherever he lives for the rest of his life and choose to be buried next to her when he dies. Her name is Evelyn Chmura, Marlowe's one and only wife. He played around on her.

Marlowe never was truly domesticated. He always lived the lonely life, spending much of his time hearing the creative hum of silence. He socialized like a whirlwind, but he was most comfortable at the typewriter and inside his own mind, as he admitted to a friend late in life. "The older I get, the more noise distracts me, and I never had a very high threshold to start," he wrote. "I wouldn't have made a good parent."

He made his life, instead, out where the hard-boiled writers worked. Think of Jim Thompson, author of *The Killer Inside Me*, knocking out his first novel on a borrowed typewriter in a cheap hotel room, his hand trembling around a glass of the straight stuff; Chester Himes, creator of Coffin Ed Johnson and Grave Digger Jones, doing a stretch for armed robbery at Ohio State Penitentiary, watching 300 fellow convicts die in a fire; Charles Williams, living alone in a trailer near the state line between California and Oregon, the plaudits for *Hell Hath No Fury* long behind him, unable to get a new novel going, sliding toward suicide.

Marlowe, outwardly, was the most conventional of the lot, but he'd traveled the fringes of society and came naturally to the hard-boiled style: low-rent writing full of ass-kicking men and yielding women, whiskey sluicing across the pages, the smell of cigarette smoke curling off the prose.

In his first *One for the Road* column published in the *Harbor Beach Times* on Jan. 5, 1967, shortly after he was elected to the Harbor Beach City Council, Marlowe touched on the occupations of his pre-writing life, and assessed his position in the literary world. He was 52, and had been writing mystery and suspense novels, short stories, articles, book reviews and columns for eight years.

"Prior to taking up writing," Marlowe wrote, "I had been—neither in order of importance or succession—a bookkeeper, an insurance agent, a bartender, an office manager, an assistant manager in country clubs (a man has to be careful not to be promoted to manager of a club; managers receive all the complaints, while assistant managers get to hire the waitresses), an accountant, a gambler, a credit manager at the wholesale level, a timekeeper, a public relations man, an advertising agent, and latterly, a politician." He hesitated to call himself a writer. "I'm far more a story-teller than I am a literary man. My agent says I'm the living proof that stories don't care who writes them. He also says I'm the most impatient man he ever saw, and it's true I'd rather knock you down than walk around you. All my life I've been in a hurry."

Although we have few sources on Marlowe's early life, and the information is sketchy, we do know he was born Daniel James Marlowe on July 10, 1914, in the home of his parents at 18 Forrest St., Lowell, Massachusetts. Marlowe's father, Daniel, was a printing press mechanic for Babcock Printing Co. Babcock, Marlowe later wrote, manufactured printing presses from "newspaper size" on down. The presses were assembled and checked at the factory, then broken down and sent to the site where they would be operated. His father went to those sites, reassembled the presses and got them running. After

Babcock went bankrupt in the 1930s, Marlowe's father made an even better living on his own maintaining and repairing the presses the company had sold. He continued to do so into the 1950s when, at 74, the "traveling finally got to him" and he retired, Marlowe told a friend. Marlowe's uncle, his father's younger brother, had a brief career as a prize fighter, the novelist said in a 1985 letter: "He could hit like a man three or four weight classes heavier, but he was a pretty boy who didn't care to get hit back...He taught me to box when I was nine or ten which stood me in good stead around the schoolyard. And occasionally since."

Marlowe's mother, whose maiden name was Helen E. Gilogly, had been born in Boston. Her birth name was Ellen Elizabeth Keohane, but after her parents died, she was adopted by a couple named Gilogly, and at some point changed her name to Helen. In 1920, when Dan Marlowe was 5, he lost his mother, who was 34, to pneumonia complicated by influenza, a casualty of the world-wide flu epidemic that began in 1918. Subsequently, Dan and his brother Don, who was two years younger, were raised by their grandmother, Ann, and two aunts, Florence and Esther, in Woburn, Massachusetts.

In Woburn, Dan attended St. Charles Parochial School, where he met Henry "Hank" Power, his best friend as a boy, according to Power's son Jed, a bartender and novelist who now lives in Peabody, Massachusetts. Marlowe lived at one end of the small downtown on Main Street; Hank Power lived a half mile away across from the school, which bordered on the Italian south end of the city.

"Apparently Dan wasn't too tough-looking a kid and that, along with being a new kid in town, caused him to have some trouble with these south enders," Jed Power said. "I was told that in the course of one of these confrontations, during the first days of school, my Dad came to Dan's aid and told these kids to back off. They did. Dan was never bothered again. Probably not so much because anyone was scared of my father, but more likely they had a healthy respect for his five older brothers standing behind him, who all went to the school, too. After that, Dan would spend after-school hours across the street at my Dad's house."

From time to time, Marlowe would write about his school days. He also recalled the relatives who influenced him as a boy, specifically his grandmother and his aunts. In fact, he devoted his March 2, 1967 *One for the Road* column to his grandmother, who he said was born in County Mayo, Ireland.

> I used to have a terrible temper, but in middle age I've mellowed.
>
> I might knock you down today, for instance, but I probably wouldn't kick you.
>
> I came by my temper naturally enough, since I inherited it from my grandmother, who raised me. My father was her oldest child, and since she had eight, I had uncles and aunts not much older than myself, which furnished me many opportunities to witness my grandmother's temper at close range. She had a short fuse and a remarkable ability to create pyrotechnic displays of awesome proportions.

Marlowe then tells the story of how his grandmother, catching his youngest uncle playing pool, rushes into the pool hall, shoves the players aside and flips the pool table over on its back ("a feat powerful men have failed to emulate"). He says he played pool there, too, but his grandmother—fortunately—never caught him at it.

> No question about it. My grandmother shaped me to face the world. After lying to her, getting caught, and facing the consequences, all subsequent face-to-face confrontation with school, church, or civic authority was as nothing at all. Hanging tough with a boyhood foe came as naturally as breathing, since I had been hanging tough in more difficult circumstances ever since I could remember.
>
> I owe her a great deal. She had the sharpest eye for a phony I've ever seen, and I either inherited that, too, or she pounded the recognition ingredients into me. It has kept me out of trouble many times since. Not invariably, of course, because my grandmother had a maxim: "If the game's worth the bloody candle, take your best shot."
>
> It hasn't been the most peaceful life in consequence, but then my grandmother always preferred a bit of excitement, too.

It's hard to say how much truth there is in this account. Genealogical records turned up by the Marlowe family show the writer's paternal grandmother, Ann Marlowe (nee Lavin) was born in New York, not Ireland, and that she died in 1922 when Dan was only 8, a bit young for him to have been playing pool downtown. In any case, it made for a good story.

He told stories of being raised by his aunts, too, whose supervision he at times found irksome. One of his women friends said Dan was a fine dancer, but hated to dance because his aunts made him take dancing lessons as a boy. He also mentioned them in recalling his boyhood love of books. "Quite often I'd hide books outside in the shed for the days when my aunts would boot me out of the house for some air," he said in a 1968 interview with Dick Allen, news editor of *The Advertiser*, a Michigan newspaper.

Still, the Marlowe boys were lucky they had caring family members. None of the Marlowes had much money, and Dan's father was often traveling for work, according to Dan's half-sister, Mary Jones. Several years after the death of Dan's mother, his father met and married Helene Pendergrast, a schoolteacher in New London, Connecticut. Dan and Don joined him there, and the boys attended Bulkeley High School.

After high school, the lives of Dan and his brother diverged. Don earned bachelor's degrees in physics and mechanical engineering and a master's degree in solid mechanics at The Catholic University of America in Washington, D.C. He went on to become one of America's most distinguished scientists, serving as president of the American Society of Mechanical Engineers, dean of engineering at Catholic University, and director of the Office of Science and Technology of the U.S. Food and Drug Administration. Dan never went to college. Instead, he received an accounting certificate from Bentley School of Accounting and Finance in Boston in 1934. Little is known about Dan Marlowe's education in accounting, but it apparently had its moments of levity. He recalled in a newspaper column years later that he joined a business fraternity, and, on the final night of Hell Week, the pledges were dropped off 30 miles out in the country, penniless and with their faces, hair and clothing smeared with limburger cheese. The smell discouraged motorists who might have given them rides, so they had to walk back to town.

On a resumé Marlowe produced more than three decades later, he said he spent the seven years following graduation working as the assistant manager of two country clubs in Connecticut—the Wethersfield Country Club in Wethersfield and the Brooklawn Country Club in Bridgeport. Among other duties he hired waitresses and swimming pool personnel and filled in for other employees when they were absent: bookkeepers, bartenders, billing clerks and cashiers. It wasn't lucrative work. He started at $55 a week and ended at $65 a week. Marlowe said he lost that employment when the advent of gas rationing in World War II severely damaged business at the clubs.

Though Marlowe gives the impression on the resumé that the two country club jobs occupied all his time during that period, he actually spent most of it as a professional gambler. He wouldn't have wanted to tell potential employers that, but he didn't hesitate to tell readers and interviewers. In a *One for the Road* column published in 1967, he refers to "the late 1930s and my days of roustabouting around the racetracks of the country." In a column headlined "Horses and People" in the *Washington Post* on April 12, 1960, the racing writer Walter Haight said Marlowe had sent him "an interesting collection of major race programs from coast-to-coast and border-to-border." Marlowe had written Haight: "They represent golden hours, aesthetically if not financially. In 27 years of watching them run, I've tried to see the good ones at the expense of a few more miles."

In the 1968 *Advertiser* interview, Marlowe recalled that after graduation he had a hard time making a living. "With no job available, I spent some seven years doing nothing but gambling," he said. "I played cards, rolled dice and booked the horses; anything to make a buck during those lean years." His gambling period later fed his fiction, he recalled on a Los Angeles-based TV talk show not long before he died: "(I) met a lot of different people," he said, "and had a lot of background experiences that all became grist for the writing mill."

Johnny pushed his thousand dollars toward the dealer. "Let 'er rip." He stacked up in front of him the twenty white chips, sixteen reds and ten blues he received in return. He ran an appraising eye around the table. At five dollars for a white chip, twenty-five for a red, and fifty for a blue, he could see a conservative twelve to fifteen thousand dollars in chips on the table. He drew his chair in a little tighter beneath him. His nostrils tested the familiar electricity in the air. He wished he had a cigar.

—From *Shake a Crooked Town*, by Dan J. Marlowe

Where Marlowe was living during this period isn't clear, but apparently he was spending time on the East Coast, based on passing references in articles he wrote. In a December 1977 piece for *Ford Times*, he tells the reader, "One winter I lived in Brooklyn, New York, above a saloon called—naturally—The Backstretch." In the article, he describes his passion for horseracing.

> When I like a racehorse, I adopt him and play him in all his races, each time he goes to the post. I've been known to follow a horse through 18 consecutive losing wagers. Stubborn? I consider it persevering. I catch the losing streaks, and I catch the winning streaks.
>
> When a horse of mine is running, I like to be right there on the rail, rooting him home, wherever the horse may be running, if it's in the continental United States. This desire has occasionally conflicted with my employment of the moment, and whenever that happened, it's been the employment which suffered. On this particular subject I've never claimed that I've played with a full deck.

During at least part of 1941, Marlowe was pursuing his obsession while living in or near Boston. In the manuscript of an article called *The Bad Old Days*, found among his personal papers, he describes how every weekday afternoon that summer he would take the "race train"—a train devoted to people going to the races—from the old North Station in Boston to Rockingham Park in Salem, New Hampshire. Marlowe rode in the last car with the professional and semi-pro gamblers, most of whom played in the dollar-a-point knock rummy games conducted from 4 a.m. to 10 a.m. at the Faneuil Hall

Market, the "barboodi" games (actually "barbudi," a casino-style dice game also known as Barbooth or Even-up Craps) in Lowell, Massachusetts, or the poker games in Jamaica Plain. The article tells how a group of Asian gamblers known as "the China Boys," who were placing heavy bets on races at Rockingham Park, were set up to lose in a fixed race. Marlowe, who knew or figured the fix was in, collected $3,920 on a $200 bet, "a small fortune in those days."

It's not clear why Marlowe wasn't drafted into the military during World War II, since he fell into the eligible age range. Perhaps his history of migraines had something to do with that. Starting in 1941, so his resumé says, he worked for four years for hourly pay as a night timekeeper at United Aircraft Corp. in Stratford, Connecticut. He monitored the performance of 24 departmental timekeepers and correlated time sheets for the payroll department, working 12 hours a night, sometimes for as many as 40 days straight.

During this period, he also renewed his relationship with his brother, who was living in Washington, D.C. In 1941, or thereabouts, Don's wife Corinne was downtown shopping with their youngest child. As she was returning home, one of her neighbors called to her. "You've got company...He says he's Don's brother." Corinne rushed into her house, picked up the phone and called her husband at work. "Do you have a brother named Dan?" she asked. Don said yes. "So that's how I met him," Corinne recalled years later. "My first impression was that he was strictly a Marlowe: reserved. Dan could sit in a room with you for an hour, two hours, and not say a word. He could be very quiet."

He could also be quite outspoken. He explained in his resumé that he left his job as a timekeeper because of "an argument with the night supervisor."

In 1945, when he was 31, Marlowe appeared to be settling down, taking a job as an office manager and credit manager for Washington Tobacco Co., a wholesale tobacco firm. At the time, he was living in an apartment in the district and indulging his lifelong interest in sports. Sportswriter Shirley Povich noted in a *"This Morning"* column published on July 20, 1945, in *The Washington Post* that "The Detroit Tigers' four-and-a-half game lead notwithstanding, Mr. Dan J. Marlowe of 736 22nd Street N.W. refuses to be stampeded into the belief that the Tigers will win the American

League pennant. He writes a very excellent letter setting forth his own ideas about the pennant race."

On the job at Washington Tobacco, Marlowe started at $75 a week, ran a 14-person office, kept the books, issued credit, supervised salesmen's collections, and did all the office hiring and firing. And he felt he was good at it. Years later, on his resumé, he said, "I can hire and fire with acuity and no qualms... I can issue credit at both retail and wholesale levels and supervise collections. Any damn fool can issue credit or say no. The trick is to say yes and make the customer live within the guidelines."

Also in 1945, he married Chmura, a 24-year-old secretary. Corinne Marlowe, the widow of Dan's brother Don, described her as a big woman, "a beautiful broad" whose physical type, at least, might have served as the model for Hazel Andrews, the long-time girlfriend of Marlowe's bank-robbing creation, Earl Drake. To many people who knew Marlowe, Evelyn was his one great passion. But he admitted years later to a friend that he had affairs during his marriage. One of these trysts was with a friend of his wife who shared his interests in theater and literature. Another was with a woman in the Swiss legation in Washington.

Marlowe's personality differed from that of his wife, according to his half-sister Mary, who was 16 years younger than Dan. Mary saw the Marlowes often after the early 1950s, when Mary landed a secretarial job in Washington. She worked for the Welfare Fund run by labor leader John L. Lewis—a job Marlowe helped arrange. "Evelyn was very quiet, very kind, very good but not really outgoing," Mary said. "Dan always had a story to tell when he stopped by to see us. He was very into life, he liked people." Mary said her half-brother was a considerate man, always ready with advice or aid. "He would go out of his way to help you," she said. "I could call him any time if I was upset about something."

Marlowe was very busy at this point in his life. To supplement his income from his day job, he started running an insurance agency evenings and weekends out of his home on New Hampshire Avenue in Colesville, Maryland, often putting in 16-hour days. And he was already considering a new career. "I remember him telling me he wanted to get to the point where he could write and make a living," Mary says. He hadn't totally given up his rambunctious ways. He was still betting the horses at tracks in Laurel and Bowie, Maryland. "I built a house seven miles from Laurel and my wife always claimed afterward that I chose the site with malice aforethought," he later wrote.

> "I've been known to make a bet once in a while," I humored her.
> "That's more like it," she said briskly. "A working man you're not. What's your action? Horses?"
> "Horses," I agreed.
> "Is that right?" She straightened up as though someone had turned on an electric current in the booth bench. "D'you remember old Northern Star? I saw him one time at Delaware Park run five an' a half furlongs in a tick less—"
> So we sat and played Remember When.
> It's a damn small world sometimes. Hazel's first husband had been Blueshirt Charlie Andrews, the man who bet 'em higher than a duck can fly.

—From *The Name of the Game Is Death*

Things might have gone on like this for quite some time, Marlowe managing an office, selling insurance policies in his spare time, working holidays to catch up on the paperwork for his home business, hitting the horse tracks for fun, trying to find time to write. Despite his aspirations to write fiction, he apparently had produced little at this time. But on July 31, 1956, Evelyn suddenly fell ill with acute hemorrhagic pancreatitis, a malady that causes severe stomach pain that radiates to the back.

It wasn't clear what had caused it. Not long before, she and Dan had been on the way to Mary's wedding, crossing Connecticut Avenue on foot, when Evelyn was injured in a minor auto accident. Mary later wondered if the incident might have been linked to Evelyn's illness. That's unlikely. Acute hemorrhagic pancreatitis is not known to be brought on by physical trauma. Eight out of 10 times, it is caused by heavy consumption of alcohol or gallstone disease. Mary said she never knew Evelyn to drink at all, reducing the likelihood that alcohol was the cause. In any case, Evelyn did not last long. Taken to Suburban Hospital in Bethesda, Maryland, she died three days later, and was buried on Aug. 7, 1956, in St. Michael's Cemetery in Stratford, Connecticut.

Her death was a great blow to Marlowe. In fact, it uprooted him. In an article he wrote for the December 1960 *Writer's Digest*, he described the aftermath of his wife's passing: "When I had recovered a little from the first shock, I wasn't long in discovering that my new status had made pretty meaningless everything I'd been attempting to do. I told my employer I'd stay with him until he had a satisfactory replacement, and then I'd move on. I didn't know where I was going to work, or live. I just knew it wasn't going to be in the same neighborhood."

Four years after Evelyn's death, Marlowe's tone sounds matter-of-fact. But according to his sister-in-law, Corinne, the loss put him into a tailspin. He was so distraught that he couldn't deal with disposing of his house in suburban Washington, or with the possessions he and his wife had shared. "He wanted nothing to do with anything," said Corinne. "Absolutely nothing to do with it…The things in the house he just more or less gave away." Marlowe rented an apartment downtown for a while, gave Don and Corinne the key to the house, and took a trip across the country. After he left, they handled the sale of the house. Never much of a drinker before, he began to hit the bottle. "He loved her very much and was absolutely devastated when she died," Mary said.

Marlowe's sensitivity wouldn't have surprised the one real tough guy among his friends, bank robber Al Nussbaum. "Dan's a funny guy," Nussbaum said in a letter written decades after Evelyn's death. "He writes such hard-boiled, unromantic stuff (he really excels in the action scenes, I think) and I don't think there is a hard bone in his body."

> The huskiness in his voice surprised him; it hadn't come out sounding quite as flippant as he had intended. A long time ago— well, six or seven years ago—Ellen Saxon had been married to Johnny Killain. Temporarily. Two short years temporarily, he reminded himself. Yeah, and one of you has never gotten over it.

Ellen Saxon lay on the bed where he had left her; for a long moment Johnny stared in disbelief at the twisted limbs, the out-flung arm with which she had sought in vain to protect herself, the so-well-remembered face that was now a death mask of hor-ror...Ellen—he still couldn't believe it ...He fought his way back up to the surface; he couldn't seem to get off dead center mentally.

—Excerpts from *Killer with a Key,* by Dan J. Marlowe

CHAPTER 3:
Doom Service

APRIL 1, 1957. IN A SMALL HOTEL IN NEW YORK CITY, MARLOWE FED a sheet of paper into his ancient portable typewriter and typed "Chapter One." He'd arrived in New York the month before, having spent the seven months since his wife's death on the road, picking up jobs here and there. Exactly what those jobs were, no one could recollect later, but indications are that he worked as a public relations man, an advertising agent, a salesman or a bartender—possibly as a bartender in some Navy facility. He'd spent some of that time in California.

From what he said later, he'd been hitting the bottle too much, staying up late at night in motel rooms, reading paperback thrillers with a glass of Seven Crown whiskey and 7UP close to hand, thinking that he could write at least as well as this, or better. All it took, he believed, was determination and industry, and he had both of those.

So he'd gone where many would-be writers go, to New York, a city he didn't particularly like. "The living is too expensive, the pace is too fast, and the accumulated heartburn is too great," he said years later in a column describing this 18-month period in the city. What he did love, however, was being able to take in a play or musical whenever the mood struck. Marlowe loved the legitimate theater. And he must have enjoyed, also, the proximity of the publishing industry, which gave him a direct line to the career he was hoping to form. He'd taken a job as a credit manager for a jewelry importer in the Diamond Mart, but his real focus was never in doubt.

"In my working life I'd put in more sixteen-hour days than I had eight, and now I had more time on my hands than I'd ever dreamed possible," he wrote in a November 1960 article in *Writer's Digest* magazine. "All my life I'd had the idea that I'd like to write, if only I had the time. I had the time now, and to spare."

As to what he would write, there was no doubt. It would be a suspense story, not an effete Agatha Christie-style mystery. The 1950s had offered a plethora of tough-minded popular novels, and Marlowe was drawn to the genre. From a practical standpoint, his idea was to write for a living, and this stuff was selling. His rough-and-tumble existence as a professional gambler had also supplied him the knowledge this kind of novel demanded. Finally, he read suspense stories and his mind was attuned to the nature of what he read.

Marlowe read constantly, and was always commenting to friends on the latest thrillers or mysteries. Later in life, he would judge many mystery competitions. Moreover, when he was forced to take on an unfamiliar genre—the supernatural thriller—late in his writing career, he methodically examined and summarized books by many of the significant writers in that field. Therefore, when he jumped into the writing racket, it's likely his reading became analytical. And he had a lot to analyze. During the decade Marlowe launched his writing career, the suspense field was rich. William McGivern had turned out *The Big Heat* and Mickey Spillane had produced *Kiss Me Deadly*, both in 1952. In 1954, David Goodis published the drifting, paranoiac tales *Black Friday* and *Street of No Return* and Jim Thompson unleashed stories of sex-crazed, homicidal criminals in *A Hell of a Woman* and *A Swell-Looking Babe*. During the 1950s, steely private eyes were kicking down doors, clutching blondes and wisecracking their way through the American landscape. Richard S. Prather's hard-boiled dick Shell Scott appeared in *Always Leave 'Em Dying* (1954) and in *Strip for Murder* (1955) and Ross MacDonald's Lew Archer made the scene in *The Name is Archer* (1955) and *The Barbarous Coast* (1956).

As he got into writing, Marlowe, whose work would soon place him among the best of these tough-minded wordsmiths, was by no means confident he could master the genre. In fact, in the *Writer's Digest* article, which is titled *Credo*, he said he was bewildered as to how to begin, and stumbled in his early efforts:

"I had no plot, no locale, no background, no story," he wrote. "I had a character. I liked suspense stories; I would put my character in a suspense story. I was living in a hotel; I put the character in a hotel locale. Plot? I wrote the entire first book without a plot, God help me. I took that character and shoved him headlong into a scene, and when it was over I shoved him into another."

This was the book that eventually would be sold as *Doorway to Death*, featuring Johnny Killain, a hard-nosed hotel bell captain and ex-government operative who gets drawn into murder cases and solves them. He's a rough customer, with "a twenty and half inch neck," a man of deep passions and great sexual appetite.

> (H)e was barely a quarter inch over six feet…Johnny had thick, unruly blond hair, and the prominent cheekbones on the deeply tanned face emphasized heavy matching brows and an aquiline nose. The rugged features tapered to a square jawline on which healthy skin fit his bones so snugly as to give an impression of leanness, an impression belied by the broadness of the shoulders in the uniform. The lean mouth, abrupt facial angles, and the frostily pale eyes all contributed to a hardbitten ensemble.

—From *Doorway to Death*

From the beginning, Marlowe's writing was character-driven, as he recalled in an August 1963 article in *The Writer* magazine. "I've always tended to put my stories together in terms of my characters, the shape of the principal character in effect determining the shape of the story. I 'live' with my characters for considerable periods before they ever appear on paper. I build them up in my mind a dimension at a time, endeavoring to endow them with plus and minus qualities, so that the hero is not all good and the villain is not all bad. I do this before I have much more than a general notion in which direction the story is going."

Getting a feel for the story was, of course, most difficult with his first effort. All summer Marlowe wrote and rewrote, and by fall he'd pulled together a half-dozen chapters. He'd also struck on a strategy for writing the book that appealed to his accountancy-trained mind. He realized that he wanted to write a 60,000-word suspense novel, which he broke down as 210 typewritten pages with fourteen 15-page chapters. Each of those chapters broke down into three five-page scenes.

The 60,000-word length of the book catered to the economics of paperback publishing. The fixed price of the paperback book (*Doorway to Death* cost 35 cents) meant that a longer book would cost more to print, cutting into the publisher's margin. The formula of three five-page scenes per chapter fit the suspense story, which demanded pace, vigor and movement.

"In my trial-and-error days, before I had the plan, I found myself quite often becoming bogged down in one scene, or with one set of characters. The action became static," Marlowe wrote. "By limiting a scene to five pages and (preferably) introducing a different setting for each of the three scenes in a chapter, I found that a sense of movement was created which carried the reader onward and prevented him from losing interest. If to this is added the effort to give each individual scene maximum move-ment and an impact of its own, then the desired effect is more easily obtained."

Marlowe settled on the first-person point of view for his main character, Killain, after trying the multiple point-of-view approach and failing. But even with his novel-writing plan in place, he needed some feedback to tell him if he was going in the right direction, so he applied for admission to New York University's evening Novel Workshop group. Asked to provide a sample of his work, he sub-mitted the six chapters. Dean Warren Bower called him from the university a couple of days later and invited him to join the Workshop, taught by Henry Myers under Bower's direction. The group, Marlowe said, was "a revelation."

"It gave me a tremendous lift mentally to be with people strug-gling to accomplish the same thing I was," he wrote. "The chance to pass judgment and have it passed was for me an unparalleled oppor-tunity. By nature I'm an opinionated, contentious individual. I thrive on competition…In the group I threw off sparks, and absorbed a few. I listened, observed, argued, and learned."

The students in the group, numbering 10 to a dozen, read their works in progress and invited comment from the instructor. Early on, Marlowe noted that each handled some aspect of writing well, and sometimes expertly. He worked to analyze their effects and how they accomplished them.

"One man in the group had a truly remarkable sense of *place*; when he described an after-midnight train pulling into a back-country station you could feel the blackness and hear the locomotive," Marlowe wrote. "When he described a bricked-in rose garden as seen from a second-story bedroom window, you could see the grain in the bricks and touch the dew on the roses. In the story he was telling I sometimes felt that not enough *happened* to people, but they saw, heard, smelled, touched, and tasted, and so did you right along with them. My character in my own book immediately began to do likewise."

Similarly, a woman in the group used vivid imagery in her stream-of-consciousness story construction. Marlowe found much of the imagery obscure, but he experimented with the technique nonetheless, and learned from the experience.

He also learned a great deal, he said, from the "after-hour coffee-klatches" in which group members discussed, and tore apart, each other's writing efforts. Myers usually presided over these sessions, which Marlowe felt promoted group camaraderie and kept the less dedicated members of the group writing "more or less steadily."

Motivation wasn't Marlowe's problem, however. When he completed the first semester of the evening class in February 1958, he left the employ of the jewelry importer and took the gamble of spending a year writing full-time.

"I felt I had to do something to close the gap between myself and the people who had been writing for years," he wrote. "I also felt a driving urge to find out if I could make it commercially. I had had encouragement from the various group members, a great deal from Harry Myers and from Warren Bower, but I knew of course that I was some distance removed from publication. I felt I had to find out the extent of that distance, and what I could do about it. And if I could do nothing about it, I could always go back to what I had been doing."

Three weeks later, through a member of the NYU group, Marlowe landed an introduction to James Reach, the agent for the literary department of Samuel French, Inc. Marlowe found him an experienced writer and excellent advisor. Reach, a graduate of Texas Christian University, had written suspense novels, short stories and plays. He'd written for radio and television, worked for publishers, done editing. A 1949 *New York Times* review of his first novel, *Late Last Night*, had described him as an "ingenious" writer whose work was for "the aficionado who likes his puzzle on the cryptic side." Reach read Marlowe's manuscript and called him in for a discussion.

"His opening remark set the pattern for our relationship," Marlowe wrote. "'You're going to publish one of these days, Dan, but this isn't it.' And then he told me why. Clearly and concisely he pointed out the flaws in the story line, the flagrant over-writing, the excessive use of adjectives, adverbs and slang. He went over the manuscript in detail. He crossed out whole chapters, scenes, paragraphs, sentences, phrases and even individual words, and he had a briskly pungent reason for each. I knew no agent did this, that no agent could take the time to do it.

"Finally he said, 'You feel I haven't left you much? It's only because of what's left that I've taken the trouble to do this. I'm betting that you're one of those really rare birds, a natural story-teller. You have a feel for people, for action and for dialogue. It comes through despite the straitjacketed technique. I'd like to see you make this into the book I know you can.'"

Far from letting the agent's critique get him down, Marlowe left elated. He realized he had found a knowledgeable professional who believed in him, and who had gone out of his way to offer helpful criticism. Marlowe wasn't going to let the opportunity slip away. Back in his hotel, he made a check list of Reach's critical comments, set it next to his typewriter and began to write. In twelve 14-hour days, he rewrote the whole book. He was determined to show Reach he could improve.

"When Jim called me back to the office after reading the revision he just shook his head. 'If I hadn't seen it, I wouldn't have believed it. Not that it's a masterpiece, understand, or even a finished product. Even in this version, I'm not sure that we can sell it, but you've improved it enough to warrant sending it out for a reaction.' He looked at me. 'What are you going to do for the next one?' I hadn't had the first stray thought about the next one, but this was the professional, whose twin gods are flexibility and productivity. 'You've still got more of a character in this thing than you have a book,' he said, 'but I like the character. Let's do a series on him.'"

That afternoon, Marlowe started on his second book, which was to be titled *Killer with a Key*. He completed it in half the time it took him to write *Doorway to Death*. He then pulled back that first book, which had been making the rounds of editors, and rewrote it again.

Don Preston, who, as an editor at Gold Medal Books, had initially turned down *Doorway to Death*, acquired both the rewritten version and *Killer with a Key*—most likely in late 1958—for his current employer, the Avon Book Division of Hearst Corp. By then, Marlowe had left New York, at least temporarily. Though the evidence is scant, it appears he was spending some time in Arizona ("He was in Phoenix when his first book sold," his friend Al Nussbaum would write in an article published years later in the *Boston Herald*'s Coloroto Magazine.) But he didn't stay there. He also lived in Connecticut and New Hampshire.

Shortly after striking a deal for his first two books, Marlowe met suspense master Cornell Woolrich (*The Bride Wore Black, The Black Path of Fear*), according to Francis M. Nevins Jr., who related Marlowe's account of their meeting—meetings, actually—in his 1988 biography *Cornell Woolrich: First You Dream, Then You Die*. Marlowe apparently believed he had met the troubled novelist shortly before the death of Woolrich's mother, Claire, but Nevins thought he had got the timing wrong.

In a letter dated Nov. 26, 1968, (provided to me by Nevins) Marlowe said he had met Woolrich in a publisher's office only a day or two before Claire's death:

> "I was an unpublished writer at the time," Marlowe wrote to Nevins, "although I had sold the first two books of what became a series of softcover originals to Avon. Don Preston (now executive editor at Bernard Geis) was my editor there, and he was working with Woolrich on a collection of short stories. We met in Preston's office one morning, and Woolrich invited me to visit

him (he was then staying at the Hotel Franconia near Central Park). I was flattered, since I was a great admirer of his work. I know now—or think I know—that he merely wanted to find out from me what my advance from Avon was in comparison to his own. Woolrich had a genius for suspicion, both founded and unfounded."

Nevin pegs this first meeting, assuming the accuracy of Marlowe's memory, at the very beginning of October 1957.

"I was living at the time in Connecticut," Marlowe's letter goes on, "but we arranged that I would come down four days later for dinner and an evening on the town. In the interval, his mother died, and I walked into the apartment to find Woolrich, his aunt, and a couple of cousins milling around. When I learned what had happened, I was astonished to find that he still proposed to go out on the town with me. His aunt was furious, and they engaged in a verbal battle in which they said stinging things to each other. I could see that she was trying to establish domination over him (at the time I didn't know the background of the mother-son relationship) and that he was resisting it. Eventually he practically pushed me out the door with the whispered assurance that he would call me."

Nevins believes it's unlikely this actually occurred in October 1957. Neither Marlowe's first novel nor the Woolrich short story collection he refers to, *Beyond the Night*, were published until 1959, and Nevins finds it hard to believe that Avon paid advances on those books and then delayed publishing them for well over a year. He speculates that Marlowe actually met Woolrich in October 1958, not October 1957, and that Woolrich's aunt was upset that he was going out for a good time on the first anniversary of Claire's death, not shortly after she died. Nevins said Marlowe fell victim to amnesia, "that most common *noir* element," before he could ask Marlowe whether his guess was correct.

In any case, as Marlowe recalled in the 1968 letter, Woolrich did call him, roughly six months after their failed first get-together.

"Out of the blue, when I had forgotten all about him, my phone rang one afternoon and there was Woolrich asking when we were going to have our evening together. I drove down to New York at once, and we had our evening, which turned out to be a disaster. He didn't drink much, but I learned quickly that any amount was too much for Woolrich. He simply went to pieces, and I learned later that this was his pattern. In his defense it should probably be said that at this time he weighed perhaps 120 pounds and every drink probably hit him three times as hard as it did a larger man.

"I got him back to the Franconia (or had the hotel changed by that time? I don't remember) finally, and had an unpleasant three minutes with the aunt, who was in residence, before I was able to deposit Woolrich and take my departure. I never saw him again, although we did exchange a few notes from time to time. There was a wit in his notes sadly lacking in his person…"

Marlowe was enjoying small-town surroundings during this period. The article in the *Boston Herald* magazine says Marlowe "lived in Keene, New Hampshire, summers while working to establish the Johnny Killain series." In New Hampshire, he apparently had the kind of female companionship that Killain favored: the giving kind. Years later, in a letter to a friend, Marlowe said his unidentified companion, 15 years younger than he was at the time, was an intellectual ("which repelled me") and extremely high-strung, but "she had a four-on-the-floor in a power-pack not yet approximated by Mr. Ford."

Both the first two Killain novels were issued in 1959. Over the next two years, Avon published three more Killain novels, *Doom Service*, *The Fatal Frails*, and *Shake a Crooked Town*. The Killain series was successful enough to keep Marlowe going, but the books aren't highly regarded by mystery aficionados. For instance, Josef Hoffmann, a crime-fiction critic, isn't a big fan of Killain.

"Killain is a character very typical of the 'hard-boiled detective story': of massive physique, aggressive, cool, reckless, a survivor," Hoffmann wrote in an article called *Playing With Fire: Dan J. Marlowe, Al Nussbaum and Earl Drake*, first published in the Australian magazine *Mean Streets* in 1993. "He is bubbling with sarcastic wit and, of course, is a great man for the women. Although the Killain novels contain some of the quality of the 'Black Mask school' of the 20s and 30s, today they seem in parts to be full of clichés and straining after effect. For Marlowe, they provide a good basis for his later writing."

The Killain stories, though told with great vigor and speed, sometimes read like self-satires of the tough-guy genre. This comes through strongly during the tiresome episodes with Lt . Joe Dameron of the New York Police, who did dangerous undercover work with Killain in Europe for the OSS. Dameron needles Killain with over-the-top descriptions of how brutally Killain beat up enemy operatives. And, of course, Killain's success with women would make Mike Hammer blush. He beds practically every good-looking woman he encounters, then brags about it to his regular squeeze, Sally Fontaine, who he calls "Ma." One day, after having sex with Sally in *Doorway to Death*, he says to her, "I try them all but I come back to you." That's one way to make a woman feel appreciated.

The hard-guy dialogue in these books can be stilted and almost impossible to follow. For instance, again in *Doorway to Death*, Killain is explaining to Sally why he has a beef with Dameron: "I don't think he really thinks I killed Max, but he's perfectly willing to hold it over my head and guarantee to keep his bloodhounds off if I'll do what he wants. When I figured his angle, I put it to him straight. I made him admit that if and when I colddecked the set up for him around here, the umbrella was gone. I don't need the umbrella, you understand, but I got mad anyway and told him what I thought of people workin' with collapsible gear." Huh?

Despite Marlowe's reworking of *Doorway to Death*, it lacks a strong plot. Basically, bad guys are trying to take over the Hotel Duarte for unspecified reasons and want Killain to play along. When he doesn't, the results are nasty: fist fights, gun fights, knife fights, even meat cleaver fights. Beneath its crudeness, the book reveals Marlowe's abiding obsessions: gambling and spanking.

Killain suspects Shirley, the boozer girlfriend of Hotel Duarte owner Willie Martin, is also a heroin addict. One night when Willie is traveling, Killain takes the drunken Shirley home, strips her, finds needle marks, and gives her a swift crack on the ass: "... anger and disgust boiled over and he exploded a hard palm upon the pale blue fragility." As the Marlowe canon wore on, dozens of women's fragilities, amplitudes and behinds were to be sorely tested.

Killer with a Key, the second in the series, is a more intriguing novel because Killain has to deal with the murder of his ex-wife, which suggests a working-out of some of Marlowe's feelings of grief over the sudden death of his own wife. Even so, there's really not a lot of soul-searching on Killain's part. His feelings are quickly channeled into action.

> Sally broke the little silence. Her voice was quiet, but there was a note of constraint in it. "I realize how this must have shaken you, Johnny."
>
> "Shaken me?" His lips drew back mirthlessly from his teeth. He picked up the refilled shot glass and gulped half its contents, then looked up at Sally on the arm of the chair. "You're the only one in the world who knew how I felt about that kid. I never blamed her for rackin' up on me when she did. I was a hard rock still livin' too close to those days overseas, an' she just couldn't understand. I hadn't seen her three times in the last five years, but it wasn't ever any different with me...I'll tell you one thing, I'll find the guy who did it if I have to live to be a hundred and four. I'll get him. . ."

Killain does get him, of course, in 159 pages flat.

In 1960, Avon published *Doom Service* and *The Fatal Frails*. In *Doom Service*, Killain is out to avenge the death of his girlfriend Sally's boxer brother, a pug with the unlikely name of Charlie Roketenetz. It's just as well Charlie died young: how many ring-side announcers could have pronounced a last name with that many bumps in it? *The Fatal Frails* boasts the best hard-boiled title of the Killain series, and also the best cover. It features a frightened nude blonde clutching a robe to her bulging chest, a hotel room key with a tab inscribed "Killain," and inset head shots of a redhead and a brunette. The plot of the book, too, is more ambitious, with overtones of *The Maltese Falcon*. People get murdered as they search for property of the Catholic Church, four "exquisitely jeweled" monstrances made in the 13th century which have disappeared.

Apparently the February 1961 issue of *Men* Magazine carried a 25,000 word abridgement of *The Fatal Frails*. This would have been one of Marlowe's early appearances in men's magazines, for which he would freelance over the years.

Shake a Crooked Town hit drugstore racks in January 1961. This adventure takes Killain to Jefferson, a city of 100,000 in upstate New York, to investigate political corruption. He is drawn in by the murder of a former Jefferson police chief who had served with Killain in the clandestine services. The book has some of the flavor of Dashiell Hammett's 1929 novel *Red Harvest*, though it's not nearly as violent. *Shake's* exploration of vicious small-town politics also foreshadows the theme of one of Marlowe's best novels, *The Vengeance Man*, published five years later. The (relatively) small community in which *Shake* was set also reflects Marlowe's growing interest in the societies of small towns, such as those in which he was living during this period: Keene, New Hampshire, and Funkstown, Maryland.

Later in 1961, *Backfire* was issued by Berkley, a new publisher for Marlowe. The book tells the story of Marty Donovan, a troubled police investigator who falls for his partner's wife, then is suspected of killing the partner.

Set in an unnamed large city, it has the feel of the Ed McBain 87th Precinct novels, which take place in the fictional city of Isola, based on New York City. The first of McBain's novels, *Cop Hater*, had come out in 1956, and Marlowe—who always kept up on the current mystery field—would have been well aware of it. Since he never shied away from a salable type of story, Marlowe wouldn't have been reluctant to imitate McBain's approach. *Backfire*, while by no means a great novel, is a more complex story than the Killain adventures. But it couldn't touch the book that followed it. That novel not only made Marlowe's reputation; it changed his life forever.

CHAPTER 4:
The Name of the Game Is Death

IT'S NIGHT. A LIGHTED TELEPHONE BOOTH FLOATS IN THE GREAT Void. Outside we see the silhouette of a man bent slightly forward, his face obscured by his hat shadow. Red flame spikes from a pistol in his hand, cracking into the phone booth and into the body of the big man collapsing inside, the phone receiver dangling as he goes down. If you want a hard-boiled paperback cover, this is it. Copyright 1962. A Fawcett Gold Medal. *The Name of the Game Is Death.*

Twenty-two years later, on a TV talk show in Los Angeles, Marlowe would call it "the novel that's done the most for me." (It almost did even more for him. In 1969, he wrote author Francis M. Nevins that "MGM optioned *The Name of the Game Is Death*." Unfortunately, the option never led to a movie.)

In his *"Criminals at Large"* column in *The New York Times* on Feb. 11, 1962, critic Anthony Boucher wrote, "This is the story of a completely callous and amoral criminal (bank robber and murderer), told in his own self-justified and casual terms, tensely plotted, forcefully written and extraordinarily effective in its presentation of a viewpoint quite outside humanity's expected patterns."

The book has stood the test of time. A writer synopsizing Marlowe's work in the April 1977 issue of *The Armchair Detective,* one of the most influential mystery-commentary magazines of its time, wrote, "*The Name of the Game Is Death* is certainly one of the finest crime novels ever written." In a 1993 article in the Australian crime magazine *Mean Streets*, German critic Josef Hoffmann proclaimed, "With this book Dan Marlowe takes his place among the great American crime writers." Veteran crime novelist Ed Gorman, founder of the magazine *Mystery Scene*, said, "I still remember reading *Name* for the first time. I'd never read anything like it, not even Jim Thompson. The protagonist wasn't spiritually redeemed (or excused) by insanity nor was he an anti-hero acting out his rage against society. He was a criminal, possibly a sociopath, and Marlowe courageously offered no excuses for him."

Given the accolades for the novel, it's frustrating that not much is known about how Marlowe wrote the book, though more is known about where. He was moving around.

A Jan. 26, 1961, article in *The Daily Mail* of Hagerstown, Maryland, said he had been living part of each year with Mr. and Mrs. Floyd Davis of nearby Funkstown, and "is presently in Hollywood, Fla., where he teaches a workshop class in the short story and the novel in the evening adult education program." That's where he finally got up a head of steam on the book, according to a letter Marlowe wrote to his agent, Jim Reach, several years later. "...I keep thinking back to *The Name of the Game Is Death*," he said. "There was a story we couldn't sell in outline to Dardis at Berkley and to at least one other editor, on the basis of 60 pages and an outline, but when I got another whack at it in Florida and got it a little more than half written, Gold Medal took it immediately."

Marlowe finished writing the book at the home of his childhood friend, Henry "Hank" Power, a lineman and later an auditor at Boston Edison who lived at 17 Hilltop Terrace, Woburn, Massachusetts, about 12 miles north of Boston.

This information comes from Power's son Jed, who has written a novel, *The Boss of Hampton Beach*, featuring a bartender protagonist named Dan Marlowe. Marlowe used Jed's first name for the character Jed Raymond, a good-natured real-estate salesman in *The Name of the Game Is Death*. Jed Power, then 12, recalls that his prim

Irish-Catholic schoolteacher mother wasn't pleased by that. She liked Marlowe, but considered his books racy.

While at the Power home, Marlowe and Hank visited two of Power's brothers, both Woburn police officers, apparently so Marlowe could gather law-enforcement information.

This was a period of experimentation for Marlowe. He had tried an Ed McBain-type novel with *Backfire*, and was massaging two plots he would rework for years without success. One was for a book called *Cold Cash* about a confidence woman. Another, *Traitor*, concerned the adventures of an American turncoat working as a spy for the Russians in Washington, D.C., another city where Marlowe spent part of 1961, living at 1208 Crittenden, N.W. In an Oct. 10 letter to Reach, Marlowe noted he'd offered *Traitor* to Gold Medal, but had been turned down. Undeterred, he continued to develop information that would enhance this and other espionage stories. He told Reach he was having lunch with a retired military officer who had worked for the CIA, the lunch having been set up by a *Newsweek* editor who was a friend of Marlowe.

Even with several projects going at once, Marlowe worked hard developing the main character for *The Name of the Game Is Death*. In an August 1963 article in the *"From Our Rostrum"* section of *The Writer* magazine, he discussed how he produced a detailed profile of the character, a progression from his earlier practice of doing rudimentary biographical sketches.

"Out of curiosity, I checked my origins file on *The Name of the Game Is Death...*," Marlowe wrote. "I found that my biography on the protagonist ran to some 8,000 words. In the development of the story, I used perhaps only a third of this, but the point is that when I began the story, I *knew* the character. I knew him to an extent that made it difficult for him to do something in the course of the story that wasn't in character."

The protagonist is a remarkable departure from the tough-but-simple Johnny Killain or the guilt-tortured detective Marty Donovan of *Backfire*. He is cold, a loner. He feels his attitude is justified by the way he was treated by others, but it's obvious he has a savage streak. When he's 10 or 11, a fat bully kills his kitten, Fatima, then laughs at him for crying. He beats up the fat boy repeatedly, turning aside all efforts at reconciliation, until the boy's family leaves town. As a high school student, the character is roughed up and hurt seriously by corrupt police officers. He won't allow his father to file charges. Instead, he lays for the brutal cops one at a time and works them over with his feet, his fists, and a steel pipe, making sure he won't be caught.

Several years later, while working the overnight shift in a gas station, the character is befriended by an intellectual young man named Olly Barnes. Barnes gets railroaded by a police lieutenant named Winick for a child molestation he didn't commit. This is a key turning point for the character, as emphasized by the back-cover copy for the original edition of *The Name of the Game Is Death*:

> On the day they sentenced Olly Barnes to fifteen years I quit the human race. I never went back to my job and I've never done a legitimate day's work since.
>
> I bought a gun in a hockshop and was surprised to learn how easy it is to knock off gas stations. The money piled up and I bought a second-hand car and drove the 180 miles back across the state. Back to Winick, the guy who railroaded Olly Barnes.
>
> I rang his doorbell one night and shot him in the face, four times. He went backward in a kind of shambling trot. "That's for Olly," I told him. But he didn't hear me. He was dead before he hit the floor.
>
> Winick was the first.
>
> He wasn't the last.

The character is obviously as hard-nosed as they come. And, to the reader, he retains an air of mystery. We never learn his real name, not in any of the dozen books Marlowe would write about him.

In *The Name of the Game Is Death*, he calls himself by the false names Roy Martin and Chet Arnold. Early on, he tells his partner to write him in care of "Roy Martin" in Phoenix, and follows up later by saying, "I had a wallet full of crap identifying the nonexistent Roy Martin." Later, after he kills a highway robber masquerading as a Texas Ranger, he switches identities. ("I cleaned out my wallet and started from scratch. When I put it back on my hip again I was Chester Arnold of Hollywood, Fla. I had business cards in the wallet identifying Chet Arnold as a tree surgeon.")

In the 1969 sequel, *One Endless Hour*, we learn that the bank robber has also used the false name "Earl Drake." Now he assumes it again. ("Seven years ago I had passed as Earl Drake, itinerant gunsmith, during my stay with Tom. Earl Drake had never been in trouble with police anywhere. It was as good a name as any.") From that point on, he is known as Earl Drake. The character, under that name, would become well-established in a series of books issued by Fawcett Gold Medal.

This caused some problems when *The Name of the Game Is Death* was reprinted. In 1973, Fawcett Gold Medal reissued the book in a revised edition that, among many other changes, substituted "Earl Drake" for the "Roy Martin" alias ("I had a wallet full of crap identifying Earl Drake.") When Black Lizard reprinted the original version of the story in 1988, the name "Earl Drake" appears nowhere in the text, but does appear in the copy on the back of the book ("Earl Drake, Marlowe's toughest character, is a professional thief...Listen to Earl Drake's side of the story. . "). The 1993 Vintage Crime/ Black Lizard edition gets it right, reprinting the original story and referring to the character in the back copy as "the man who calls himself Roy Martin."

Since it's easiest to refer to this many-named protagonist as "Earl Drake," I'll do that. Drake shows many contrasts with Johnny Killain, Marlowe's other series character. Killain, though by no means a goody two-shoes, typically winds up seeking more-or-less conventional justice and upholding the law. Drake, in the first two novels about him, is a criminal who shows no remorse for killing his enemies, or for disposing of a physician and a fake cop who intend to rob him. Killain is a sexual athlete who beds new women at a rapid clip and can always return for comfort and coitus to his regular girlfriend, Sally Fontaine. Drake, on the other hand, is sexually damaged goods. Tough and masculine out of the sack, he often has a hard time performing in it, so he tells tavern owner Hazel Andrews when they wind up in bed in *The Name of the Game Is Death*. On the first go with Hazel, he can't perform. She asks if he's just not sexually excited by her. He says she isn't the problem.

> "You're not a queer." She said it as a statement but with an implied question.
> "I don't think I'm a queer," I said.
> "But this happens? Often?"
> "About half the time."

When Hazel asks him what allows him to complete the sex act, he says "excitement," but nearly says "guns." He implies to the reader that he also is jacked up by killing. "With the air crackling with tension and a gun in my hand I'm nine feet tall and the best man you ever saw, right afterward. There's another time, too, but I'm not so proud of that."

The rewritten version of the novel issued in 1973 by Gold Medal softens this exchange to make Drake appear less impotent and certainly not homosexual and to remove the idea that killing turns him on.

> "You're not a queer." It was a statement, not a question.
> "No."
> "But this happens?"
> "Yes. Not all the time."

The ensuing comment by Drake is reworked so that he says, "With a gun in my hand and tension crackling in the air, I'm the best damn man right afterward that you ever saw." The rewrite deletes the final line.

While Marlowe thoroughly rewrote the book, this was one of the few significant changes. It fit the character of Drake as most readers knew him from the several "Operation" novels published by that time: as a quasi-secret agent who had regular sexual romps with Hazel and other women, and as a man who was still steely tough, but not a wanton killer.

It's hard to say why Marlowe chose to make Drake prone to impotence in the first book. Most likely it was simply to create a more complicated character than Killain. As an artistic decision, the impotence accomplished its purpose. However, those seeking a more personal reason for its inclusion might note that Marlowe suffered from a condition that can make erections and sex painful: phimosis, a tightening of the foreskin over the head of the penis that prevents the foreskin from being pulled back. On July 10, 1969, eight years after *The Name of the Game Is Death* was published, a urologist diagnosed Marlowe as having "severe phimosis" and performed a circumcision, which presumably solved the problem.

Whatever personal experiences Marlowe drew on while creating the bank robber—such as betting on horse races and dealing with gamblers and low-lives—he created a compelling character and a story with a pitch-perfect tone.

"In that one," Gold Medal Editor-in-Chief Knox Burger told Marlowe, "you did something I don't see enough of: You struck a note and held it."

The two editions of *The Name of the Game Is Death* differ in many details, but, with the exceptions noted above, don't change the main character or the story.

Some mystery readers believe the 1973 version was considerably "softened," taking the edge off the brutality of the original. That's not really true. The later version has one less chapter, but that's simply because chapters VIII and IX were combined. Marlowe did the revisions. "It's the book I had to revise the most often from edition to edition, although it still carried the same copyright," he said in a 1984 interview with French author Roger Martin, who at the time was publishing a fanzine focused on American crime writers called *Hard-Boiled Dicks*.

The language and the flow of the sentences between the two editions differ slightly. In the 1962 version, the paragraphs are longer and the style is rawer. Sometimes extraneous words are thrown in. The story feels hot from the typewriter. Still, you have to read closely to notice the differences.

Here are the first two paragraphs in each.

From 1962:

From the back seat of the Olds I could see the kid's cotton gloves flash white on the steering wheel as he swung off Van Buren onto Central Avenue. On the right up ahead the strong late September Phoenix sunshine blazed off the bank's white stone front till it hurt the eyes. The damn building looked as big as the purple buttes on the rim of the desert.

Beside me Bunny chewed gum rhythmically, his hands relaxed in his lap. Up front, in three-quarter profile the kid's face was like chalk, but he teamed the car perfectly into a tight-fitting space right in front of the bank.

From 1973:

From the back seat of the Olds I could see the kid's cotton gloves flash white on the steering wheel as he swung the car from Van Buren onto Central Avenue. The strong, late-September, Phoenix sunshine blazed off the bank's white stone front till it hurt the eyes. The damn building looked as big as the purple buttes on the rim of the desert.

Beside me Bunny chewed gum rhythmically, his hands relaxed in his lap. Up front the kid's face was like chalk, but he teamed the Olds perfectly into a tight-fitting space in front of the bank.

With the exception of a hyphen and a few commas, and the removal of the extraneous phrase "in three-quarter profile" in the second version, the two passages are quite similar. This is fairly representative of the changes between the two versions.

For further comparison, here are two passages from later in the same robbery.

From 1962:

Inside the railing with Bunny, two big-assed women huddled together against the door leading into the cages, empty trays in their hands. Right where they should have been at two minutes to three. Bunny motioned with the gun at the cage door. They stared at him, cow-eyed. Inside the cages there wasn't a sound. Bunny whipped the flat of his automatic up against the jawline of the nearer woman. She fell over sideways, mewling. Someone inside opened the door. Bunny stepped in quickly, herding everyone to the rear. He began yanking out cash drawers. Bundles of hundreds and twenties went into the sack. Everything else went to the floor.

From 1973:

Two big-assed women huddled together inside the railing with Bunny. They stood against the door leading into the tellers' cages, empty trays in their hands. Right where they should have been at two minutes to three.

Bunny motioned with his gun for them to open the cage door. They stared at him, cow-eyed. He whipped the flat of his automatic up against the jawline of the nearer woman. She fell sideways, mewling. Someone inside opened the door. Bunny stepped inside quickly and herded everyone to the rear. He began yanking out cash drawers. Bundles of hundreds and twenties went into his sack. Everything else he tossed on the floor.

The viciousness of the robbery comes through in both versions. No "softening" there. But rewriting makes the beginning of the second passage more staccato, and the breaking up of the long paragraph makes the narrative punchier. Otherwise, we mostly see editing for clarity: "Bunny motioned with the gun at the cage door" becomes "Bunny motioned with his gun for them to open the cage door."

Was Earl Drake based on real-life research? We don't know. But Marlowe did manage—perhaps merely by chance—to come up with a protagonist whose life paralleled that of a real bank robber. This robber was not Al Nussbaum, with whom Marlowe was to have a decades-long friendship, but Nussbaum's partner in crime, Bobby "One-Eye" Wilcoxson. The lives of Marlowe, Nussbaum and Wilcoxson were set on a collision course in December 1961, shortly before *The Name of the Game Is Death* was published, when three men carried out a bank robbery in Brooklyn, New York, and the robbery went bad.

CHAPTER 5:
The Real Hard Men

"The only thing I could hear was the whimpering of the woman on the floor and the clatter and bang as Bunny emptied and dumped drawers. On my left something moved. I turned and the movement stopped. Dead ahead on the balcony overhead I caught a rapid blur of gray. I belted the guard over backward with the first shot I banged up there. Bunny never even turned his head."

—From *The Name of the Game Is Death*

BOBBY "ONE-EYE" WILCOXSON HAD PULLED BANK ROBBERIES, but he'd never killed a man. Today would be the day. It was clear and cold in Brooklyn, nearing 10 a.m., Dec. 15, 1961. Wilcoxson was 31, small but hard, at 5-foot-9 and 155 pounds. Under his tan Sears Roebuck raincoat, he cradled a Thompson .45 caliber submachine gun. His backup weapon was a 14-round Browning Hi-Power 9-millimeter pistol. Live hand grenades nestled in his pockets. His raincoat and neck scarf concealed a business suit, which covered a wire for the walkie-talkie clipped to his belt. Through an earplug, he could receive warning messages from Al Nussbaum at the wheel of the getaway car, a 1960 Ford station wagon. Nussbaum had a good vantage point. He was parked 125 yards away in an alley west of Schenectady Avenue.

Wilcoxson slid out of the second robbery car, a stolen Oldsmobile, and the Negro kid, Peter Columbus Curry, took the wheel. As Curry swung the Olds around the other side of the brand-new Lafayette National Bank at 4930 Kings Highway, Wilcoxson pulled his slouch hat lower over his dark brown hair. Then he set off toward the entrance, shifting his head about to take full advantage of his good left eye. The habit gave him an antsy, suspicious look. His right eye was artificial, replacing an eye blinded in a childhood accident (a razor-sharp shard had slashed into the eye when his stepfather, doing auto repair, had hammered a piece of metal).

At the bank's main entrance on Kings Highway, Wilcoxson looked through the glass door. Across the lobby, through the drive-in teller windows, he could see Curry approaching the side entrance on Utica Avenue. Curry was wearing a red corduroy cap and a tan car coat and carrying an Army duffel bag. Pasted on his upper lip was a black crepe mustache. The false mustache was Nussbaum's idea: He was the disguise expert. In Curry's hand was a revolver— Wilcoxson couldn't tell if it was the .32-caliber or the .22.

Curry plunged through the Utica door. At the same time, Wilcoxson slapped sunglasses over his eyes and shouldered into the Kings Highway vestibule. Wilcoxson took two quick strides, pushed through the second glass door, and pivoted to his left, knowing he'd see the bank guard. And there he was, sitting down, his revolver holstered low on his hip, his chair leaning against the wall. The guard would fight; he'd told Wilcoxson that. He wasn't ready for a fight, though, and Wilcoxson was. Well, not exactly a fight. "I am here," Wilcoxson said, and swung the Thompson up.

* * *

Curry was a throw-in for the robbery. The veteran heisters were Wilcoxson, the muscle, and Nussbaum, the brains. In time, Wilcoxson would be called "the most wanted man since Dillinger" and Nussbaum (by no less a figure than J. Edgar Hoover) "the most cunning fugitive in the country." They touched off bad things in each other, Marlowe said in an unpublished article called *Anatomy of a Crime Wave.*

"Separately, neither man had shown a particularly dangerous potential in previous skirmishes against society," Marlowe wrote. "Together, after meeting in federal prison at Chillicothe, Ohio, they fused like nitric acid and glycerine (sic) to form an equally explosive compound."

By the time Wilcoxson and Nussbaum hit the Brooklyn bank, they'd knocked off at least four others over the course of a year and taken down nearly $200,000. They were giving J. Edgar Hoover ulcers, and putting the fear of God into bank tellers and bank officers up and down the East Coast. But the two were odd brothers in crime.

Wilcoxson was a head case, although he was able to keep the psychiatrists guessing about his competence by trotting out big words and phrases he didn't entirely understand. His sense of grandiosity would lead an attorney many years later to describe him as "a guy who thought he knew what he was talking about all the time." Formerly a picker and a crew boss in the fruit groves of California and Arizona, Wilcoxson had sun-tanned skin, leathery and coarse. Once he'd gone after a man's face with a broken beer bottle in a bar fight. He liked fast cars and expensive women, but couldn't hang on to either.

His juvenile record began in 1943 with a conviction for running away in Salinas, California. Other convictions also marked his adolescent life in that state—in Salinas, Santa Clara and Carmel—and in Phoenix, Arizona: statutory rape, battery, petty theft, disturbing the peace, passing bogus checks. As an adult, he was a fuck-up, failing at just about everything he attempted: burglary, safecracking, car theft, auto sales. He was constantly in and out of jails. Marlowe quoted a friend of Wilcoxson's as saying, "Before he met Nussbaum, all you needed to know about Bobby was that he got caught at everything he tried." He had little formal education, but, possibly because of his success with Nussbaum, was full of pretension. In testifying about how he cased the Brooklyn bank, he said, "It was a place of procuring employment because my profession at that time was a bank robber."

Nussbaum, then 27, was more complex. Raised by middle-class restaurant owners in Buffalo, New York, Nussbaum had great technical skills and intelligence. Marlowe asserted he scored 140 points out of a possible 150 on the Army's Binet Intelligence Test, "a near-genius rating." Federal prison files say his IQ was 118—above average though not "near-genius"—based on information from the New York State School of Applied Arts and Sciences, where he studied drafting.

In any case, he was crafty, with a taste for crooked ways. Later, he would tell a judge: "Crime has always been a combination game and livelihood for me. Ever since I was about sixteen, I've made my living, at least partially, from some kind of illegal activity. It was usually profitable and always exciting, like a chess game for cash prizes, and that's the way I thought of it. I can't say which held my interest more, the fun or the money, but I enjoyed playing the game."

His efforts to beat the system were creative. Years later, he told an acquaintance that when he drove on bank jobs he'd sometimes take a large, vicious black dog he had specially trained. If a police officer noticed Nussbaum waiting near a bank and came over to check out the car, the robber would signal the dog to go berserk, jumping between the back and front seats and attacking the windows. The startled cop would back off.

Nussbaum's FBI Wanted poster noted that he had blue eyes and light brown hair and, on his upper left arm, a tattoo of a snake curling around a dagger. He stood 5-foot-7, two inches shorter than Wilcoxson, and, at 170 pounds, carried more weight. An expert locksmith and gunsmith, Nussbaum could also pilot and repair airplanes, and had a good working knowledge of electronics and explosives. He was not only sharp, but independent. He later would say he studied for two years to get his Class A Radio Operator's License so he could be an engineer in a radio station, then dropped out two weeks short of completing the course when he realized he never wanted to work for someone else.

Nussbaum played chess, took part in gymnastics, and was a member of the National Rifle Association. At one time, he had been a casino employee in Las Vegas, Nevada, and he loved playing the angles. When he was young, he worked in a gas station. When a customer drove up, asked for a fill-up and went into the station,

Nussbaum would throw the car's gas cap into the bushes. Told the gas cap was missing, the driver would buy a new one. After he left, Nussbaum would retrieve the discarded gas cap and sell it to someone else.

At 18, Nussbaum was arrested for carrying a concealed weapon and given probation. Six months later, he was picked up again, for auto theft, carrying a revolver, and attempting to steal a diamond ring. Then, for a while, he seemed to settle down. He worked as a draftsman for the Sylvania Electric Co. in Buffalo at $85 a week for three years, but found the work too tame. On Jan. 25, 1955, he enlisted in the Army and spent a couple of years stationed at Walter Reed Army Medical Center in Washington, where he bought guns from several dealers. According to Marlowe, he sold them to "acquaintances" at South American embassies.

Nussbaum was making so much money, Marlowe said, that he was able to maintain two expensive apartments. He also scored some cash from a bank robbery in Maryland he pulled with someone else in 1956, though details are scant (He would testify briefly about this in 1964 when he was tried for multiple bank robberies.) In Alexandria, Virginia, Nussbaum bought a half-dozen submachine guns made inoperative by having their barrels welded closed. Honorably discharged from the Army on Jan. 24, 1957, he went to Las Vegas, opened a gun shop, bought new barrels for the guns and made a tidy profit selling them.

Nussbaum, working intermittently as a casino floorman and draftsman in Las Vegas, then began smuggling guns to Mexico for sale, Marlowe asserted. In court testimony much later, Nussbaum denied ever running guns, and said he never sold as many as 50 guns to any one person. Marlowe, although he didn't provide details, said Nussbaum not only ran guns to Mexico but smuggled them to Fidel Castro, who in the late 1950s was coming to power in Cuba.

In any case, Nussbaum's career in the arms trade was suddenly interrupted when he got caught twice in California with submachine guns in his car. (Though he was never arrested in the state for more serious crimes, many years later, when he and author Joe Gores were driving around San Francisco, Nussbaum suddenly started laughing and told Gores they had just passed a bank he had once robbed. Nussbaum didn't say when the robbery had occurred.) The California gun-possession sentences took Nussbaum, in 1958, to a federal lock-up in El Reno, California, then to the federal prison in Chillicothe, Ohio. There, he met Wilcoxson and Curry, who was only 18. In late 1959 and early 1960, all were paroled within a few months of each other.

Wilcoxson had served the last of his sentence in Florida, where he had family. On the street, he immediately embarked on an ill-fated round of burglaries and safe-crackings, got bagged while loading a safe into the trunk of a car, but beat the rap with a good lawyer. Nussbaum went to Buffalo, where he worked in an ironworks run by a friend, producing ornamental scrollwork for iron railings and fire escapes. He also sent a couple of his outdoorsy friends—including the owner of the ironworks—to Mexico on a wild goose chase: Nussbaum told them he'd buried a quarter of a million dollars from a gun-running deal there under headstones in a cemetery. Off they went for a week or two. They came back empty-handed. Nussbaum had just wanted them out of the way. While they were gone, he brought Wilcoxson in from Florida to help steal and crack safes.

Wilcoxson and Nussbaum made their names as bank robbers, but both had entrepreneurial instincts. Nussbaum, in particular, used bank robberies to raise the money he needed for various business enterprises. One of those continued to be arms dealing. He also set up a print shop specializing in advertising and promotional literature, and an importing business that sold cameras, field glasses, radios, walkie-talkies and other goods.

The two men also were turning to domestic pursuits. Bobby was living with a slender blonde from Delray Beach, Florida, named Jacqueline Ruth Rose, who he presented as his wife. She was only 17, but, according to Marlowe, managed to look considerably older by virtue of an upswept hairdo and heavily applied make-up. The cosmetics helped conceal burn scars from elbow to shoulder on both of her arms and from her neck to her waist, the result of a childhood encounter with an exploding kerosene stove. In October 1960, Rose and Wilcoxson took an apartment at 190 Olympic Street in Buffalo. By then, Nussbaum had married his high school sweetheart, Alicia (Lolly) Majchrowicz, on July 26,

1960. Nussbaum and Lolly moved into an apartment over that of her parents and soon she became pregnant.

With a baby on the way, Nussbaum stepped up his business activities, legal and illegal. He couldn't resist demonstrating his criminal prowess. One day, as described by Marlowe in *Anatomy of a Crime Wave*, Nussbaum and a friend called "Hart" (not his real name) went to an office supply store to buy equipment:

> When the purchase had been completed, the proprietor tried to sell them a safe. Nussbaum glanced at the safes lined up along the far wall. "You couldn't give me one of those tin cans," he said.
>
> "What d'ya mean!" the proprietor sputtered. "Those are good safes!"
>
> "They're tin cans," Nussbaum repeated, turning to Hart. "Take the card with the combination numbers off that one so I can't see it," he said, pointing. He drew up a chair and sat down in front of it, fingering the dial lightly and drawing a graph on a sheet of paper while the proprietor grinned sardonically.
>
> In eighteen minutes, Nussbaum opened the safe. The outraged proprietor rushed up and snatched the paper from his hand to compare it with the combination on the card Hart held. "You didn't use the right combination!" he accused.
>
> "Is the safe open?" Nussbaum asked him, smiling his pleasant smile.
>
> Whereupon he went down the line and in nine more minutes opened two more safes.
>
> "With the last number of a safe combination known to him," Nussbaum informed Hart as they left the store with its bug-eyed proprietor staring forlornly at his line-up of safes, "even an average safe mechanic can open just about anything. And the last number is the easiest to find. All it takes is time."

In the unpublished article, Marlowe implies that Nussbaum (presumably helped by Wilcoxson) pulled at least one safe job in Buffalo, bashing a hole in the roof of a large wholesale grocery, making his way inside and tapping the safe for $25,000. But the two men already were working on a more ambitious scheme.

On Oct. 30, Wilcoxson bought a 1948 International "Step-In" van. He and Nussbaum cut holes in the sides of the van and glassed them in. Then they set up surveillance of a number of banks, particularly branches. All through November, they watched the banks and laid plans. Finally, on Dec. 5, the Shiller Park branch of the First Federal Savings and Loan Association got two visitors who worked quickly and efficiently. Nussbaum, wearing a gauze mask and brandishing a .380 caliber semiautomatic pistol, and Wilcoxson, who carried a sawed-off shotgun and didn't bother with a disguise, cleaned out the tellers' cages in three minutes. They fled in a vehicle rented from Vega Rentacar Service at the Buffalo Municipal Airport.

Marlowe wrote that the getaway car driver was said to be a "tall, slender young blonde," suggesting this was Jackie Rose, though Nussbaum later denied that. The robbers dumped the rental car not far from the bank. The take wasn't great: a little more than $5,709 in cash, plus $13,740 in negotiable traveler's checks, which they buried and retrieved much later.

Because the proceeds were so small, Nussbaum and Wilcoxson waited only a bit more than a month before striking again. On Jan. 12, 1961, they took down the Manufacturers and Traders Trust Co. in Buffalo. This time, both wore sunglasses. While Wilcoxson covered the people in the bank with his shotgun, Nussbaum approached the tellers' cages. When one of the tellers held out a sack of "bait" money—easily-traced cash with recorded serial numbers—Nussbaum knocked it to the floor. "Clean out those cash drawers," he commanded. Meanwhile, Wilcoxson sent the manager into the vault to get more cash. They made a big score this time: $87,288.

Finally, Nussbaum had enough money to get rolling on his various business enterprises. In March, he set up a radio- and electronic-equipment importing firm, N and W Unique Services Corp., at two locations in Buffalo. Later in the month, he incorporated his printing shop as Power Promotions.

The stage was set for Nussbaum's real business—arms dealing—and he began to buy up weapons, many automatic. He also wanted to trade in aircraft. His plan was to buy planes in Arizona for $5,000, arm them and sell them in Central and South America for 10 times that to governments, revolutionaries, or both. To further this enterprise, he bought a used plane. His pilot friends flew him around the country in it, and he began learning to fly it himself. Meanwhile, he was planning still another venture: a chain of restaurants he intended to call Prospector Pete's.

On March 31, the Nussbaums had a baby girl, Alison. The child, Marlowe said, increased Nussbaum's "feeling of responsibility." The pressure was on him to provide income, his life was getting crazier, and he began to pump Benzedrine into his system every day to keep up.

He and Wilcoxson needed more cash, and in June, they got it in Washington, D.C. Nussbaum planned to set off a homemade bomb to distract police while he and Wilcoxson carried out a bank robbery. He exploded two test bombs, "sending police scrambling," according to an FBI account, but a third test bomb failed to detonate, and investigators lifted Nussbaum's prints from it. Although the distraction plan hadn't worked, on June 30 the robbers went ahead with a bank job. They hit the Brightwood Branch of the Bank of Commerce, within a few blocks of Walter Reed Army Medical Center, where Nussbaum had served in the Army. Inside the bank, Nussbaum threatened the customers with a .45 automatic and Wilcoxson kept them in line with a 9-mm Schmeisser submachine gun, backed up by his nickel-plated 9-millimeter pistol, a P-38. They rolled out of the bank with $19,862.

By now, Wilcoxson and Nussbaum were diverging in their approaches to personal lifestyle and business. While Nussbaum kept trying to build up his legitimate or semi-legitimate businesses and to settle into domestic life, Wilcoxson was running wild, burning his money on gambling, fast cars and stupid investments. He was also having trouble with his girlfriend, who was pregnant. With a child on the way, Jackie Rose discovered Bobby's divorce to his current wife hadn't gone through. Furious, Jackie ran off with a truck driver. Bobby chased after her. Meanwhile, he was losing heavily at the Las Vegas dice and blackjack tables and risking as much as $5,000 on the horses.

Much of the rest of his cut of the robbery money went to feed his passion for wheels: He bought a Thunderbird and a Corvette, a Porsche Golden Spider and a customized Chevrolet Aztec. He paid

$4,000 for the Aztec and dropped $4,500 on modifications. The money was going quickly. He burned off thousands more by investing in Midway Motors, a used-car lot in West Virginia run by a friend from prison. When an embezzler grabbed the proceeds and ran, Bobby was left holding the bag.

Nussbaum's operating funds weren't stretching as far as he'd hoped, either. Solution? Bank robbery. On Aug. 31, 1961, Nussbaum and Wilcoxson took down the Browncroft Branch of the Lincoln-Rochester Trust Co. in Rochester, New York, and made off with $57,197. Then they headed for Las Vegas, where Wilcoxson began to burn through the loot at the gambling tables. Nussbaum, disgusted, soon headed back to Buffalo.

The stars were beginning to align for the convergence of the career paths of Nussbaum and Marlowe. That August, Marlowe completed *The Name of the Game Is Death* and submitted it to Fawcett for publication. The fictional bank robber who would come to be known as Earl Drake was about to be loosed upon the reading world.

As 1961 drew to a close, Marlowe was also looking for a change of scene. He had been moving around, mostly on the East Coast, and found himself in Connecticut. There he picked up a national magazine and saw an advertisement from Helen Hamilton, an elderly lady in Harbor Beach in northeastern Michigan. She was seeking a quiet tenant, preferably a writer, to share her pleasant, rustic home. Marlowe had been told Michigan was a nice place to live by his friend Hank Power, who had served there in the Coast Guard. Marlowe, seeking inexpensive living circumstances while he pursued his writing, responded to the advertisement.

As Marlowe's world began to slow down and smooth out, Nussbaum's was becoming more frenetic. Despite a few big scores, Nussbaum couldn't get over the hump financially, and he had to rely on an increasingly out-of-control Wilcoxson. Bobby, perhaps in imitation of Nussbaum, was still trying to get into legitimate business, but it was no go. He spent September in California buying and selling cars and part of November in Phoenix trying to open up a "speed shop" to sell race car accessories. But, on Nov. 15, Bobby had to run. The FBI was looking for him, presumably for bank robbery.

There was more bank robbery on the way. Shortly after Thanksgiving, Wilcoxson and Nussbaum were looking for another big score, this time in New York City. For reasons not entirely clear—perhaps because Nussbaum had begun to worry about shooting someone inside a bank or getting shot—they brought in help for this job. Two of Wilcoxson's friends considered the job and declined, but Peter Curry, the young Brooklyn native Wilcoxson and Nussbaum had met in prison, decided to go along. The robbers settled on the Lafayette National Bank in Brooklyn.

In early December, Wilcoxson and Curry were casing the bank, going in to inspect the interior layout, analyzing the surrounding neighborhood for a getaway route, and timing the escape. One excellent vantage point for watching the front of the bank was a diner across the way, the GIP Luncheonette. One day, Wilcoxson was sitting in the diner having breakfast when he noticed another customer wearing uniform trousers, a dark overcoat and a snap-brim hat. The robber also noted a station wagon parked at the curb. Two guards left the bank and approached the car. The customer in the uniform pants walked to the door of the restaurant, pulling back his overcoat to reveal a holstered pistol on his hip. Indicating the station wagon, he shouted to the guards, "Go on in, boys. I will watch it."

Wilcoxson realized this was a bank guard. In fact, he was the chief security guard, Henry Kraus—a friendly man who was a marksman with a pistol. As Kraus turned back from the door, he found himself face-to-face with Wilcoxson.

"He said something to me," Wilcoxson would later testify. "And I felt just a little bit shaky at that time, being as my intention was to case the bank. And I says, 'It looks as though you would use that gun.'" Wilcoxson couldn't stop himself. He asked, "What would you do if I walked into the bank with a gun?"

"Either I would shoot you or you would shoot me," Kraus replied calmly.

"And at that time I was trying to drop the conversation," Wilcoxson recalled. "I didn't—I'd—I'd just as soon not talk to the man at all."

As soon as it was reasonable to do so, Wilcoxson left the diner and joined Curry in a car across the street. Wilcoxson was still jumpy.

"We got a real Wyatt Earp there to contend with," he told Curry.

"What do you mean, 'Wyatt Earp'?"

"There's a man we are going to have trouble with," Wilcoxson replied.

* * *

Kraus was as good as his word. When Wilcoxson barged into the bank, the guard had been lounging in his chair, tipped back against the wall. As he saw the muzzle of the Thompson swing up to cover him, he leaned forward and his chair legs thumped the floor. He blurted, "No!" and began to rise, reaching for his gun. Wilcoxson, a man who knew the value of saving his shots, had his chopper set to semi-auto—one shot each time he pulled the trigger. He fired, and a heavy .45 caliber bullet ripped into the guard's chest. *That should do him*, Wilcoxson thought. A .45 bullet is supposed to knock a man down and out. But the guard continued to rise, still clutching at his gun. Amazed at Kraus' toughness, Wilcoxson fired again. Kraus fell. The robber leaned over, popping two more bullets into the guard, then wheeled to the stunned bank customers and employees.

"This is a hold-up," he shouted. "I don't want no trouble out of nobody, or you'll get what the guard got! Don't move, and nobody will get hurt. I mean business!"

One customer panicked and dashed for the door. Unwilling to shoot up the place, creating chaos and alerting people outside, Wilcoxson let him go. The customer slammed through the doors to Kings Highway. Meanwhile, Curry ran down the length of the tellers' counter, gun in one hand, canvas duffel bag in the other. He vaulted the counter, pointing his revolver at two bank employees. "Get over there," he told them, indicating the rear wall, "or I will kill you." Curry scooped currency into the bag from the nearest teller's drawer, then began jogging back toward the Utica Avenue entrance, stopping at one teller's cage for more cash.

Suddenly, Nussbaum's voice crackled over the receiver in Wilcoxson's ear. A man was coming in the Kings Highway entrance. Now Wilcoxson saw him. A customer, looked like. "Step right over there," the robber ordered, and the man moved over to join the other customers. The situation was tense. There had been gunfire, and the hostages were uneasy. "Just stay where you are," Wilcoxson told them. "Don't put your hands up. Just stay where you are." Wilcoxson noted a little boy, his face quivering with fear. "Everything's going to be all right," Wilcoxson told the boy and the man next to him, trying to keep everything calm. But, damn it! Things wouldn't stay calm. A bank employee behind the counter kept flexing the fingers of one hand, making reaching motions. He looked like he was trying to hit a hidden alarm button or grab a telephone. "Straighten up and fly right," Wilcoxson growled at him, lifting the muzzle of the Thompson to make his point. "No more monkey business."

For the robbers, things just kept getting worse. Outside, the customer who had escaped from the bank, a man named Wisotsky, flagged down a motorist. Wisotsky directed the driver to a police call box a block away. His choice was good. New York City Patrolman Salvatore Accardi was already at the box, and Wisotsky told him the robbery was going down. Accardi acted quickly. He caught a ride with the driver back to the bank, and stepped out nearby, his approach covered by a bus that had stopped in front of Nussbaum.

The cop slipped into the Kings Highway vestibule, revolver out. Wilcoxson, following Curry's gaze, turned and saw him. Accardi fired. So did Wilcoxson, swinging the submachine gun from his right hand to his left and snapping off three quick shots. The first two smashed the glass of the inner door; the third whacked the policeman's chest. Accardi flew back through the outer door, shattered glass tinkling around him. The cop thought he was badly wounded. He scrambled to the luncheonette and raised the alarm by phone. The bullet, however, had struck Accardi's badge, saving him.

By now, though, the police radio in Nussbaum's car was coming alive with bulletins about the bank robbery. "Let's go," Nussbaum said into the transmitter, his voice tight. Wilcoxson turned to Curry: "Let's make it." Without waiting to see Curry's reaction, Wilcoxson dashed through the Utica Avenue entrance, expecting to have to shoot it out with more police. Curry came after, running so quickly he spilled $10,000 in cash on the floor. Both jumped into the Oldsmobile and headed off to rendezvous with Nussbaum in the getaway station wagon. Wilcoxson dumped the Olds behind a garage a few blocks away. The men, walking via separate routes, reached Nussbaum's car and piled in. Curry hid under a blanket in the back.

Nussbaum drove smoothly to Flatbush Avenue, found an area with heavy foot traffic, and dropped Curry there, saying he'd call him in a couple of days. Nussbaum and Wilcoxson headed back toward Manhattan. As they approached the Brooklyn Bridge, they stopped to put signs for N and W Unique Services in their rear side windows. It was a small disguise, but it might help. At least it changed the station wagon's appearance, signaled it was a harmless business vehicle. Then they drove into Manhattan.

Nussbaum and Wilcoxson needed cover. They found a moving police cruiser and pulled in behind it. Sticking close to the cop's bumper, they proceeded out of town. Then they headed for Buffalo, carrying more than $32,000.

They'd turned a profit, but it had been a bad and bloody day. In the past, Nussbaum and Wilcoxson had infuriated their FBI pursuers, had made sport of them and outfoxed them, but nobody had gotten hurt. Now the robbers had raised the stakes. Today, they had turned the chase into a game of death. Now, the feds would be on them like a pack of wild hounds; they wouldn't quit until all the robbers were bagged.

CHAPTER 6:
The Town on the Lake

AROUND THE TIME THE SOUND OF GUNFIRE AND THE SCREAMING OF the police sirens faded away in Brooklyn, Dan Marlowe was enjoying a leisurely stroll to the Corner Drug Store in Harbor Beach. He liked the community. It was quiet, reserved and amiable, and it suited his nature perfectly. As a boy, he'd lived in small towns in Massachusetts; this was like coming home. Harbor Beach, founded in 1837 as Sand Beach, comprised 2,000 residents on the shore of Lake Huron two hours north of Detroit. It was both a resort community serving rich Detroiters and a village where life unfolded at an easy pace. Freezing cold in the winter, it was cool and sunny in the summer.

Flanked by farmlands and woods, Harbor Beach was home to acres of lush parks and the largest freshwater man-made harbor in the world. On the north side of the harbor stood a lighthouse built in 1885, extending 54 feet above the water, its foghorn audible a mile away through the mists of winter. At the end of Pack Street was the Coast Guard station built in 1935, staffed by as many as 100 men during World War II. The town had known seafaring disasters on the large and sometimes treacherous Lake Huron. The closest to home was the wreck of the tugboat Searchlight, on April 23, 1907, which took six lives—four of them Harbor Beach residents.

The architecture of Harbor Beach was a mix of Victorian and American eclectic, and some of the most prominent buildings were churches. The place didn't bother with pretension. City Hall had been used as a garage and a flour-storage facility before being renovated in 1947. The town valued its Rotary Club, its American Legion, its Masonic Lodge, and its sports teams. The community was virtually all white, and its politics were conservative, as Marlowe's were. Current and former Harbor Beach residents had made their marks in many ways. "Automatic Jim" Brieske had been a star placekicker for the University of Michigan's football teams in 1942, 1946 and 1947. Frank Murphy had held office as Michigan governor, U.S. attorney general and U.S. Supreme Court justice. Gen. George Lincoln and his brother, Lt. Gen. Lawrence Lincoln, had served in three wars. Sanburn Smith, who owned Smith's Department Store, had organized the Harbor Beach Gun Club.

Gordon Gempel, a swarthy, thick-set man with big eyes who ran the Gempel Insurance Agency, was a fixture in the community. The agency had been established by his grandfather, who also farmed and ran a butcher shop. Gempel, the classic big-hearted American guy, could have stepped out of a Norman Rockwell painting for the cover of *The Saturday Evening Post*. An outspoken man with great common sense, he was generous and kind, especially to elderly people. He was an active Republican and a great fan of University of Michigan football.

Gempel could be feisty, too. Years later, he would knock heads with federal tax collectors and refuse to file tax returns for several years, though he estimated his taxes and paid them during that period and kept his books open to the government. Gempel loved a drink, male conversation and sports, both as a participant and a spectator. He bowled and played tennis. He was an enthusiastic supporter of the Detroit Lions, the Detroit Tigers and the hometown Harbor Beach Pirates football team. He sang in the Men's Glee Club, and was a member of the Jaycees, the Touchdown Club and the Rotary Club. And he was always on the lookout for people he could welcome into his community.

Marlowe entered the drug store and began to check out the display of paperback books. Gempel bought a cigar and asked the druggist if he knew the identity of this baby-faced man (who at the time was pushing 50). He's the writer, the druggist said, the one living in the Resort Association near the lake. Gempel knew the story of how Marlowe had gotten there, and it was mildly intriguing. Helen Hamilton had advertised for a writer to rent the upstairs room in her rustic, cabin-like home. She already was renting space to an elderly man and wanted another quiet tenant, this time a woman. Instead, the applicant turned out to be Marlowe: an upbeat but reserved widower who made his living churning out tales of blood and thunder. She had taken to him immediately, and the relationship proved congenial.

A great situation for a writer, Gempel thought. Even if he's not making much money, he's living in the nicest part of town. The 75 acres of the Harbor Beach Resort Association community extended three-quarters of a mile along Lake Huron with magnificent views of the harbor and breakwall. Large oak trees and towering pines shaded the 42 split-level cedar log cottages, which carried sumptuous (some might say pretentious) names, such as "Al Araf," "Eagle Lodge," and "Broadhearth." It was said that Henry Ford had summered there in the 1920s and Gempel was fond of saying that the Wurlitzer family, of calliope fame, had a cottage there. Residents were given to the kind of celebrations seldom seen in a small Michigan town. A few years after Marlowe moved there, the Resort Association put on a "Fiji Island Fiesta," decorating the interior of the clubhouse with real and artificial flowers, building an outdoor grass hut surrounded by flaring Hawaiian torches, outfitting waitresses in sarongs and instructing them to perform native dances. Female guests wore muu-muus, men cutaways and stovepipe hats.

For day-to-day recreation, the community offered a swimming pool and tennis courts. The golf course lay across the former Chesapeake and Ohio railroad tracks, near the 1898-vintage clubhouse, where most residents ate their evening meals, and some enjoyed the regular Friday night dance. Many owned sailboats, and enjoyed sailboat races in the harbor. A number of the cottages there had been owned by the same families for generations and the Resort Association board ensured people who bought in were worthy. You had to be approved as a member, and once you were in, you owned your cottage but not the land it occupied. If you wanted to sell, lease or rent your cottage, you had to get permission from the board. The community had its own security force, with an armed guard at the entrance.

When Gempel saw Marlowe in the drugstore, the insurance man didn't approach the writer, but did decide to ask him to speak at the Rotary Club. The chance to do so arose a few days later when Marlowe came to Gempel's office to buy car insurance. Gempel made his pitch and Marlowe, a gregarious man always seeking ways to promote his work, agreed. With that conversation, they began a friendship that flourished for nearly 20 years. Yet, there was a secret side to Marlowe that Gempel would look back on with suspicion.

"Dan came here under false pretenses, I found out many years later," Gempel told the author in 2005. "We were close. We shared rooms at Republican meetings, motel rooms. He had a key to our office. He used our office equipment whenever he wanted. He was just a real good friend. But I found out later, no question, he was tied in with this Nussbaum…and when he left Harbor Beach, he left with Nussbaum, who wouldn't even stay for dinner because he wanted out of here."

Gempel apparently thought Marlowe had known Nussbaum— and had been involved in nefarious activities—before the writer showed up in Harbor Beach. While that probably was not true, Gempel's misgivings suggested a thread that ran through Harbor Beach's attitude toward Marlowe. On the one hand, members of the community embraced him. On the other, they were puzzled and intrigued by his obscure connections to the larger world. Years later, after he left Harbor Beach, the true feelings of many local residents surfaced, said Jamie Iseler, a copy editor at the *Jackson Citizen Patriot* in Jackson, Michigan, whose father Don typed manuscripts for Marlowe.

"Rumors ran wild, since he fostered a sort of mysterious air when it came to his background and his life outside Harbor Beach," Jamie Iseler said. "I recall hearing years ago that he was somehow involved with the CIA, and also that he had to leave town quickly because he was being hunted by mobsters."

K. Don Williamson, who was city engineer for Harbor Beach during the time Marlowe was there, said he had heard, possibly from Gempel, that Marlowe was "a bagman for the mob." Marlowe never talked about his life prior to moving to Harbor Beach, Williamson said.

David Krueger Sr., a mechanic and owner of a NAPA Auto Parts store who later served on the City Council with Marlowe, also felt that the writer was not very forthcoming.

"He was quiet, pretty secretive," Krueger said. "He kind of impressed me as having a shroud of mysteriousness about him—how he came to town, when he left town." But Krueger wasn't put off by Marlowe's personality. "I liked him," Krueger said. "He was a kind of quiet, friendly, smooth type person. He would listen and nod his head, but if you said something he didn't think was right, he would step in. He wasn't a guy who dominated a conversation. I would call him a quiet-spoken person, a gentleman. He could fit in with the elite, or with a guy like me who greases cars and changes oil."

In addition to speaking to the Rotary Club, Marlowe took on at least one other engagement early in his stay in Harbor Beach. On Feb. 15, 1962, the *Harbor Beach Times* ran a photo of him, backed by shelves of books, holding a paperback copy of *The Name of the Game Is Death*, and looking uncharacteristically grim (and rather porcine). The short article imparted that he would describe "a few of his experiences in the world of publishing" to the local Book Review Club on Feb. 19. The piece noted the favorable review of the novel in *The New York Times*.

"Marlowe, a member of both the Mystery Writers of America and the British Crime Writers Association, is currently working on a book dealing with the fast-paced adventures of a young and attractive confidence woman," the article said. That plot referred to *Cold Cash*, a book Marlowe never sold.

Though Marlowe kept to himself to get his writing done, he was anything but a recluse. Socializing in public was his preferred form of entertainment. Several years later, he would say he didn't own a TV and rarely went to movies. When he was out and about, he plunged into the life of the community. He joined the Rotary Club, did a great deal of research on the history of Harbor Beach, composed a slide show to send to a sister city, and created an exchange-student program. He was "a darn good" Rotarian, Gempel said. Marlowe sold tickets for the spaghetti and chicken dinners the club sponsored to raise money for community functions, loved to attend the football and basketball games at Community High School in Harbor Beach, and volunteered to sell tickets to those games, too.

He also became a fixture downtown at Smalley's Bar and Grill. There, he spent his evenings at "the longest bar in Huron County," smoking, talking sports and politics, periodically lifting a single finger to order another 7 and 7 (Seagram's Seven Crown whiskey and 7UP), and playing pool ("Hell of a shot!" he'd exclaim whenever an opponent sank a ball).

"He was always interesting, never ran out of something interesting to talk about," Gempel said. "He had a wealth of knowledge, a mind that wouldn't quit." Marlowe was always up for a trip to Detroit to watch Tigers baseball or Lions football, and he hadn't lost his love for gambling, though he didn't play the part of the high roller.

Gempel played poker with him at Smalley's Bar, at the local country club and at Gempel's home, mostly five-card stud and seven-card stud, occasionally with wild cards. The game was dollar-limit, fairly cheap even for a small town in the 1960s. ("A guy would say, 'I had a bad night, I lost $30,'" Krueger said of similar games played in the 1970s). Marlowe was a good poker player, Gempel recalled, but not flashy. He never revealed whether he had won or lost in a session. Marlowe still apparently got down bets on big sporting events and horse races, too, Gempel said, sometimes using "connections" in Las Vegas, possibly through Joe Capling, who owned Smalley's Bar. Occasionally, when Capling went over to Canada, he'd take money from Marlowe and buy Lotto tickets, Krueger said.

For the first year, Marlowe lived the easy life among his fellow Harbor Beach residents, secluding himself in the morning to concentrate on his writing, venturing forth in the afternoon and evening to socialize. He was a bit of a phenomenon locally; though he was one of the guys, he stood out. In a small town in which casual dress was the rule, he often wore a sport coat and tie. Unlike the local men, who occasionally neglected their duties with the razor, he was always clean-shaven. Though he was different, he might not have become fascinating had it not been for lurid events elsewhere.

Al Nussbaum and Bobby Wilcoxson had gone to ground after the fatal Brooklyn robbery. The FBI had picked up Curry on Feb. 13 near his mother's home in Brooklyn, and Curry had spilled the whole story of the Brooklyn bank job. With that information, agents had found Nussbaum's stash of weapons in Buffalo. Nussbaum had been equipped to go to war. Agents confiscated two Finnish-made Lahti anti-tank guns equipped with armor-piercing ammunition, a Thompson submachine gun, 14 Schmeisser submachine guns, dozens of handguns, four bullet-proof vests and thousands of rounds of ammo.

Even with the pressure on, the robbers had to make a move. They needed more money. Wilcoxson was trying to raise it by passing Bank of America travelers' checks they had stolen. He and his girlfriend Jackie Rose, who had dumped the truck driver and returned to Bobby, visited the Teplitzski Hotel in Atlantic City, New Jersey, and cashed 19 checks. Then they traveled to the World's Fair in Seattle, Washington, to pass more. Checking into the Hungerford Hotel, they set to work quickly, but flunked their very first check-passing attempt and had to leave town.

During part of this period, Nussbaum was also away from his usual East Coast haunts, hiding out in Juarez, Mexico, just across the border from El Paso. During this sojourn, he told Marlowe, he crossed the border, bought a gray kitten he named "Gringo," and brought him back to Juarez. The kitten died a week later. This story would have seemed almost too pat, a retelling of the boyhood loss of a kitten by the protagonist of *The Name of the Game Is Death*, except that Nussbaum turned out to be a cat lover later in life, when he was living in Los Angeles.

By late June, 1962, Wilcoxson and Nussbaum were in Pennsylvania. On June 26, they robbed the Fidelity Federal Savings and Loan Association in Philadelphia. Wilcoxson crashed the bank himself, brandishing a .45-caliber automatic, while Nussbaum hovered in the car, also armed with a .45, as well as with an M1A1 carbine with a 30-round banana clip. They got only $160. Wilcoxson later provided that version in court testimony.

For some reason, however, Marlowe offered a different account in *Anatomy of a Crime Wave*, saying Wilcoxson carried out the crime spontaneously and alone. The robber did so, Marlowe said, because he had been infuriated by an FBI-inspired *Reader's Digest* article about him and Nussbaum. Marlowe wrote that the *Digest* splashed Wilcoxson's photo in promo ads in newspapers such as the *Philadelphia Inquirer*, which ran it June 26. The magazine called Wilcoxson the "Most Wanted Criminal Since Dillinger." And it offered a $10,000 reward for information leading to the capture of the pair. Why this might have upset Wilcoxson isn't clear. After all, he prided himself on his "profession," and getting top billing like this over other slam-artists would seemingly have been to his liking. Later in his life, he would brag about the article to anyone who would listen.

Bobby was always hair-triggered, however, and, according to Marlowe, this was one of the occasions when he went off.

"I got mad," he [Wilcoxson] said, "and decided to show them."

He "showed them" by going downtown without saying a word to anyone and walking in on the Fidelity Savings and Loan Association and conducting a one-man stickup. With his bad eye and so many people to watch he couldn't control the action, however, and was frightened off before he was able to get his hands on any substantial amount of money, the association's loss having been variously estimated at amounts ranging from $120 to $420.

The account is puzzling. Court records show Wilcoxson often worked alone inside a bank, so it's not clear why his physical limitations would have affected his success on the Fidelity job. Marlowe reports the story as if he got it from Wilcoxson, but it's unlikely he even spoke to Wilcoxson. If he had, Wilcoxson's ego most likely would have kept him from admitting he had been "frightened off." In fact, in court testimony, Wilcoxson tried to put the best face possible on the debacle by commenting, "Even the best make mistakes."

Bobby was a braggart, but, for the most part, he had gotten good at heisting. On June 29, three days after the Fidelity job, he competently handled the inside-the-bank role all by himself when he and Nussbaum hit the Western Pennsylvania National Bank in North Versailles Township near Pittsburgh. Nussbaum drove one of the two getaway cars. The official take was $4,373.

During this period, Wilcoxson and Nussbaum had rentals in the Philadelphia area. Nussbaum was living in the Germantown section, seldom leaving his room except to buy food or hair dye. To explain his reclusiveness, he told everyone he was a free-lance writer. True to his nature, though, he wasn't content with a simple cover story. Throughout his life of crime, he put a lot of time into inventing clever ruses for throwing off witnesses and police. Nussbaum had placed a spirit-gum-attached mustache on Curry to disguise him for the Brooklyn robbery, but the veteran heister used subtler strategies, too. Later in life, he told a friend he sometimes would commit a robbery in a particularly noticeable suit, throw that suit away and keep a similar suit a couple of sizes too small for him in his living quarters, so that if he were ever caught, the size of the suit wouldn't fit the evidence against him. His thinking apparently was along the lines of the argument about the glove in the O.J. Simpson case, "If it doesn't fit, you must acquit."

In regard to his cover story as a writer, Nussbaum added pieces here and there to make it more believable. To some degree, he was forced to do so. People kept asking about the writing life, and he had to put them off with vague answers. Realizing this sounded suspicious, Nussbaum bought half-a-dozen books about writing and several on the biographies of famous writers. He also subscribed to writers' magazines and allowed them to protrude conspicuously from his mailbox.

Being a detail man, Nussbaum also bought a desk, a used typewriter and a ream of paper, and situated them in his apartment so that anyone who happened to come to the door would be able to see them. He bought a tape recorder, prepared a tape of himself banging away at the typewriter, and played it most of the day, so that anyone passing his door would hear it. He even dressed like a writer, in a tweed coat with leather elbow patches.

"Then a funny thing happened," Nussbaum later wrote in an article called *Turning Sentences into Words: Writing in Prison* for a collection of articles published by the Mystery Writers of America called *I, Witness: Personal Encounters with Crime by Members of the Mystery Writers of America*. "I was so immersed in writing lore that I began to identify with real writers. I was able to appreciate many of the difficulties they had faced and overcome; and, alone as I was, it wasn't hard to imagine how a writer might feel, sitting alone in front of his typewriter, confronting miles of blank paper and the danger of snow blindness."

A couple of weeks after that, Nussbaum was back in his hideout in Philadelphia, reading to pass the time on a rainy day. He polished off *The Name of the Game Is Death*, and the book resonated with his life. The main character was as cold as Wilcoxson; that's what grabbed him. He decided to write a fan letter to the man whose name was on the cover, so he called Marlowe's publisher in

New York, tracked down the writer's agent, and got Marlowe's address. But then Nussbaum, uncertain he had the skills to write a well-crafted letter, decided instead to call Marlowe in Harbor Beach. He did so, using the pseudonym "Carl Fischer."

To Marlowe, getting a call from a fan was not unusual.

"My fan presented himself on the telephone as a frustrated writer who had made a few unsuccessful attempts to get his ideas down on paper," Marlowe wrote in an article called *Odyssey* for *I, Witness*. "He dissected the story line of my book intelligently, inquired how I had created some of my effects, and asked where I had obtained some of my information.

"I answered in some detail, all the more so since my caller was cheerful, incisive, and irreverent, qualities I happen to appreciate. Within a week, I received a follow-up letter from him, going over much of the same ground. I answered the letter, heard nothing more, and forgot about it."

(Marlowe later told mystery writer Joe Gores a different version of this story: In this one, Nussbaum also called using a false name, but told Marlowe, "I've always wanted to be writer, I'm always sitting around hotel rooms with my partner." Marlowe asked, "What do you and your partner do?" Nussbaum answered, "We rob banks. We're going to rob a bank tomorrow.")

The robber's career was moving fast—downward. On Sept. 19, 1962, a couple of months after he spoke to Marlowe, Nussbaum teamed with Wilcoxson to rob the Western Pennsylvania National Bank branch they'd hit for $4,373 in June. Once again, Nussbaum declined to go into the bank with his partner, but this time it cost him. Wilcoxson reported that he carried off $31,000 (the official take was listed as $28,901), but gave Nussbaum only $500, showing contempt for what he saw as his partner's lack of moxie.

"I said if he was not man enough to go in with me, he wasn't man enough to share equal gain in the robbery," Wilcoxson explained in testimony at their later trial for bank robbery and murder. "I said, 'You either go in and rob the bank or I will go in and rob it. But I am not—I won't rob the bank twice with you sitting in the car.'" According to Marlowe's account, Nussbaum "reacted explosively: a shoot-out was narrowly averted." The bad feelings lingered, and two days later Wilcoxson and his girlfriend left Philadelphia.

CHAPTER 7:
Be Careful About Brazil

LOOKING AT THE RECORD, THERE'S NO EVIDENCE MARLOWE EVER crossed the line legally, unless you go to extremes and count the dirty stories he published, sometimes under arch pseudonyms. For the most part, Marlowe was a jovial public-servant type, a face among the community leader faces displayed at City Hall. Was there a genuinely shady side to Marlowe? Some thought so. To the burghers of Harbor Beach, Marlowe's reticence gave off the whiff of sinister doings. He had been a professional gambler, a man familiar with the fast shuffle, the fixed race, the set of weighted dice. But there was no evidence he ever used those ploys himself.

Those concerns might have lurked forever on the perimeter of his public persona if it weren't for a visit he received in 1962 at his cozy retreat near the lake. He was, as usual, hard at work conjuring criminal fictions, when the rattle of his typewriter was interrupted by a knock on the door downstairs. He told the tale in *Odyssey*:

> In November, I was summoned from my typewriter in the upstairs workroom to meet two men who had come to the house to see me. When I descended the stairs, the men were in opposite corners of the room I entered, as far apart as they could get.

"We're from the FBI," the younger man said, showing me his opened billfold.

I have friends who play practical jokes as a way of life. I didn't think they were from the FBI. I examined the Department of Justice gold shield carefully, then changed my mind. They were from the FBI. "What can I do for you?" I asked.

The agent produced two Post Office circulars of the Man Wanted type. "Do you know either of these two men?"

I looked at the circulars. "No, I don't."

"We think you do."

"Then think again. I don't."

"We think you do," the older agent said, "because this man telephoned you from Philadelphia in July." He pointed to one of the circulars.

I laughed. The most prominent words on the circulars were WANTED, BANK ROBBERY and DANGEROUS. "Called me? You're mistaken. Certainly no bank robber ever called—say, I did get a long-distance phone call from Philadelphia in July."

"We know you did. We checked it out. And we'd like to hear about it."

I explained the circumstances of the fan telephone call. "That's all there was to it," I said. "Except that he wrote me a letter afterward."

"We'd like to see the letter," the younger agent said.

I found it in my files, and only after both men had read it did the atmosphere begin to relax slightly.

Al Nussbaum had been run to ground, and investigators tossing his apartment in Philadelphia had turned up the Marlowe connection. After years on the run, doing banks up and down the coast, Nussbaum had been snared through the involvement of people close to him. The perfect noir denouement. It had occurred about a week before Marlowe got his visit from the FBI, and Marlowe might have written the final scene himself. If he had, he might have done it this way:

Nussbaum hit the brakes on the blue Chevrolet and it cornered hard, the Chevy's tail end bucking, its tires skidding in the November snow-slush as he swung down a one-way street the wrong way. He punched the accelerator, saw the needle on the speedometer tickling 70 per. Ahead of him, brakes squealed, headlights bounced, metal swerved, civilians scrambled for safety. He glanced at the loaded .22-caliber rifle on the seat next to him, felt the live grenades nuzzling his sides through his fatigue jacket. This was where it was going to end, where it had all begun. Buffalo, New York. He shouldn't have come back. Three hours with his wife on two long drives between Buffalo and Niagara Falls. A chance to ask about his baby, Alison, 19 months old. His shot at conventional happiness, but it was all fading now.

He cornered, checked the rear-view. The FBI cars had somehow dropped away, he had the jump on them for just a moment. Now, to try to duck out completely. He doused the headlights, snapped quick right into a parking space, trying to keep the tires from screeching, killed the engine. It was quiet, the edged wind hissing outside the windows. Time to make his move: the rifle, the grenades. He thought it over quickly and decided, no. No more blood. Maybe that's what he had been thinking all along, when he'd stopped rushing into banks with Wilcoxson. No more blood. No more life. He shook a bottle of Seconal tablets from his pocket, hesitated slightly, then rattled a stack of them into his palm. They struggled down his throat in a series of hard swallows. The barbiturates gusted through him like a drowsy wind. He flattened himself on the front seat. Darkness pushed into him. Muddled by the drugs, he was going to sleep, but he couldn't get there. Suddenly, the street went crazy. Shrieking tires, shouting voices, bumps on the windows. The front doors flew open and the guns were at him. Hands slapped down on him, gripped his arms, pulled him out. Pulling him toward the electric chair. The executioners squeezed a wet sponge on your head to pop the juice into your brain. He knew that. He knew machines. Through his muzziness, he felt the cold, wet sponge.

According to *Anatomy of a Crime Wave*, the events leading up to the final scene had developed this way: Nussbaum had decided to leave the country and had made arrangements to do so. In looking over the countries to which he might flee, he had narrowed down his choices. The article didn't say what his favored choices were, but they apparently were Russia and Brazil, leaning toward the latter. He had been careful about Brazil.

> "Exile in a foreign country is a trickier proposition than is generally realized," Nussbaum afterwards noted. "Countries like Brazil which would not have extradited me as a wanted man in the U.S. might easily have deported me on their own if there had been any illegality involved in my entry into the country. The problem was to obtain both valid credentials and also assurance at the other end of the line against extradition. Forged papers were obtainable, as were altered stolen papers, but once I reached the Top Ten (on the FBI's Wanted list) both price and risk were prohibitive. I certainly didn't want to risk deportation and the publicity that goes with it for something as silly as fraudulent entry into a country. What I needed was valid credentials from an official source (not U.S.) and an assurance against extradition by an official of the country of my choice. After a hell of a lot of digging and scraping, I finally had paper and assurances good for either of two countries. I didn't make use of them immediately because there was something I wanted to do first."

What Nussbaum wanted to do was to convince his 25-year-old wife Lolly to come with him and to bring their 19-month-old daughter, Alison. He'd arranged the papers so that would have been possible. Now all he had to do was to get her to agree. On Nov. 3, he called the apartment in Buffalo where she was living with her parents. Her mother, Alice Majchrowicz, 46, answered the phone and recognized Nussbaum's voice. Without admitting she knew the caller, she passed the phone to Lolly, who had a brief, murmured conversation, hung up, threw on a coat and left, saying she had an errand she'd forgotten to complete.

Alice Majchrowicz paced the floor and wrestled with her decision, but she'd been heading in this direction for a long time. After a few minutes, she went to the phone and dialed the number for the local FBI office. She told the agents that Nussbaum had called and her daughter had gone out to meet him. They quickly responded. FBI agents arrived at the apartment shortly to await Lolly's return:

"It's not a decision I'd want to have to make more than once in a lifetime," Mrs. Majchrowicz said grimly. "I'd always had a good relationship with Al. But if he was in town, he was there for only one purpose—to talk Lolly into going away with him. I didn't think she'd be willing to settle for life on the run, but I was afraid of his reaction on her. He could always talk her into anything. I had my daughter and granddaughter to consider. That's why I made the call."

When Lolly came back, at first she wouldn't admit she'd been with Nussbaum, but before long, she broke down. He'd lost weight and looked tired, she said. That concerned her. He'd changed his appearance, was now wearing a mustache, had dyed his hair black, and wore dark horn-rimmed glasses. Twice they had driven back and forth to Niagara Falls. He'd told her he was tired of running, and he was afraid he might be recognized anywhere. When they stopped at a restaurant, he had her go in and buy two cups of coffee.

"They won't take me alive," he'd said, and he referred to some type of poison pills that he was carrying. The FBI agents saw their opening: If she didn't help them catch him, they said, he'd be killed when they did get him. Wasn't it better to have him alive and in prison? How long could he really expect to run? In the end, she gave in to the arguments. She was to meet him again at 1:15 a.m. that morning in the lobby of the downtown Buffalo Statler-Hilton Hotel. The agents came up with a plan, and she reluctantly agreed.

By 1 a.m., the trap was set. Lolly was waiting in the lobby of the hotel, with more than 20 FBI agents, most in cars, scattered around outside, waiting for the rendezvous. Near the appointed time, the bank robber's blue Chevrolet eased by on the street outside, its occupant giving the hotel the once-over. At the last moment Lolly couldn't bring herself to betray her husband. She waved him off, and the race was on.

After Nussbaum was captured, some who knew him criticized Lolly's mother for turning him in, particularly in light of the fact that she collected a $10,000 reward from a magazine for doing so. Nussbaum was more realistic.

"Lay off my mother-in-law," Nussbaum told his friends. "I had my problems; she had hers. I don't hold it against her. I knew what I was doing, or thought I did. Do you think I'd have placed my neck in the Buffalo noose for anyone except Lolly? Where I made my mistake was in underestimating how badly they wanted me and the pressure they'd put on to make the capture."

With Nussbaum in custody, but not talking, FBI agents pursued every avenue that might lead them to Wilcoxson. In Nussbaum's car, they found a number of documents, including one carrying a Philadelphia address. That led them to Nussbaum's apartment, which he had deserted some time before, leaving some of his belongings. In the letter Nussbaum had sent to Marlowe, the robber had told the writer he was going to show *The Name of the Game Is Death* to a friend who would be sure to be interested in it. That caused agents to surmise that Wilcoxson was living near Nussbaum. They put on the full-court press, doing a house-to-house search. They didn't find Wilcoxson, but they found enough.

"They shouldn't have been able to find a thing," Nussbaum said. "I'd warned Bobby to stay away from Philadelphia over three weeks before I was captured. I warned him to clean out his place, and mine, too. He wound up leaving a hot trail, instead of a cold one. He even made the mistake of buying a car for cash in Philadelphia and being seen with it at his apartment there."

The FBI found the apartment in which Wilcoxson and his girlfriend had been living most of the summer under the names Charles and Barbara Dix. Interviews indicated that the two had changed their appearances. Wilcoxson had shaved part of his hair and whitened the rest to appear older; his girlfriend had also dyed her hair. He'd started wearing a heavy black mustache and horn-rimmed glasses and had changed his alias to Robert Thomas Bronson, she'd changed hers to Gloria Banks, and was pretending to be his daughter. And, most important, they'd gone to Baltimore. FBI agents tracked them to a row house on Walterswood Road in north Baltimore. Then they conducted a 12-hour stakeout so they could snatch Wilcoxson when he emerged and was out of reach of his main stash of guns. That happened on the morning of Saturday, Nov. 10. The couple walked out and started to enter a car parked at the curb. They were swarmed. Wilcoxson was seized before he could get a hand on his .38 pistol. She was grabbed running back inside in an effort to reach her baby.

Searching their residence, the agents had good reason to be happy they had pursued the strategy they had. Inside were several more handguns, two live grenades, a sawed-off M-2 carbine, 400 rounds of ammunition, a two-way radio, various police and press badges, and a passport case. They found a loaded and cocked .45 automatic under the mattress on the bed. Neatly stacked in a suitcase was $21,000 in bills of denominations ranging from $1 to $100, obviously bank robbery loot. The agents also found keys that would unlock and start any General Motors car, an aid to stealing autos for robberies or getaways.

Though Marlowe's first contact with the bank-robbing crew was made with Nussbaum, his early focus in researching *Anatomy of a Crime Wave* was on interviewing Wilcoxson and telling his story. It's possible the writer did so because Wilcoxson's personality more clearly paralleled that of the Marlowe character who would come to be known as "Earl Drake." Drake, however, was a well-grounded sociopath, and his real-life counterpart wasn't. Drake, for instance, wouldn't have given up everything for a woman (though he at times went to great lengths to save—and get revenge for—his girlfriend, Hazel). Also, Drake had a strong, reality-focused approach to life, and Wilcoxson did not.

After his arrest, Wilcoxson called on a high-powered Florida attorney he had used in the past, Joseph Varon. Varon wasn't pleased with the approach the robber was taking to a situation that might result in his execution. Wilxcoxson was telling FBI agents everything he'd done. "He used to be the most close-mouthed man on earth about things that mattered," Varon told Marlowe in an interview for *Anatomy of a Crime Wave*. "I asked him why he thought he needed a lawyer if he was prepared to admit everything. 'They said if I talked they'd let Jackie go,' he told me. 'That's all that matters. I'll pay for what I did. You just get Jackie off.' His conversation rambled and backtracked, and I frankly didn't think he was making a hundred percent good sense.

I went back to Florida and told his father that after Bobby's performance to date I'd be fortunate to save his life."

Wilcoxson and Jackie wound up in the Erie County Jail in Buffalo. Nussbaum, who was being held there, was shortly transferred down to Brooklyn to plead. A second attorney was appointed for Wilcoxson to help with the Buffalo charges. This lawyer talked to his client and began to doubt his sanity. A court-appointed psychiatrist found that Wilcoxson showed a strong tendency toward psychosis. At a court hearing in Buffalo, the head-shrinker testified that the robber demonstrated "the suspicions, distrust and grandiosity of the paranoid." He was, the psychiatrist said, "an abnormal individual with emotional disturbances." Even so, the court found him competent to stand trial.

Marlowe had planned to cover this hearing to gather material for the *Anatomy of a Crime Wave* article he had already successfully pitched, but, as he described in *I, Witness*, the FBI gave him the fast shuffle.

In December 1962, I drove from my home on the shore of Lake Huron in Michigan across Canada to Buffalo, New York. The purpose of my trip was to attend a preliminary hearing in federal court in Buffalo. The hearing was for one of a pair of bank robbers who had been captured the previous month after a two-year assault upon the banks of the country during which they had staged brazen daylight robberies at more banks and escaped with more money than John Dillinger during his entire career.

I arrived in Buffalo a day early and went around to the local office of the FBI, where I introduced myself as a writer who had been assigned by *The Saturday Evening Post* to do a lengthy article on the bank robbers, one of whom in a bizarre circumstance had involved himself in my life.

The hearing was scheduled for 11:00 A.M. the following morning. At 9 A.M. I received a phone call in my hotel room from an FBI agent who informed me that the hearing had been postponed until 2 P.M. He suggested that we have lunch together in the interval.

I agreed, and after a leisurely meal I walked to the courtroom where I found that the original hearing, far from being postponed, had taken place at the originally scheduled time. The FBI, it appeared, had wanted no writers present for a hearing in a case in which the FBI appeared none too favorably even in their own eyes. Twice during the robbers' two-year run, the FBI had had its hands on one of the pair only to have him talk his way loose.

Marlowe goes on to say that he complained to the prosecutor, but wasn't allowed to interview Wilcoxson, despite having permission both from Wilcoxson and his attorney to do so. It appears the writer never did get to talk to the violent bank robber. In his stories later in life, Marlowe subtly conflated Wilcoxson with Nussbaum, so it often wasn't clear which he was discussing. For instance, he says the FBI twice "had its hands on one of the pair only to have him talk his way loose." It's not evident to which robber he is referring in each case (or to what incidents he refers). Later in his *I, Witness* account, Marlowe says of Nussbaum that he, with his partner, "had been written up in *Reader's Digest* as "Most Wanted Criminal Since John Dillinger." The *Reader's Digest* stories, however, show the "Most Wanted" designation was pegged to Wilcoxson, not Nussbaum.

However, by the time Marlowe wrote the *I, Witness* article, his relationship with Nussbaum was well developed, and Marlowe may have wanted to give Nussbaum featured billing. Nussbaum's exploits were, after all, a professional plus for Marlowe. He wrote in *I, Witness* that: "The fact that my novel about a fictitious bank robber had received a written testimonial from a real bank robber created a small stir in the literary world. It gave my writing career a boost at a time when it badly needed a boost…"

Marlowe was making the most of the connection during 1963, while Nussbaum, Wilcoxson and Curry were awaiting their fates. Nussbaum and Wilcoxson had escaped the risk of a death sentence by agreeing to plead guilty to many of their crimes and testify against Curry, the small fish in the bank-robbing crew. Curry, after initially cooperating with the police, decided he wasn't being offered a good enough deal, so he fought the charges and asserted he was only a tangential player in the Brooklyn bank robbery. Without his testimony, prosecutors were forced to turn the tables on him and get help from the really bad guys.

All this drama provided plenty of grist for Marlowe's promotion mill. A June 20, 1963, article in the *Harbor Beach Times* noted that Marlowe had recently been in Chicago to be interviewed on "Tony Wetzel's breezy CBS radio program" originating from McCormick Place on the Lake Michigan waterfront.

"Under discussion was Marlowe's forthcoming *Saturday Evening Post* article on the bank robbers...which was provoked by Nussbaum's reaction to Marlowe's Gold Medal book about a bank robber, *The Name of the Game Is Death*. Discussed also was his next from Gold Medal, *Strongarm*, due on the stands in August or September."

The article went on to say that Marlowe had appeared as one of six writers on "At Random," Carter Davidson's three-hour open forum television program on WBBM-TV. The participants had discussed "The Writer and His Place in Contemporary Society."

Marlowe's appearance on the program had been arranged by a friend, Alexandra Jane Benchly, a member of the Publicity Club of Chicago and also executive editor of the *Totem Pole*, the publication of the Seven Arts Club, of which Marlowe was "an honorary council member." Marlowe also was a house guest of Benchly while in Chicago. A fiction writer and founder of the Quill Pushers Round Table in Chicago, Benchly later garnered credits for at least two short stories in mystery magazines: "The Glass Casket" in the December 1964 issue of *The Saint Detective Magazine* and "Albert Wept" in the March 1966 issue of *Edgar Wallace Mystery Magazine*. Her novel, *If the Heart Be Hasty*, published in 1969, was praised by Marlowe as a "warmly rendered recollection-tale of Chicago and an unspecified area of the Michigan north woods country in the 30's and 40's."

In September 1963, Gold Medal published *Strongarm*, Marlowe's first novel since *The Name of the Game Is Death*, which had come out a year and a half before. It had been a long drought for a writer of paperback thrillers, whose book advances were only about $1,500 each. *Strongarm* (working title: *Karma*) is among Marlowe's best. The "*Criminals at Large*" column in *The New York Times Book Review* said: "Espionage effectively crosses the path of the gangster novel in this one. When you intend a simple heist and find you've lifted the briefcase of a secret courier, containing $720,000 in cash and a packet of secret plans, you become a focus of interest for forces quite outside the mobs you're used to dealing with. An elaborate and somewhat mad story told with enough vigor and bite to make it highly satisfactory reading."

The book follows the adventures of Pete Karma, a Korean War vet and all-around tough guy who works as the night bartender in a mob joint in Detroit. Karma, who has done time after being set up for a murder he didn't commit, winds up with the courier's briefcase. He and his girlfriend Lynn—and eventually her cousin Gussie—flee across the country with foreign agents on their tail. Patriotic mobsters help them beat the foreign bad guys. Also, we get the first sample of the spanking fetish that would pepper much of Marlowe's work when Karma, discovering a naked Gussie rummaging through his closet, gives her an open-handed smack on the rear.

The quality of the book kept Marlowe on top of the market, and the publicity about Marlowe's relationship with Nussbaum kept the writer in the minds of mystery publishers. That was true even though *The Saturday Evening Post* never published *Anatomy of a Crime Wave*. Josef Hoffmann, writer of *Playing with Fire: Dan J. Marlowe, Al Nussbaum and Earl Drake*, said the *Post* editors backed off for political reasons:

"Publication was stopped…as a result of objections made by the FBI to the editors," Hoffmann wrote. "Apparently the FBI was afraid that the documentary about the bank robber, written as it was with such exactitude and verve, could lead to imitations or to the creation of a legend."

That appears to be more or less what happened. Marlowe retained in his files a copy of a letter from an unidentified *Saturday Evening Post* editor rejecting the piece. In it, the editor cited not only the FBI influence but the severe financial distress the *Post* was experiencing after being hit with a libel judgment of more than $3 million (later reduced) by Georgia Athletic Director Wally Butts. On March 23, 1963, the magazine had accused Butts of conspiring with Alabama football coach Bear Bryant to fix an Alabama-Georgia football game. The libel judgment followed. On Sept. 3, 1963, the editor wrote to Marlowe:

I have bad news for you; I've been instructed to reject the article. As I probably don't have to tell you, things have deteriorated rapidly around here since the Butts judgment against us. We had anticipated that we—as well as all magazine publishers—would be leaning over backward against the threat of a libel suit in the future, but in your particular case there was an unforeseen by-product that killed us. The judgment encouraged the FBI to renew the—I don't like to say "threat"—adjuration against publishing your article which, as you know, I barely succeeded in heading off once before. This time it's final. I have to regret to inform you that at the moment, at least, your article has no future with this magazine, and it would be manifestly unfair to keep you dangling.

You have worked hard on this story, and I'm sorry to see it turn out this way. I'm sure you will have no difficulty in replacing it elsewhere, although I'm also sure it's a small consolation to you at the moment.

I have enjoyed working with you on the article (and this is NOT just a stereotyped sign-off), and I hope our next project will work out more successfully.

I am putting through your guarantee immediately.

Though politics and fear of libel killed *Anatomy of a Crime Wave*, Marlowe had found a new friend, Nussbaum, who in time would collaborate with him on short stories and help Marlowe with his books, offering technical and criminal expertise. During this period, the writer also connected with another collaborator who would become far more significant in his writing life, though often hidden from public view. Marlowe, who was not a man of action, had formed a relationship with a bad-man adventurer in Nussbaum. Now he would form a much more productive relationship with a modest war hero: an action-loving aviator named William C. Odell.

CHAPTER 8:
Shadow Writers

THOUGH MARLOWE DID WORK BACKGROUNDING HIS NOVELS, HE never liked it. "I tend to shy away from research as much as possible (sometimes it isn't possible, of course) since time spent researching is time you can't spend writing," he once told a friend. This approach stemmed from two different attributes of Marlowe's personality. One was the usual writer's love of getting caught up in the dream of writing, the zen-like state of feeling the words, sentences and paragraphs notching together and flowing along. The other, oddly, was Marlowe's businesslike approach. As a businessman allocating resources, he realized that his strong suit was writing, and research was a task he should delegate to a partner less expert at the typewriter.

His discipline during the writing process followed a set pattern, which he described in a letter to a friend: "My daily routine is basically as follows: I'm a lifelong early riser, so I'm usually at the typewriter by 6:30 a.m., sometimes earlier. I work through then to 10:30 when the mail arrives. About half the time I get in a couple of hours in the afternoon. In the evening I seldom do original manuscript, unless I'm pressed for time, but quite often I do final drafts then. When I'm going well on a project, this routine can go on for 40 days or more. Then I get cabin fever and take off a few days."

Though this was his usual pattern, his letters indicate that at times he wrote for 16 hours straight while rushing to meet a deadline. And he wrote a lot: suspense novels, adventure stories, erotic stories and novels, newspaper and magazine articles, book reviews, columns, anything to keep the money flowing.

Research for the journalistic work, of course, mostly fell to him. Often, though, he simply didn't have time to do it for his novels, which required a great deal of fact-finding. Because they were action yarns replete with guns, planes, cars, radio sets and other gadgets, settings foreign and domestic, and military procedures, someone had to dig hard for authentic details. Marlowe solved this problem, sometimes for better, sometimes for worse, by working with collaborators.

One of these was Al Nussbaum. Many years later, Marlowe would write: "I haven't written a word for years about weapons and ballistics that he hasn't vetted for me. Ditto with locks and bolts and their manipulation. Ditto with safes, vaults and alarm systems. It's not every writer who is fortunate enough to get his technical information from the horse's mouth." Nussbaum also wrote drafts of short stories that Marlowe refashioned, worked with Marlowe on the never-published article *Anatomy of a Crime Wave* and reportedly talked him into writing *One Endless Hour*, the sequel to *The Name of the Game Is Death*, by churning out a 60-page outline of how the story should go.

Marlowe's collaborations didn't always go well, however. In 1962, he spent two months of his summer working with a former U.S. Marine captain on a novel to be sold to an editor at Doubleday named Lee Barker, who was acquainted with the Marine. The book, set in the Virgin Islands, dealt with military diving techniques and the attempted recovery of stolen government gold. Barker accepted an outline and appeared to be on the point of giving Marlowe and the Marine a contract. Then the Marine went through a messy divorce, and the project went bust.

A far more productive and long-lasting collaboration for Marlowe—in fact, the most important of his career—began two years later, a month before Nussbaum was sentenced for several bank robberies. In this instance, the collaborator would again be a former military officer, this time a U.S. Air Force veteran. His name was Col. William C. Odell, and his exploits would have fit right into a Marlowe novel. Consider the following scene (taken from life, but courtesy of yours truly):

> It was chilly barreling through the night sky over northern Luzon in the Philippines, but shortly it would be hot on the ground. March 13, 1945. Col. William C. Odell punched the bomb release in his P-61 Black Widow, heard the clicking and whirring of the unlatching process, knew he was releasing descending death. A few seconds passed as the Black Widow rushed on. Then, far below, a building shattered and exploded outward, the "whump" of the bomb sending wood and steel—and parts of men—cartwheeling outward and up. Odell swung the Black Widow toward the Japanese airstrip as the anti-aircraft fire sparked up from the ground—deadly yellow blossoms reaching out for him and the rest of his volunteer crew. This was where night fighting got hairy: you were able to sneak in, but trying to maneuver out in darkness could get you killed.

Dealing with this kind of situation was not a problem for Odell, a Mansfield, Ohio, resident with the charismatic look of a movie actor—Jeff Chandler or Clark Gable, perhaps. Odell glowed with savoir faire. A solid 5-foot-10, 180 pounds, he was good-humored but self-assured, able to immerse himself totally in his job in World War II because he didn't expect to return. Three years before the Luzon raid, when he was 27, he'd flown one of six bombers on a daring low-level raid against German airfields in the Netherlands. One of their escort fighter planes failed to return, but Odell made it through. "I knew if there was any action around he'd find it," his mother commented.

In his 23 years of military service, Odell collected 15 decorations and campaign medals, including the Legion of Merit, Distinguished Flying Cross and the Purple Heart. He flew 98 missions and had been scheduled to make the last air raid on Japan, a mission canceled when the Japanese surrendered.

His wartime service began in England in April 1942 as a member of the 1st Pursuit Squadron (Night Fighter) of the Eighth Air Force. He fought not only in Europe, but in Algeria and

Tunisia, Luzon and the Southern Philippines. He went on to command the Army's 420th and 547th Night Fighter Squadrons during the war, and later served as commandant of the Air Force's instrument flying and all-weather interceptor schools. In addition, he had spent several years running a cryptography department for the National Security Agency, a Defense Department intelligence agency responsible for analyzing and monitoring foreign communications. His retirement announcement also noted discreetly that he had "served overseas in Greece" from May 1953 to June 1956, a period in which he—one way or another—became quite familiar with intelligence activities.

Odell's efforts after the war to write fiction met some success in 1957, when he won the Air Force's annual short story contest. After that, he continued to work on his fiction, and finally got a break in January 1964, when he was 48. At the time, Odell was living in Ohio, running an advertising agency called Odell and Associates. One of his fiction manuscripts, a full-length thriller called *The Puppet Master*, had landed on the desk of Jim Reach, Marlowe's New York agent. Reach found the writing clunky and the dialogue stiff, but saw potential in the story, which was set in Washington, D.C. and involved an intelligence operation much like the technology-oriented National Security Agency. He told Odell that help from an established writer might get the story off the floor. Odell agreed. On Jan. 24, 1964, Reach wrote to Odell:

> Thank you for your letter accepting my suggestion for a collaboration on the rewriting of THE PUPPET MASTER; I hope and believe that the results of it will amply justify your decision.
>
> As is customary in such arrangements, our commission (10 % of all domestic sales) comes off the top, and the remaining 90% is shared equally between you and the collaborator.
>
> Your manuscript is going off today to our client in Michigan. If, after reading it, he agrees to undertake the revisions, I shall then tell you more about him and put you in touch with him personally.
>
> May events prove this to be the beginning of a fruitful relationship for all of us concerned.

Events eventually did so, but not in connection with *The Puppet Master*. Meanwhile, Nussbaum's future looked grim. He and Wilcoxson were to be sentenced in February. The system was deciding Nussbaum's fate, trying to calculate his personality and potential. Nussbaum told the U.S. Probation Office employee who prepared his pre-sentence report, Wilbur S. Clarke, that he spent his leisure time playing chess and engaging in gymnastics.

"Defendant was poised during the interview, was a glib talker, and appeared to possess above average mental intelligence as reflected by his score of 118 on Intelligence tests administered in school and at Federal institutions," Clarke wrote. This report, which went out over the signature of Chief U.S. Probation Officer Peter E. Saxon, was analytical, not judgmental. In that respect, it avoided the condemnation of Nussbaum issued by Peter Curry's lawyer. The lawyer contended that Nussbaum had lured Curry remorselessly into the deadly bank robbery. "Nussbaum may have a lot of good in him," the lawyer said, "but it is a perverted mind, put to ill use, shrewd, cynical, and will do whatever suits his purposes."

Nussbaum knew that justice officials could easily reach this conclusion, too. He couldn't make much of a case for himself, but he wasn't going down without a fight. In a letter quoted in his FBI file, he wrote to the sentencing judge, J.F. Dooling Jr., of the Eastern District of New York:

> I'll be thirty years old in a few months. I want you to keep in mind that I will have to serve almost all of the sentence you give. I want you to leave me some future to live for.
>
> I haven't always told the truth or, when telling the truth, told all of it, but all that I have written here is true.
>
> Take a chance on me.
>
> Give me a sentence that I can live with!

In the end, Dooling didn't cut Nussbaum much slack, but didn't destroy him. On Feb. 7, 1964, Wilcoxson got life in prison, as did Curry. Nussbaum did better, but not much. He was handed two consecutive sentences of 20 years for eight bank robberies and other offenses. That meant 40 years inside if he served the full terms. However, he only had to do eight years to be eligible for parole. That was something.

As for ever seeing Wilcoxson or Curry again (as if Nussbaum wanted to), the system put the kibosh on that. Wilcoxson was sent to the federal lock-up in Atlanta, Georgia, Curry (eventually) to prison in Lewisburg, Pennsylvania, and Nussbaum to the Federal Penitentiary in Leavenworth, Kansas. Even with years inside facing him, Nussbaum still showed his individuality. "The first act of Nussbaum upon his commitment to Leavenworth was to shave his head," noted the writer of the account in the FBI file. "Whether it was intended as an act of contrition or another gesture of defiance remains for the future to tell."

Marlowe continued to correspond with Nussbaum as the prison gates slammed shut. But the author was also having to devote a great deal of time to making a living. He and Odell slugged away through 1964 trying to get the manuscript for *The Puppet Master* in shape, but Reach was not always pleased with their efforts. Publishers were even less satisfied. On March 19, Reach criticized Marlowe's handling of dialogue between two characters named Carter and Weston: "I'm not very happy with the way this is going—Carter and Weston talk-talk-talking—need more action. You've taken Odell's solid exposition and put it into solid dialogue and made it less interesting."

The agent also felt Marlowe was including too much detail. Even so, on April 13, Reach said an editor at McGraw-Hill was "drooling" for the story. This apparently was David Segal, associate editor of the Trade Book Department. But before Segal passed judgment on *The Puppet Master*, it went to Thomas C. Wallace, an editor at Holt, Rinehart and Winston, as being the work of Dan J. Marlowe and "Arthur Hunt." Wallace turned it down on April 29. The editor said the Washington background was good, but "the characters seem pretty stock; the frustrated wife, the ambitious civil servant…The authors are missing the nuances and elaborating on the obvious." Reach, too, noted that Marlowe had slipped into a bad writing habit. Instead of simply using "said" and letting the context supply how the line was being delivered, the writer was adding adverbs like "acidly," "uneasily," and "thoughtfully."

Despite the turndown from Holt, Rinehart, and Winston, Marlowe told Reach on May 5 that he and Odell were "together for the long haul" and he wanted to continue to work on *The Puppet*

Master while also working on "the SCUBA story," presumably a reference to *Death Deep Down*, which would be published the following year. Segal at McGraw-Hill wasn't any happier with *The Puppet Master*. He rejected it on June 3, saying it contained no "good guy" to cheer for and that the story was too complex, with too many characters and subplots. "Also, just between you and me, the writing is pretty punk—they (the writers) are the masters of the cliché adjective."

At this point, Reach thought it was time to dump the project and move on—either that or cut it drastically and try again. The agent was disillusioned with the literary partnership. "Maybe you've let Odell's unprofessional ideas influence you too much," he told Marlowe in a June 5 letter. (Earlier in the year, Reach had similarly expressed uneasiness about Marlowe's ex-Marine collaborator on the novel about stolen gold. Reach said Marlowe had run off the track by including boring passages on military training: "I can see what happened: you got seduced by your collaborator's expert knowledge of diving techniques—which must have seemed fascinating to you.") But, in regard to the partnership with Odell, Marlowe was undeterred. He told Reach that he and Odell had decided to strip the story down, recast it and come up with a version running 70,000 to 75,000 words. Over the next few years, they would continue to rework and resubmit *The Puppet Master*, but without success.

Marlowe, who always seemed to be on the lookout for collaborators and material, wasn't neglecting Nussbaum as a possibility in both areas. He was already looking forward to the former bank robber winning his freedom. In the same letter in which he told Reach about the effort to slash *The Puppet Master*, he said he was outlining a fiction story based on Nussbaum's career. "The 'I' of the story would be the protagonist who sponsors Nussbaum's parole from prison," Marlowe wrote, possibly seeing himself in that role. It's not clear whether anything ever came of this.

In 1964, Marlowe was still five years away from publishing *Operation Fireball*, his first adventure featuring "Earl Drake" as a bank robber-turned-government-operative. But the seeds for the transformation may already have been planted in a July 23 letter from Reach to Marlowe in which the agent suggests the writer should try an espionage story. "Incidentally, since the success of

[John Le Carré's] *The Spy Who Came in from the Cold*, all publishers, hard- and soft-cover—also TV and movie people—are clamoring for more espionage stories. With the dope you've got from Odell on the inner workings of NSA, can't you come up with an idea for a book, or maybe a series? How about a top NSA (or CIA) operative, maybe a general on loan from the Army and his aides (including a sexy female) who gets assigned to the big trouble spots anywhere in the world?"

The "espionage agent" series, as such, didn't gel for years, but elements of it were beginning to come together in *Never Live Twice*. Published in 1964, the book was notable for exploring two subjects central to Marlowe's personal story: the amnesia he would experience 13 years later, and his obsession with spanking. In the story, Ted Blaine, a bloated, hard-drinking businessman in south Florida, survives an attempt by his wife to kill him. She propels his car, with him in it, into a roadside canal. When he surfaces in the water, he's shocked into the realization that he is actually a former government operative named Jackrabbit Smith. That identity had been erased from Smith's mind 19 years before in 1945 during a violent incident while he was on assignment in northern Italy.

Following the car crash, an all-mixed-up Smith/Blaine is treated by Dr. Jessica Weldon, a beautiful, prim female physician who has been trained in psychology. She suspects his condition is that of "retrograde amnesia," a repeat of a previous memory blackout. Now that Smith knows who he is again, his government handlers, learning he isn't dead, send him back to southern Florida under his "Blaine" identity. It turns out "Blaine" is doing business with people they suspect are involved in gunrunning.

Dr. Weldon (who is "Jessica" to Smith by this time, as he increasingly tries to get her into bed), accompanies Smith to south Florida. Her role is to convince the people who tried to kill him that he's forgotten the murder attempt because he's suffering from alcohol-induced amnesia. So, amnesia is piled on amnesia. The plot is outrageous, but Marlowe makes it work.

On the trip, Smith tries to convince Jessica to have sex. His argument is novel: "I'm a man who's meeting his wife tomorrow and doesn't remember ever having been in bed with a woman in his life. For all I know I could be as queer as a four-dollar bill." (An interesting nod to the impotence discussion in *The Name of the Game Is Death*.) Jessica still resists, but Smith doles out a lusty spanking. She succumbs.

The latter part of the book is filled with detailed information about firearms and other weapons, subjects with which both Odell and Nussbaum were familiar. It's possible that either, or both, contributed to the book. Four years later, an item in the *News-Journal*, Odell's hometown newspaper in Mansfield, Ohio, would say Odell and Marlowe had worked together on six novels up to that time, which would have made *Never Live Twice* the first of these.

Arguing against Odell's participation, however, is the fact that he and Marlowe weren't introduced until the book was well along in the creative process. Also, a list Odell wrote late in life noting his writing credits did not include this book, or two others of the six supposed collaborations. In the same vein, it's unlikely Nussbaum offered gun advice for *Never Live Twice*. During most of the writing of the book, Nussbaum's fate in the legal system was undecided, so he probably didn't risk upsetting authorities by feeding weapons details to Marlowe. Still, it's possible he had a hand in the story. Like many other things about Marlowe's life and work, this question remains unresolved.

By the time Marlowe and Odell got together, Marlowe had already published nine genre mysteries and was 50. Increasingly, he was seeking a success that would put him on solid financial ground. The best chance for this, of course, would be a breakout novel that would earn some serious money and lead to big advances for subsequent best-selling novels. The book that brought him the most critical acclaim, *The Name of the Game Is Death*, had not sold well, and his Gold Medal books were earning only modest advances. Marlowe was always a hard and productive worker, churning out freelance articles for Michigan newspapers, book reviews, the occasional horseracing article for one mainstream magazine or another, and racy stories for men's magazines. But he yearned for the big money a smash-hit hardcover novel would bring, and exchanges between him and agent James Reach in the years after he met Odell clearly show how hard he worked to make such a novel happen.

Even as he did so, however, he was beginning to be plagued by the kind of physical problems that eventually would throw his career into disarray. In late September 1964, he suddenly developed a swollen ankle that made it difficult to work. On Oct. 8, he wrote to Reach that "Two weeks (ago) tomorrow I climbed out of bed in the morning with an ankle mysteriously the size of a football." The pain was agonizing, but his physician couldn't figure out the cause. Marlowe suspected booze: "I suggested delicately to the M.D. that just possibly the bourbon might finally be catching up with Marlowe," the author told Reach, "but he said no, he didn't know what the hell it was, but it wasn't that."

These vicissitudes slowed Marlowe down, but didn't stop him, and he and his agent continued to brainstorm possible blockbusters. In mid-November 1964, Reach came up with a wild idea for a suspense novel, a Cold War story eventually titled *As Good as Dead.* In the book, a former soldier winds up impersonating himself. The plot was this: Russian spies are casting about for someone to play the role of a former soldier named Joe who disappeared during the Korean War 15 years previously. They want the fake "Joe" to return to his former wife, the daughter of a scientist engaged in a hush-hush government project, to kidnap her and get the scientist to reveal the details of the project. As the Russians seek a look-alike among the winos of New York, they hit on the real "Joe," who has been disgraced, hit the skids, and changed his name. He joins up for the scheme, but turns the tables on the Russians and is reunited with his former wife.

Marlowe jumped into the project and slugged his way through a partial manuscript and plot summary, but was hampered by psychological twitches. On Dec. 5, he told Reach he simply didn't know what was the matter with him and joked lamely that perhaps he was going through the "change of life."

> You know I've never had a nerve in my body; well, if I'm not nervous now, I'm certainly irritable. I don't know whether my mental condition is affecting my physical or vice versa. My concentration span is short; my thinking is cloudy; decisions seem impossible to make; in short, as I just said above, nothing I'm doing feels right.

By Dec. 15, Marlowe and Odell had knocked out a few chapters of a rough draft, but Reach wasn't pleased:

> This is probably okay if you want to settle for a Gold Medal sale; but if you want to aim for better things, it's all wrong: the pulpy dialogue; the fisticuffs; the agents speaking Russian among themselves and using foreign words and expressions.

The agent told Marlowe to "de-pulp" the writing. Over the next few months, Marlowe tried to do so, and improved the manuscript enough to send it out. Editors weren't enthusiastic. One negative reaction came from Clayton Rawson, editor of *Ellery Queen's Mystery Magazine*. By Feb. 28, 1965, Marlowe was writing to Reach about another project:

> As a hedge against a total reaction similar to Clayt Rawson's on *As Good as Dead*, I'm putting together a Gold Medal-type story, downbeat in about the same proportions as *Name*, based in South Carolina and with a background of a sophisticated version of the unwritten law.

Reach wrote back quickly, saying he liked this story, and Marlowe replied that he'd move right ahead. By May 3, editor Knox Burger at Gold Medal had agreed to buy it. This book, originally called *Nobody Laughs at Me*, would be published the following year by Fawcett as *The Vengeance Man* and is considered Marlowe's second-best novel after *The Name of the Game Is Death*. The relative ease with which Marlowe threw this story together and polished it off, in contrast to the big-picture thrillers with which he struggled, demonstrates that the fast-moving pulp story was his natural medium. It also might show he would have done better artistically if he had relied less on collaborators, but it's easy to sympathize with his motives. Working on more commercial novels gave him at least a shot at financial independence. That wasn't a hope that proved out with *As Good As Dead*, however.

On April 5, Helen King at William Morrow and Co., who had considered *Dead* on the basis of a partial manuscript and outline, gave it a thumbs-down. "A lot depends on the man-wife relationship," King said, "and we're not confident he [Marlowe] can do it."

On June 9, Jeanne F. Lloyd of the E.P. Dutton and Co. editorial department also turned it away. Her rejection, though, shows that Marlowe was held in high esteem as a genre writer, and that hardcover publishers were expecting him to break through at any time.

> Now, I am more than a bit unhappy—as we all are. You see, we just do not think that this is a sufficiently strong work for Dan Marlowe's hardcover debut. It begins extremely well, but the whole (idea) of the kidnap scheme is a somewhat stale one. And of course the perfect coincidence which triggers the plot is a little hard to take even though Mr. Marlowe does his best to explain it. We hope that he will pick a new idea and develop that for his entry into the world of the permanent cover.

As Marlowe's collaboration with Odell bogged down, the author was also having trouble getting respect for the man who would become another of his key co-writers: Al Nussbaum. On June 8, Marlowe asked Reach to assess a 60,000-word novel manuscript that Nussbaum had written and rewritten four times in the 2 1/2 years he had been locked up. Marlowe had done some edits, but said it was "105 percent" Nussbaum's story. Because of Bureau of Prisons rules, Marlowe didn't think the novel could be sold, but he believed it was of salable quality, or close to it.

> So why am I bothering you if you can't sell it? Because I think this boy is going to write a real book one of these days, Jim. He's done more in less time than I did, if you want a personal comparison. What I wish you'd do for me, if you disagree about its present salability, is to write me an anonymous strictly hardboiled note saying why. He's perfectly prepared to rewrite it four more times; in fact, is looking forward to it. He's now working on the outline of what he calls a "humorous" book. He's going to be out in six to eight years, and if he continues to improve he's going to be a selling writer by the time he hits the street. Outside of muscle-building, it's all he does in there: write, write, write. At this point I'll leave it with you. Don't pull any punches if you don't like what you see: he laps up criticism.

Reach, in fact, really did not like what he saw, as he told Marlowe on June 18:

> I don't think this stands the remotest chance of being published: and I think he has a long, long way to go before he can be published, if ever.
>
> The best thing I can say about his writing is that he does visualize well; the scenes, most of them, sound real. The present story, however, lacks incident and, especially in the early parts, is over-detailed. The plot is thin and creaky in spots. For instance, I could never believe in a character as completely evil and without redeeming traits as he makes Dwyer out to be...But the most serious defect is the level of the writing itself: about that of a senior high-school class in English comp. It's what editors call "pedestrian," and badly so: no spark, it never soars. And he hasn't got the drive, the guts, that compels a reader to read on and overlook a lot of faults. With those two assets—vivid writing and narrative drive...you can build; without them, you have two and a half strikes against you. Those are the two things you had when you didn't have anything else, what I saw in you and built on; in N. they're almost completely lacking.

It's not clear how frank Marlowe was with Nussbaum about the agent's scathing critique. Whatever Marlowe said, it didn't stifle Nussbaum's devotion to his new craft. At this point, Nussbaum had been trying to write salable fiction for two years, and it would be another year before he sold a short story. Over time, however—and he had a lot of time—he would succeed in molding himself into a professional writer.

As 1965 neared an end, Marlowe was having considerably more trouble with another of his collaborators, the former Marine captain with whom he was writing the novel about stolen government gold, tentatively titled *Red Gold*. Marlowe never identified the man in his letters to Reach, probably because the ex-captain didn't want military or government authorities to know he was involved. On Oct. 11, Marlowe told Reach the man had "disappeared," and had been gone for four days. Finally, the man wired on Oct. 19, asking Marlowe to telephone him in Alexandria, Virginia. The number turned out to be the Alexandria hospital. "He's in there with four broken ribs and two ligaments strained in his back, cause unspecified," Marlowe reported.

The implication was that the ex-captain was now doing clandestine government work and had been beaten up on the job. More troubling, after a routine polygraph test, the Marine had admitted he was collaborating on a novel describing his past experiences. "His bosses didn't like it and want to see the manuscript to approve it, which means they'll bury it under a ton of other stuff and forget it," Marlowe asserted. The novelist decided to drop *Red Gold*, and told the Marine to explain to their Doubleday editor, Lee Barker, who Marlowe intended to approach separately. By now, the Marine was hinting he wanted Marlowe to give up his copy of the manuscript and outline. Marlowe wouldn't do it.

"So there it is," Marlowe told Reach. "I wouldn't call it wasted effort, since I'll find a way to use it eventually somewhere, but it's surely frustrating." As it turned out, Marlowe's opportunity came soon, and his maneuvering would show the former gambler's cleverness and boldness in dealing with a fast shuffle.

Still, 1965 had been a miserable year for earnings, as Reach noted, apologetically, in a letter in mid-December. But Marlowe, who knew the dice could run both hot and cold, reassured him in a return letter:

> While it hasn't been a good year financially [Marlowe wrote], part of it was due to taking calculated risks in an effort to improve the product, and the fact that the initial effort wasn't successful is no indication we weren't on the right track. Fairly early in 1966 it may become necessary to lower our sights a bit, but for the time being I'd like you to continue doing exactly what you're doing, giving us exposure in the better markets. We might find an editor who agrees with us, and if we don't, then it will be time to pull in our horns...
>
> Don't worry about the present situation. We've had a long run of good luck, and a little belt-tightening might be good for the soul as well as the figure. I'm not hurting right now, and I'll let you know in plenty of time before it becomes necessary to lower all boats. And in the meantime I have every intention of making '66 the best year ever.

CHAPTER 9:
The Dirtiest Book in History

ON MARCH 20, 1966, THE *DETROIT FREE PRESS* RAN A BOOK REVIEW by Marlowe in which he didn't name the author or the book. Why? Because the novel was "pure filth," he told his readers. In fact, the review was headlined: "The Dirtiest Book Ever Written."

Marlowe began the review by recalling his appearance two years previously on *"At Random,"* an early morning TV talk program in Chicago on which participants discussed book censorship. The subject of the show, broadcast on WBBM-TV and hosted by Carter Davidson, was "The Writer and His Place in Contemporary Society."

Also on the panel were Herbert Gold, novelist and critic; Shel Silverstein, cartoonist and author; the Rev. Thomas Calkins, O.S.M., author and missionary; Claire Cox, an author of non-fiction; Charles Beaumont, a writer of TV and movie scripts, and magazine editor Paul Krassner. In the group, Marlowe said, he took the strongest position against book censorship. Furthermore, Marlowe wrote, he was no stranger to "dirty" books at the time, having sampled the wares of such writers as Richard Burton, Octave Mirbeau, John Cleland, Frank Harris, Henry Miller and Louis-Ferdinand Celine, and having read a pirated edition of *Lady Chatterley's Lover*.

Even so, he asserted he'd been brought up short by the book he was currently reviewing, which 18 months previously had been described in a capsule review in a national publication as "the publisher's extra-special dirty book for the fall line." Marlowe had been captivated by the book. The material was cruel and shocking, but the writer was like a musician with perfect pitch, a writer of superb dialogue. Given these positives, should this work of art be promoted to the public at large? Marlowe's conclusion: No way.

It's an extraordinary performance, an extraordinary talent, but—recommend the book? Are you kidding? Recommend it to whom? Not to any woman I ever met, certainly, and to few men. Only to writers could I honestly recommend it, to fellow workers with words, and then only to those with strong stomachs.

For the book is pure filth. It's life, granted, but it's filth. I never thought I'd live to see the day when I'd back away from endorsing a well-written "naturalistic" novel, but that day is here…At this point let me say don't bother to write or call to inform me that I inadvertently forgot to include in this "review" the name of the book, the author and the publisher; I didn't forget; I omitted them deliberately…it is this opinionated man's opinion that this is a book that definitely should have been written but just as definitely shouldn't be read.

Figuring out the title from extraneous clues more than 40 years later was a challenge, though, as it turns out, Marlowe was just bluffing when he told readers he wouldn't reveal the name of the book to them if they called. The key was the phrase about the "extra-special dirty book." A Google search turned up a review from *Time* magazine for Oct. 30, 1964. The review, headlined "Borderline Psychotic," showed that the book in question was *Last Exit to Brooklyn* by Hubert Selby Jr., a tale of the waterfront slums of Brooklyn published by Grove Press. The *Time* reviewer was expansive about the rawness of the incidents in the book:

A fist in the face or a knee in the groin are routine asides. The climaxes occur when a gang of hoodlums beats a stray soldier nearly to death, with every kick, blow, chipped tooth, broken bone, and gout of blood and vomit described in detail; when a gang of transvestites and their boyfriends get high on gin, Benzedrine and morphine, with every ensuing act of sodomy and fellatio described in detail; when a gang of dockworkers, derelicts and degenerates inflict multiple intercourse upon a prostitute in a parking lot so savagely that she is killed, with every drop of beer, blood, spittle and semen described in unrelenting detail.

As it turned out, Marlowe's mysterious review may have churned up more interest about the book among *Detroit Free Press* readers than did the *Time* reviewer's work. Among Marlowe's papers at Boston University is a 1982 letter to a New York agent in which the writer said he had once thought newspaper readers should be protected from the rawer aspects of life and literature. He acknowledged that he may have been wrong.

> ...16 years ago when I was reviewing for the Sunday *Detroit Free Press*, one of the books that landed in my mailbox was Hubert Selby's *Last Exit to Brooklyn*. Truthfully, I thought the *Free Press* book editor, a rather frisky female, was pulling my leg, so I sat my ass in the typing chair and delivered a 350-word review announcing the arrival of the dirtiest book ever written (to that point) but pointing out that it did have some redeemable social value. And I sent in the review without naming either the book or the author. And—more leg pulling?—they ran the review exactly that way, with a big question-mark in the space allotted for the book's cover. And the next day my phone rang off the hook with calls from the *Free Press* people wanting to know the title so they could tell *their* callers, and calls from all over southern Michigan from people who knew me wanting to know the title, too. I guess the times they were a-changin' then, too.

The incident was fascinating from a number of standpoints.

For one thing, it showed Marlowe was struggling financially: He had to write book reviews to help make ends meet. He also had to write columns and newspaper copy. Among other gigs, early in 1966, he had landed a position as a columnist for a large weekly in

Michigan, and he would wind up doing a weekly column for five newspapers in the state. This sort of piecework, added to Marlowe's book-writing income, didn't amount to much. When Marlowe's career collapsed due to amnesia 11 years later, he wrote a resumé saying his annual income during his writing years ranged from $15,000 to $25,000 a year, but this may have been an exaggeration. In a column written in early 1969, he noted that he grossed only about $8,900 the previous year.

Marlowe's putdown of the book reviewed in the *Detroit Free Press* also exemplified a conservatism that helped him fit in culturally and politically in the small-town community of Harbor Beach. The conservatism, however, was part of a complex personality mix. Although Marlowe—a trained accountant, experienced office manager, and Rotarian—did have the soul of a businessman, he tended to the exotic and sweaty in both his literary endeavors and personal life. While he was rejecting the lewdness of the unnamed book, he also was churning out heavy-breathing paperback epics and producing down-and-dirty sex stories for men's magazines and the adult-bookstore trade. Indeed, despite the review's puritanical surface approach, a close reading reveals it wasn't the prudish attack it purported to be. Marlowe's approach to the review, and his later description of why he took that approach, demonstrate his wry humor, a trait that doesn't always come across in his macho adventure tales.

The year 1966, marked by this lively incident, was an eventful one in Marlowe's life, characterized by the publication of two of his finer books, *Four for the Money* and *The Vengeance Man*, and a struggle to keep his literary output going while dealing with three collaborators.

Early in the year, still another publisher passed on *The Puppet Master*. This was New American Library, whose editor dismissed the book as "probably publishable but rather routine." Shortly thereafter, Marlowe wrote to Reach, "I think we're losing Bill Odell. Nothing overt, but he's drying up on me. I think he's just getting discouraged. My personal relationship with him is still good, but it's not *The Puppet Master* he wants to talk about these days."

Things were not going well with Reach, either. The literary agent remained as engaged as ever with Marlowe and his work, but he was beginning to fail physically, though he was only 56. "I'm not well," he told Marlowe. "My blood pressure has shot way up into the stratosphere and my doctor has ordered me to take it extremely easy until he can coax it back down again. But I think I can manage to get to the office for at least a few hours most days."

Reach, a clever agent with a firm hand, had guided Marlowe well in his career and the development of his writing. That would continue for a few years, Reach's physical troubles notwithstanding, but his partnership with Marlowe would end prematurely in 1970, and Marlowe would never have the same level of success after that.

In 1966, Marlowe was in very good voice, and his instincts were excellent. Of the two books he published this year, *The Vengeance Man* came closest to equaling the quality of his classic *The Name of the Game Is Death*. The protagonist of *The Vengeance Man*, construction company owner Jim Wilson, demonstrates a ferocity matched only by Marlowe's character Earl Drake. The kinky overtones of the sex-and-power relationship Wilson has with his murdered wife's best friend provide the most offbeat example of Marlowe's heavy-breathing eroticism. The corruption of virtually every important character in the book is thorough, and the theme of betrayal is relentless.

The Vengeance Man starts with a bang, ends with a bang, and gallops like a desperate racehorse in between. The book, set in South Carolina, is built around Wilson's driving, vicious personality—a prickly character hinted at by the book's working title, *Nobody Laughs at Me*. At the beginning of the book, Wilson murders his wife Mona during a tryst she's having with the mayor's son, and shoots her lover twice in the buttocks. Wilson claims he was drunk and impassioned. The coroner's jury lets him off.

He then blackmails his wife's closest friend, Ludmilla Pierson, threatening to make public a movie of her and Mona having sex with each other. His object is to get her to convince Mona's father, the violent Judge Tom Harrington, not to kill him for murdering Mona. Wilson escapes Harrington's vengeance, collects Mona's substantial estate, marries Ludmilla—who is more than his equal in viciousness and manipulation—and begins to rise through corrupt political circles in the state. His progress is interrupted by another double-cross, one that finishes the book in a blaze of violence.

Perhaps because he thought *The Vengeance Man* tapped the primal creative force that had produced *The Name of the Game Is Death*, Marlowe kicked around the possibility of having *Name* reissued, and ran the idea by Knox Burger, his Gold Medal editor. "Knox Burger called me last week and told me about your suggestion that they re-issue TNOTGID," Reach told Marlowe on Feb. 17, 1966. "Knox said that, although the original edition hadn't sold well enough to justify it, he'd see if he could persuade the top brass to go along, and that he'd let me know. I haven't heard from him since." Gold Medal would in fact re-issue *Name*, but not for another seven years, after Earl Drake and Marlowe's "Operation" series starring Drake were in full swing. Reach would never live to see it happen.

Four for the Money, also published by Gold Medal in 1966, is a much different book, but quite effective. The story deals with four men who, locked up in prison in the East, hatch a plan to rob a casino in "Desert City" between Las Vegas and Reno. After they leave prison, they move to Nevada and put the plan into practice. The story is told by James Quick, a "card mechanic" (card cheat) who first gets hired as a draftsman by the county, then buys a motel to serve as a front operation for the team as they plan the heist. Quick starts up a romance with a girl who works in a casino, and everything is going smoothly. Then the robbery turns into a burglary, and everything goes to hell, with two of the gang shooting each other to death. Even so, the story has a surprisingly upbeat ending for a Marlowe novel. The legal heat dies down, Quick marries his girlfriend, and they settle in to run the motel as a legitimate, and successful, business.

Critic Anthony Boucher gave it a thumbs-up in his *"Criminals at Large"* column in *The New York Times*: "Dan Marlowe comes up with a fresh variation of the Big Caper novel in *Four for the Money* (Gold Medal, 50 cents), in which four ex-cons plan a major operation on a Nevada gambling town. Shrewd, tough writing; vigor and ingenuity in plot; some fine poker and con games; and a gratifyingly unconventional final outcome."

Marlowe was showing his versatility in these two books—one about a corrupt, politicking businessman, the other about cons with fevered ambitions—and he would go in yet another direction with a third one he would write this year dealing with military adventuring.

In the summer of 1966, Marlowe had been telling Reach in vague terms about a writing project he was working on that hadn't come to fruition. The agent was intrigued, and not terribly happy, because in the past Marlowe had occasionally gone around him and dealt directly with publishers. In fact, these maneuvers by Marlowe had been relatively innocent. The writer networked constantly, chatting and corresponding with publishers, newspaper editors and magazine staffers about book ideas, articles and stories. He had been doing it for years. Inevitably, he wound up kicking projects around without first consulting his agent. However, this current "mystery project" would be a major departure from the author-agent relationship, and Marlowe was concerned about the reaction when he finally revealed the facts to Reach on Aug. 10.

> …Now for the "mystery" about the new project, and I hope you and Samuel French don't blow your collective stacks. I had to wait until I had the loose ends nailed down. You remember the Virgin Island story that the ex-Marine hung on me twice when it looked as though we had a winner going? Since he has the morals of an alley cat, I've had a friend looking over his shoulder ever since. Seven weeks ago that friend told me my boy was trying to write it himself (you remember that we ended up with a solid outline and a fair amount of manuscript). I wasn't about to let him do that to me, although I doubt he could have done it him-self, anyway. I got busy and ran off a skeletonized, first-person treatment of what I had here, and I sent it to Gold Medal with the word that *on this one project* I wanted them to handle it directly with me. This, as I'm sure I don't have to tell you, was because I didn't know which way my boy would jump. It could have been messy, and I didn't want to involve SF or you. I got a contract from Gold Medal, with the usual $1,000 advance (enclosed please find SF's usual end), and an Oct. 31st dating. THEN I sent my boy a registered letter telling him I'd made the sale. He was on the phone five minutes after he got it, raising hell. I told him if he gave me any trouble I'd hit him with the biggest bag of shit he'd

ever been hit with, and I reminded him that I had about eight reels of tape here on which he's the only conversationalist. He subsided in a hurry. He's going to get 25 percent instead of 50 percent since he'll be doing no more work. I sent him a check for his $225 of the advance, and I was waiting to make sure it cleared before I broke the news to you. It cleared my bank yesterday, endorsed by him, and I had on it a release that won't permit him to weasel out of what the check was for. So everything is under control, we have a contract, and you'll handle everything else in connection with it exactly as you always do. Sorry to seem to be lurking in the bushes on this one, but I had to be sure he couldn't spin me around before I knew for sure I could go ahead. Now all I've got to do is write it.

Reach took the news with equanimity. "Okay, I go along with the *Red Gold* deal, and I understand everything about it, except why you settled for Gold Medal; we probably could have gotten a nice deal from Doubleday...but that's now water under the bridge." Marlowe replied, "I'm glad you can see the box I was in with that boy...The only reason I went to Gold Medal was because I had to have an accomplished fact to hit him with, and from Gold Medal I could get it quickest..." Marlowe went ahead and wrote the book, and the novel was published the next year as *Route of the Red Gold*.

Despite this sour experience, and the continuing rough spots Marlowe was having selling material written with Odell, at least one of the author's collaborators was doing well. Al Nussbaum found success late in 1966. After three years of trying to write commercial fiction, he sold his first short story. It was published as "Viewpoint" in February 1967 by *Alfred Hitchcock's Mystery Magazine*, a publication that would treat him well in the years to come.

CHAPTER 10:
Public Servant, Public Enemy

As a writer, Marlowe transported himself across the country and the globe, robbing banks, conducting military missions, taking part in shoot-outs, sexing up attractive women, beating the hell out of people who crossed him, outfoxing shifty gamblers in poker games, mixing it up with mobsters, settling the hash of Communist agents. But in real life, back in Harbor Beach, he was a regular member of the community: chatting people up at Rotary meetings, attending get-togethers of the local Republican Party, joining his buddies for day trips to Detroit to see Tigers and Lions games, hanging out down at Smalley's Bar and Grill, shooting the bull about sports.

His best friend in town, Gordon Gempel, marveled at the writer's gift of gab. Marlowe's quick mind, ability to engage with people, and political awareness made him a natural for public service, and he was encouraged to give it a shot by Gempel, a Republican who did stints as chairman of the Huron County Republican Party and as a member of the Harbor Beach Planning Commission. Marlowe himself was an active Republican who helped with political fundraising.

In November 1966, Marlowe ran for one of two four-year terms up for grabs on the City Council, promising to pursue a program of fiscal conservation that would promote the city's growth. Marlowe won with 528 votes. On Jan. 1, 1967, he took office along with another council member and the newly elected mayor, George Scott, a 57-year-old merchant.

Marlowe would serve on the council, and fill in as mayor pro tem (temporarily carrying out the duties of mayor) for three years, before resigning on May 4, 1970. His presence on the council and the weekly column he wrote for the *Harbor Beach Times, One for the Road*, established him firmly as a key voice of the community.

David Krueger Sr., the owner of a Napa Auto Parts store, was elected to the council during Marlowe's service. Krueger said the writer appeared dedicated to doing the right thing, with little return (council members didn't get paid much, perhaps $40 or $50 a month). "It was more of a pain in the butt than anything," Krueger said. Many issues considered were economic or ecological, such as building a landfill inland to replace the water-polluting city dump near the lake. Other decisions were important, too. At one point, Marlowe addressed the Harbor Beach Chamber of Commerce about the need for a municipal water tower and how it would be financed. He supported a ballot proposal to create a Tri-County Community College to serve Huron, Sanilac and Tuscola counties, a move that would encourage industry to move into Michigan's "Thumb" area by ensuring education of the local workforce. In his column, he exulted in the delivery on Sept. 12, 1967, of the first 11,600 tons of coal for the new Detroit Edison plant in Harbor Beach, a major step forward for the local economy.

"Every businessman in the Thumb area, and indeed every individual, should put on his socks each morning a little more confident in his own future and that of his township, city, or county because Detroit Edison has so emphatically registered its confidence," Marlowe wrote.

The writer's civic-mindedness was well known. On at least one occasion, he gave a talk on "Citizenship" at a local Lutheran school. He served as a judge for the Harbor Beach Garden Club's contest for the best display of outdoor Christmas lighting. In his column, he promoted the work of the Huron County Historical Society, publicized the Mothers' March for the Muscular Dystrophy Association, and lobbied strenuously for tax increases to support Harbor Beach

Community School. To benefit schoolchildren, he presented a Rotary-produced photo slide show about the beauty, tradition and history of Harbor Beach.

On the council, Marlowe was much more than a booster, however; he was a man who knew his business. "Dan was a good man on there," Krueger said. "People kind of listened to him. When he had something to say, it was no-nonsense. Some politicians can talk and talk and talk and when they get all through, you say, 'What did he say?' Dan wasn't like that. He was likeable, but he was pretty opinionated...I got into a few little tiffs with him on the Water Commission. I was water commissioner and wanted to pour some money into this building and he disagreed with me and I tried to convince him. He was pretty tough to convince."

Jack Stickney, who was Harbor Beach police chief from 1968 to 1984 and who knew Marlowe as a fellow Rotarian, said Marlowe's intelligence and desire to build the community made him a standout council member. "He was a great councilman," Stickney said. "Very bright. He was very sharp and before he did anything he wanted to find out all the facts."

Marlowe's background in business, and his hardheaded attitude toward spending, made him the ideal person to monitor money matters for the city. And that's just where Mayor Scott placed him, appointing Marlowe finance officer and budget officer for Harbor Beach, as well as assigning him responsibilities dealing with streets, drains, sidewalks and the Civil Service Board. In one of his columns, Marlowe explained his qualifications for the finance position, noting that before he became a writer, he had been an office manager and credit manager for wholesale companies averaging 3,000 customers apiece.

"There is always more to be done in municipalities than there are municipal funds to do it, and a finance officer often has to say 'No' to a worthy proposal so that the city fathers can sleep nights," Marlowe wrote. "An ex-credit manager, of course, has had a lot of practice in saying 'No.' Perhaps because I spent so many years getting the biggest bang possible for each of the bucks spent by my employers, I have an aversion to deficit financing. I like to know where the money is for a given program, and while in municipal government there is necessarily a bit of robbing Peter to pay Paul at times, I like to see the end result clearly promulgated before the 'go' button is pushed by those in charge of pushing it."

Marlowe's fiscal conservatism, and his willingness to act on it, made him even more in demand politically. In August 1968, he attended the Republican State Convention in Grand Rapids as a delegate, served as acting chairman of the Huron County delegation, and was secretary for the Eighth District caucusing for the counties of Huron, Tuscola, Sanilac, Saginaw and St. Clair.

K. Don Williamson, who served as city engineer when Marlowe was on the council and was a friend of the writer, agreed that Marlowe was an effective communicator and public servant, and that he liked to socialize. "He really was the leader on the council, more so than the mayor," Williamson said. "A very intelligent man. Dan worked like the devil, and he played hard, too. Finish a book and he'd be down at Smalley's with his 'champagne,' as he called it: 7 and 7. And he could consume quite a few of them. Quite often after a council meeting, the whole council would stop down at Smalley's and have a drink."

Marlowe's work as a city official left less time for writing, but he still produced a blizzard of copy, only part of it fiction. On Feb. 10, 1967, he wrote to Anthony Abruzzo, medical superintendent at Lapeer State Home in Lapeer, Michigan, asking to interview him for an article he was doing for the *Detroit Free Press* on mental hospitals in the area. Marlowe told Abruzzo he was writing a weekly column for five Michigan newspapers, including the *Lapeer County Press*, plus book reviews for the *Free Press* and an occasional article for the newspaper's Sunday magazine, called *Detroit*. A week later, Marlowe tried to regularize his arrangement with the *Free Press*. On Feb. 17, he wrote to his friend Mort Persky, an assistant managing editor, asking for a regular gig. In the letter, he referred to Bill Baker, another editor at the newspaper, with whom he was working. He asked Persky:

> How would you and the *Detroit Free Press* feel about putting me on the payroll at $125 a month? I would contribute a book review a week, a conversation piece a month (no sweat, actually; Bill must have four or five possibilities in the file right now), plus a couple or three assignments and/or interviews... with the exception of three or four days a month on city business

(as councilman), I'm almost always available to go anywhere at any time…

It's not clear whether this offer was accepted, but Marlowe did continue to freelance for the newspaper. One of his regular contributions, however, disappeared. On Nov. 14, Baker wrote to Marlowe saying the Nov. 26 issue of *Detroit* would carry the last Marlowe "conversation piece." The magazine was dropping the feature, Baker said, "for reasons too complicated for me to articulate," but the editor wanted to keep seeing ideas from Marlowe for short features as well as longer articles.

Marlowe's fiction efforts continued unabated in 1967, though the year didn't begin auspiciously. On Jan. 9, Evan Heyman, editor for Avon Books, rejected both *As Good as Dead*, the former-soldier-impersonating-himself story, and *Cold Cash*, the conwoman tale, saying that *Cold Cash* "tends to drift from one caper to another, lacking focus and direction."

Even so, in the Feb. 9 paperback section of *The New York Times Book Review*, Marlowe was cited as one of America's outstanding writers of original softcover suspense by Anthony Boucher, writer of that newspaper's *"Criminals at Large"* column. Boucher's selections for the top eight softcover novelists in this genre were John D. MacDonald (selected as the best), Brett Halliday, Donald Hamilton, Richard Stark (a pseudonym for Donald Westlake), Dan Marlowe, Stephen Marlowe (no relation) and Edward Aarons.

The recognition was simultaneously a boost for Marlowe and a hint at the difficulties he faced in getting greater recognition and more lucrative book contracts. For the reader, having two "Marlowes" on the list created confusion as to which was which, and even the supportive *Harbor Beach Times* noted that the town's Marlowe was probably the least well known nationally of all those listed, though it asserted hopefully that "he is on the move."

After nine years of writing suspense novels, and with 12 books to his credit, Marlowe was still hoping for the one that would vault him into the ranks of bestselling novelists.

"I really have hopes for the one coming out in May, *Route of the Red Gold*," he told the *Times*. "That one could put me over the top if it gets the reaction for which I'm hoping. If it does not, it's back to the drawing board and a bigger and better product next time. Check back with me in another nine years and I'll let you know the box score then. Who knows—I might outlive a few of those guys (on Boucher's list)."

Marlowe was also strategizing to widen the array of publishers to which he could sell, rather than relying so much on Fawcett's Gold Medal line. On Feb. 5, a few days before Boucher's list was published, Marlowe had told Reach, "I sense Fawcett is cutting back on originals. Maybe we should shop around and broaden our base a bit." Marlowe, always the businessman, also was trying to step up production. "One of the reasons for tying up with Bill Odell is that I know he and I can do 3 books a year together, if we can get them through editorial offices." Despite Marlowe's doubts about Gold Medal, the imprint would continue to be his home base for many years, making him one of the longest-running and most prolific Gold Medal writers. His run would be extended considerably by the "*Operation*" novels featuring the bank-robbing Earl Drake as an international agent.

The springboard for that series would be supplied by bank robber Al Nussbaum, who was making good use of his time in prison. Nussbaum had made solid steps over the years in his efforts to become a writer. From November 1962, when he was first placed in prison in The Tombs in New York City, to February 1964, when he was sent off to federal prison in Leavenworth, Kansas, Nussbaum had been writing fiction on lined paper in pencil and sending his efforts to Marlowe. While Nussbaum was imprisoned in The Tombs, he and Marlowe exchanged letters two or three times a week. Marlowe critiqued Nussbaum's stories and answered the robber's technical questions about writing.

"He demonstrated from the beginning an aptitude for story construction and for dialogue," Marlowe wrote in *Odyssey*, the article included in *I, Witness*, the 1978 non-fiction collection by Mystery Writers of America. "I felt from the outset that if he persevered he could make it as a writer, even though he faced the additional complication while in the federal prison system that he wasn't allowed to write about the activities with which he had been most recently connected."

In fact, Marlowe did more than offer advice, according to *Turning Sentences into Words: Writing in Prison*, the companion piece to *Odyssey* that Nussbaum wrote for *I, Witness*.

"When I was in The Tombs, I had sent Dan a terrible 5,000-word story," Nussbaum wrote. "He rewrote it, cutting it to 2,000 words and making it end with a bang instead of a soft fizzle. He sold it to *Alfred Hitchcock's Mystery Magazine* and split the money with me."

Nussbaum's contributions to *Anatomy of a Crime Wave* were probably handled in a similar way, except that the article didn't sell. But when Nussbaum went to Leavenworth, his instruction from Marlowe and collaboration with him were abruptly cut off. Federal prison policy forbade Marlowe writing to Nussbaum because he wasn't a blood relative, though Marlowe repeatedly told Bureau of Prisons officials they should let him continue helping the robber to rehabilitate him.

In the meantime, the two men used a subterfuge to stay in contact. Nussbaum would send letters intended for Marlowe, as well as drafts of stories, to his sister Doris, and she would pass them on to the author. Marlowe would send her his critiques and comments, and she would pass them on to Nussbaum. "He not only told me where I had gone wrong, he showed me," Nussbaum wrote. "Then, if he could, he would sell the story and split the money with me." After a year, and three or four visits to prison officials in Washington, Marlowe finally was allowed to correspond directly with Nussbaum once a month. After another year, the schedule was eased to once a week.

Nussbaum made good use of the advice, and he was working hard. By the end of 1966, after writing what he referred to as "a million worthless words," he sold the first story to go out under his own name to *Alfred Hitchcock's Mystery Magazine*. He'd written and sent the story out without passing it to Marlowe for his advice, and Nussbaum was justly proud of his accomplishment. Called "Viewpoint," it appeared in the February 1967 issue. The magazine paid $42 for it, plus 25 percent for foreign magazine rights. "That $52.50 let me cross the invisible line and join the writers who get money for their work," Nussbaum wrote. "It also kept me in fresh fruit and coffee for over three months."

A few months later, in June 1967, Marlowe was already doing research in San Francisco that would find its way into the third "Operation" book, *Operation Drumfire*, which would be published in 1972. The story, in part, would involve a scheme by computer-savvy scientists to win horse races by running programs that processed data about the horses, weather conditions, and racetracks. In a letter to Reach on June 24, Marlowe noted that he had interviewed people at the Oakland Army Base and the Concord Naval Station and was "trying to get to Alcatraz."

A few days later, Marlowe's column in the *Harbor Beach Times* touched on the theme of scientists trying to make money as horseplayers.

> During my gambling days, I often encountered mathematicians who were attracted to games of chance, professorial types well versed in pure math who felt that their sometimes astounding feats of mental calculation gave them an "edge" over their less well equipped fellow gamblers.
>
> I met these professors at racetracks and gambling casinos, and some of them worked hard at it. I knew a Johns Hopkins professor who took periodical leaves of absence to follow the horses, and I never think of these professor-gamblers without recalling an incident that took place in the Washington, D.C., of World War II.

Marlowe went on to describe how scientists at the National Security Agency, some of them top bridge and chess players, tried to beat the races by programming such racetrack data as the soil content, temperature, humidity, wind velocity and direction and pollen count, as well as details on jockeys, such as personal habits, mental condition, financial status and anxiety complexes. The scientists, Marlowe noted with satisfaction, lost their money.

Shortly after Marlowe returned from San Francisco, he told Reach that henceforth income from his joint projects with Odell would be split 65 percent-35 percent in Marlowe's favor, a departure from their previous 50-50 arrangement. It's not clear why the change was made, but it wasn't because of Marlowe's dissatisfaction with Odell's work. Indeed, on July 28,

Marlowe told Reach "...for the immediate future I'm thinking of working with him toward the end ultimately of producing a blockbuster."

Late August brought both bad news and good news on this front. On the downside, Gold Medal rejected a proposal by Marlowe and Odell for a novel about a private eye to be called *The Bugle Blows a Long Cold Note*. At about the same time, however, their proposal for a novel called *Traitor* caught the eye of Howard Cady at the David McKay Company. Cady, a true player in the publishing world, had "a reputation in the trade of being one of the best editors around," Reach told Marlowe. (Cady had served in the Office of Strategic Services during World War II, which might have made him particularly interested in a book like *Traitor*. Over his 50-year career, he would edit books by Rex Harrison, William Saroyan, Leon Uris, Sophia Loren, Barry Goldwater, Bette Davis, Lowell Thomas and Norman Vincent Peale.)

Cady, said Reach, was "tremendously excited" by the proposal and commented "what a big, powerful book" Marlowe could produce if he handled the material correctly. However, the agent cautioned that Cady's boss, McKay co-owner Kenneth Rawson, would almost certainly not okay a contract for a non-name author on the basis of an outline. Therefore, Reach urged Marlowe to turn out 40 to 50 pages of manuscript for Cady, a move the agent believed would seal the deal.

This development seemed to show the wisdom of sticking with a project. Marlowe had first come up with the idea for *Traitor* in 1961, when he was living in Washington. The plan was for a suspense-spy novel built around the adventures of Carl Edwards, an American turncoat working inside the U.S. government for the Russians. Edwards moves from one Civil Service position to another in Washington by manipulating his superior, a pederast named Boland. In time, Edwards lands a position in the State Department, where he can get valuable information to feed to the Communists.

Originally, Marlowe had offered the story to Gold Medal, but was turned down. After he and Odell joined forces in 1964, they strengthened the story and produced an outline and two sample chapters, drawing on Odell's background in security work and government. This was the proposal that eventually caught the eye of Howard Cady, a development that thrilled Reach. "I believe you should drop everything else and get going on this," the agent told Marlowe. "With Howard Cady as your editor, this could be the big break that will set you up for life. If you need a Samuel French advance to carry you for a while, let me know. And do you still want Odell's name on the book? Why don't you call me collect and tell me how you feel about it?"

Reach was already worrying that Marlowe was diminishing the "brand" of his name by adding a co-author, but Marlowe was committed to the arrangement. The writer shot off a letter to Cady touting Odell's background as a plus in developing the story, enclosing a copy of *The Name of the Game Is Death* to show off his best work, and promising to send the additional scenes he wanted for *Traitor* "as soon as possible, hopefully within two weeks."

Reach continued to fuss, telling Marlowe he would have to change the title because the upcoming fall book line had a book called *Traitor!* Also, the agent advised, the novel should read like "fictionalized fact," particularly in the scenes between Boland and a U.S. senator who played a prominent role in the story.

> As you know, you have a tendency when writing dialogue between educated people, or people with important positions, to get quite fancy and have them speak in long, grammatical sentences the like of which you'll never hear in real life. And as I recall, Odell has even more of a tendency in that direction. These people, Boland, the Senator and the rest, are only human, even as you and I, and their speech tends to be just as colloquial as yours or mine.

The clunkiness of the dialogue may or may not have been a stumbling block as the project went forward, but other flaws did loom large. A reader's report from another editor at David McKay expressed concerns about a perceived lack of action and dramatic complication in the story, as well as a shortfall in emotional conflict. Reach, too, expressed doubts about a scene from the boyhood of one of the characters in which he attends a barn dance, has sex with a girl, and gets into a fight.

> ...I understand that you wanted to get some action in,
> which you do with the fight, but this just seems action for action's
> sake. Just as the sex seems sex for sex's sake. Don't forget that
> you're not writing this for soft covers; and Howard is not the kind
> of editor who's going to be impressed by big tits and so on, unless
> the tits are an integral part of your story, which I don't think these
> are.

Marlowe fired back, arguing that the early sex scene was necessary to set up "seven or eight hardnosed sex scenes" that would follow. Cady continued to stick with the book, asking for an extra page of outline that had been requested by his boss. But by Oct. 10, the project had run aground. Cady sent the partial manuscript and a rejection letter directly to Marlowe, a stunning development. "To say I was dumbfounded upon receiving it is the understatement of all time," Marlowe told Reach. "Either Rawson changed his mind completely after thinking it over, or Cady realized Rawson's hesitation and refused to lay his own neck on the line."

Marlowe didn't give up, though. It wasn't in his nature. At a writers conference in Rochester, Michigan, he'd met Alan Rinzler, senior editor at Macmillan. Marlowe and the editor had gotten on famously and now Marlowe suggested Macmillan—and Rinzler—should be the next stop for *Traitor*. Reach dutifully shipped off the partial and the outline, but it was no go. "The Marlowe (proposal) is slick, professional and well-done," Rinzler wrote Reach on Nov. 21. "The problem for me, however, is that tired-old traitor, the likes of whom I have seen too many times for too many years. I like Dan a lot and would love to publish him. But can't he come up with something fresher and more original than an archetypal 1950-type Communist spy? It's so damned old hat."

In December 1967, Gold Medal issued *The Raven is a Blood-Red Bird*, the only novel that would carry the names of both Marlowe and Odell. Like *Route of the Red Gold*, it dealt with military adventuring, this time involving Air Force Col. Russ Carlson, the pilot of a plane that leaves Greece carrying a defecting Russian scientist. The plane, damaged on takeoff by pistol shots fired by Russian agents, is finally downed behind the Iron Curtain in Albania by a violent thunderstorm and lightning strike. The crew and the scientist must enlist the help of a band of gypsies, including a beautiful female triple-agent code-named Raven, to try to escape.

Neither *Route* nor *Raven* put Marlowe in the big time, but a slight change of direction the following year would give him and Odell (and Nussbaum, operating in the background) a long-running gig in the world of Gold Medal adventures.

CHAPTER 11:
The Man With Nobody's Face

MARLOWE'S INCOME FROM WRITING FLUCTUATED SIGNIFICANTLY FROM year to year. It's hard to track it closely, except for 1968, when he charted it himself. This was a pivotal year. After finishing off the Johnny Killain series, Marlowe had written stand-alone books for years, always seeking the dream of a big-selling hardcover. Softcover sales weren't bringing him financial security, even though he told an interviewer in 1968 that his biggest-selling paperback book up to that point (he didn't specify which this was) had sold 400,000 copies, including translations in Germany, Spain, France and other countries.

Though he would continue to pursue hardback success, in 1968 he would commit to a paperback character—the bank robber-turned-foreign agent Earl Drake—and to a series—the "Operation" series—that would define most of the rest of his career. He would also move to an even closer relationship with his two main collaborators, Al Nussbaum and William Odell.

Although the year, his second on the Harbor Beach City Council, was not good for him financially, it was quite productive, he said in a *One for the Road* column published on Jan. 2, 1969. In 1968, Marlowe wrote 894,000 "commercial words," which included four letters a day, most to domestic and foreign literary agents, editors, publishers and producers. That average was down deliberately from five a day in 1967, and he'd made a New Year's resolution to go to three a day in 1969. He'd also written 50 pages and an outline of a suspense novel (*One Endless Hour*) equaling 40,000 words (first draft plus revision) and then wrote and sold the novel—two more drafts—for another 120,000 words, totaling 160,000 words for the project.

He also turned out 50 pages and an outline for a suspense novel (*Operation Fireball*), doing two drafts to complete that work. He landed a contract for *Fireball*, planning to write the final version in 1969. In addition, he went to his files, dug out an unsold novel (possibly *Syndicate Kickoff*, a novel he wrote with Odell about the Mafia fixing professional football games), rewrote it completely and sent it off to market. He wrote and sold 13 short stories averaging 3,500 words each, and churned out five others he failed to sell. Marlowe also wrote 52 weekly newspaper columns averaging 500 words each, as well as a dozen book reviews for the *Detroit Free Press* averaging 750 words each. The newspaper was on strike the first eight months of the year, he noted, "or that total would have been considerably higher."

For his 894,000 words, Marlowe had a gross income, before expenses, of slightly less than a cent a word, or somewhere in the neighborhood of $8,900. "If the foregoing set of facts prompts you to steer your boy or girl away from being a writer, I can't blame you, but I can say truthfully that I wouldn't change places with any of you," Marlowe wrote. "For a man with no financial responsibilities other than to himself, there's no life like it despite more than its share of frustrations…I make my own decisions, for one thing, and I set my own alarm clock."

Marlowe's independent nature, so obvious in this statement, led him to take an extreme position in an April 25, 1968, *One for the Road* column that many readers found offensive. Dr. Martin Luther King Jr. had been murdered a week before. Marlowe said perhaps King was a great orator and a "dynamic catalyst," but he was not a "great man" because—in Marlowe's view—he had turned away from nonviolence and had broken the law in the course of civil rights protests. "He was a martyr, true," Marlowe wrote, "but from one point of view, so was

Hitler. King believed in what he preached, obviously, but so did Hitler. King believed that the end justified the means, as did Hitler."

Having linked King in this argument to one of the most despised men in history, Marlowe then eased off. "This is not to say that his death is not a burden to us all," Marlowe wrote. "It is. He was wrong, but the manner of his going was wrong. He chose to be a warrior, which was his folly. We killed him, which was our folly... To a courageous but misguided man I say: vale, Martin Luther King. Lie light the earth above thee."

(Despite the far-out nature of this column, many people who knew Marlowe well—including a number of liberals—didn't consider him a racist, or even particularly extreme in his political opinions. "Most of the Mystery Writers of America were rabid right-wingers," said his friend Mel Cebulash, an author, editor and publisher. "Dan wasn't. He thought out his views. Dan had an open mind about everything." Marlowe's most prominent black character—included in three books—is a flamboyant gambler named Candy Kane, a brave man and loyal friend who dies fighting home-grown terrorists. On the other hand, Marlowe's personal letters after he suffered amnesia offer two examples of racial slurs: "a big black buck" and "a nigger in the woodpile," the second reference meaning something suspicious in a situation. Even pre-amnesia, he was politically incorrect in many ways.)

Marlowe wasn't consistent in his views. He defended law and order where King was involved, but ignored it in regard to Nussbaum—a multiple felon who had taken part in a crime that resulted in murder. Apparently, Marlowe saw no contradiction in that.

Marlowe's bond with Nussbaum continued to strengthen. In 1968, after Nussbaum had been in prison for four years, Marlowe was finally allowed to visit him at Leavenworth, and thereafter he tried to visit him twice a year. The visits were welcome, since prison was rough and sometimes deadly. This was underlined when Peter Columbus Curry, the young man who had taken part in the Brooklyn bank robbery with Nussbaum and Wilcoxson, died of unknown causes at 27. On Sept. 11, 1968, in the parlance of the Federal Bureau of Prisons, Curry was "released by death" from the sentence he was serving at the U.S. Penitentiary in Lewisburg, Pennsylvania.

Nussbaum could count himself lucky that he was not only surviving in prison but, to some degree, thriving. His fiction-writing efforts were picking up speed. In 1968, two more of his stories, "The Paternal Instinct" and "The Dead Past" were published in *Alfred Hitchcock's Mystery Magazine.*

Marlowe, possibly to help market Nussbaum by pretending to keep him at arm's length, sometimes wrote about his friend without fully explaining their relationship. For instance, on March 6, 1969, Marlowe wrote a column that began "Many of my friends know that a bank robber once identified himself with one of my books and involved me with the FBI. By the time that little misunderstanding was straightened out, I had met the bank robber (in custody) and a few of his friends."

Marlowe then went on to tell the tale about how Nussbaum opened a number of locked safes to show a retailer his products weren't secure. In the column, Marlowe didn't mention that his friendship with Nussbaum was ongoing and close.

On April 1, Nussbaum signed a document authorizing Marlowe "to act for me in regard to all my literary properties." There was no hint of this in a column Marlowe published on Dec. 4, 1969. In it, the novelist noted that the annual short-story collection of the Mystery Writers of America, which that particular year was titled *Merchants of Menace,* contained a story by Nussbaum: "Newcomer Al Nussbaum, with 'The Dead Past,' takes us on a startling excursion to the turn of the century when men were men and women were devious."

Despite Marlowe's reticence, his help and Nussbaum's industry were already showing results that would lead to a productive career. In all, over 20 years, Nussbaum would publish 50 stories in either *Alfred Hitchcock's Mystery Magazine* or *Ellery Queen's Mystery Magazine.* Some of the stories were published under his own name, others under the pseudonyms Alberto N. Martin, Albert Avellano, A.F. Oreshnik, and Carl Martin.

In the late 1960s, Nussbaum also began writing for Scholastic Magazines, which issued youth-oriented publications out of its offices in New York City. His contact was Cebulash, an editor and editorial director for the publisher. Nussbaum wrote to the publisher under his prison number at Leavenworth, and initially placed stories in the magazine *Scholastic Scope.*

"He published two stories with us, juvenile stories," Cebulash said. "If they were mysteries, they were just little mysteries for a teenager. I thought he was an interesting, bright fellow, and I got to be good friends with him."

Cebulash, who had done novelizations of Disney movies and would go on to write many novels (and to become executor of the estate of novelist James T. Farrell), corresponded with Nussbaum regularly from that point on and later was introduced to Marlowe through Nussbaum. Over the years, Cebulash got to know both men well, especially in California. After moving there in the mid-1970s, he inadvertently played a minor role in a bizarre scheme in which Nussbaum lured Marlowe to L.A.. He also hired both men for freelance work, socialized with them, and kept in contact with them for the rest of their lives.

Nussbaum's writing skill was growing, as was his familiarity with Marlowe's style and characters. The bank robber's entrepreneurial and literary instincts began to assert themselves. He realized, as most discerning readers of Marlowe still do, that Marlowe's best character was the bank robbing protagonist of *The Name of the Game Is Death* who goes by the false names "Roy Martin" and "Chet Arnold" but never reveals his own name.

Nussbaum urged Marlowe to bring this character back in a sequel, but Marlowe wasn't convinced, according to *Playing With Fire: Dan J. Marlowe, Al Nussbaum and Earl Drake* by Josef Hoffmann. Part of Nussbaum's effort was to come up with a name that would define the character. He chose "Earl Drake," using a version of the last name of Roy Earle, the gangster in W.R. Burnett's *High Sierra*, and the surname of Sir Francis Drake, the seafarer, explorer and pirate. Though the name Earl Drake would stick to the character from that point onward, attentive readers will note that this, again, was not the true name of the bank-robbing protagonist, but an alias he had used in the past.

The choice of a strong character name was only part of Nussbaum's lobbying effort to produce a sequel, Hoffmann says. A continuation of the story presented strong challenges. For one thing, the protagonist had sustained severe burns, especially in the head area, at the end of *The Name of the Game Is Death*, when a rifle bullet punctured an automobile gas tank and sprayed him with burning gasoline during a gun battle with police. Because of this, the character could only return as an invalid, or someone in need of permanent care, Hoffmann noted.

"Nussbaum suggested to Marlowe that he go through the novel for him, looking out for the elements which constituted the figure of the hero, and for ways in which the story might be continued," Hoffmann wrote. "Nussbaum then produced an outline of the character for the series, gave him a name and drew up a 60-page concept for the sequel. In three weeks flat, Marlowe wrote the second volume of the Earl Drake series. It appeared in 1969 published by Gold Medal under the title *One Endless Hour*."

Nussbaum's account of what happened is similar, except that he said his sample was somewhat shorter and that Marlowe took longer to write the book. "He wrote *One Endless Hour* in about six weeks, and his Earl Drake series was off and running," Nussbaum recalled in *Turning Sentences into Words: Writing in Prison*.

While all the Earl Drake books, including *The Name of the Game Is Death*, are now seen as a series, *Name* was not supposed to be a series book. It's unlikely Marlowe intended *One Endless Hour* to fit this pattern, either. There's little development of the main character's personal story beyond day-to-day survival. The protagonist is the same steely, amoral robber of *Name*, focused simply on pulling more bank jobs planned by criminal expert "Schemer" Frenz, whose detailed analyses resemble Nussbaum's real-life casing practices.

The Drake character recovers from his burns in the prison wing of the state hospital in Florida. He then bribes a Pakistani plastic surgeon to rebuild his face. To make his appearance as natural as possible, he needs to apply makeup to his reconstructed face and to wear a hairpiece after he escapes and resumes his life of crime. He pulls off one small bank robbery with part-time robbers "Preacher" Harris, a gambler, and porn-film maker Dick Dahl, but a more complex robbery—involving the kidnapping of the families of a bank manager and his assistant—goes wrong. Both Harris and Dahl are killed, leaving Drake with nothing. (A small note: While writing the book, Marlowe either forgot one of Drake's chief passions—playing the horses—or decided Drake should conceal that fact from Harris. Asked by Harris whether he's a gambler, too, Drake replied: "I might have bet fifty bucks on a horse three times in my life.")

One Endless Hour, which apparently carried the working title *The Face of Evil*, is a bizarre book. It's a quite worthy successor to *The Name of the Game Is Death* as well as a strange minor master-piece in its own right. Though the surface story is simple enough—a criminal escapes from prison and pulls off robberies—it's set apart by its atmosphere of cruelty and sexual kinkiness, punctuated by the death of one of the robbers at the hands of the assistant bank manager's idiot daughter, who has been locked up in the basement by her family for years.

Odell, Marlowe's other chief collaborator, also helped with the writing of *One Endless Hour*, though apparently his contribu-tion was minimal, at least through the early efforts to produce the book. In a July 7, 1968, letter he told Marlowe: "Thanks for the check for my share…and I'm a little chagrined to accept it since I haven't done much up to this point." After four years of Marlowe's collaboration with Odell, Marlowe's literary agent still wasn't enthused about the relationship. Reach expressed his doubts again on March 19, 1968, when he told Marlowe their *Syndicate Kickoff* novel proposal had been sent to Gold Medal, but that he wasn't happy with it.

> As before, the actual football sections are great, but some of the other parts sound like somebody trying, badly, to write for *Ladies Home Journal*. Why in the world do you need those three models at the start of Chapter 2? They don't add one whit to your story and the writing of them is oh, so, cute—and absolutely dead. And when you finally do get around to the sex scene, it's so perfunctory it *still* could go into LHJ. Better do something about your collaboration setup before it ruins you.

Some three years later, *Syndicate Kickoff*, by now a fully fleshed-out novel, ultimately failed to make it into print when four other pro football novels reached the bookstores, causing the prospective publisher for *Kickoff* to lose interest.

But, despite Reach's misgivings early in the writing of that book, Marlowe was still committed to working with Odell. The two writers had decided to leave Odell's name off their collaborations, however, believing Marlowe's name alone was more marketable. "They used Dan's name and reputation to get the sales," explained their mutual friend, James Batson. However, Odell's silent efforts were significant. The Air Force combat veteran (who also had a background in intelligence operations) would soon be making a huge contribution to Marlowe's output, with the creation of the "Operation" series. The story lines for the character Earl Drake begin to change with *Operation Fireball*, published in January 1969. Hoffmann, whose *Playing With Fire* article was reviewed in draft form by Nussbaum, put it this way:

> At the recommendation of Fawcett, his [Marlowe's] publisher... he allows the hero to undergo a change. The professional criminal becomes a sometime undercover CIA agent. Each book is given the password "Operation," even new editions of old Earl Drake novels.
>
> The reason? Commercial considerations. Since 1967, Fawcett Gold Medal had been publishing the gangster series "Parker," by Richard Stark (Donald Westlake)," the first volume of which was published in 1962, the same year as *The Name of the Game Is Death*.
>
> It was assumed at Fawcett that the market could only take one gangster series, and as Stark's novels were more established, they were given priority over the Earl Drake series. In view of the sales successes of spy and political thrillers à la James Bond, the Earl Drake series was also to be pointed in this direction (with the exception of *Operation Whiplash* in which the setting and action of the first two Drake stories are taken up again.)

Marlowe's own explanation for the change differed slightly from Hoffmann's interpretation, which presumably originated with Nussbaum. In a 1984 interview by journalist Roger Martin that was published in a French newsletter for crime readers called *No. 8*, Marlowe said editors at Fawcett did suggest the change. But they did so not because Drake was seen as too similar to Parker, but as too similar to Travis McGee, the private eye created by writer John D. MacDonald. "His books and mine were competing for the same audience, so I had to 'reinvent' Drake," Marlowe told Martin.

Perhaps, but it's obvious that Drake resembles Parker, a hard-as-nails criminal who sheds blood easily, more than he does McGee, who is tough, but often trips over his ideals.

Marlowe adapted to the change with his usual willingness to write whatever sold, but had some doubts in the wake of the first two "Operation" books; "…One of my few reservations in connection with Gold Medal's desire that I move the Earl Drake character in the current series more over onto the side of law and order is the seemingly corresponding drop in European sales," Marlowe told an executive at the Samuel French agency on Aug. 2, 1970. Whether or not the change affected European sales (which isn't clear), American sales were good enough for the publisher to keep Marlowe and Odell pumping out "Operation" books for roughly seven years.

[To be clear: Fawcett Gold Medal marketed the 12 books that featured Earl Drake as the main character as the "Earl Drake series," including *The Name of the Game Is Death* and *One Endless Hour*. But when this book refers to the "Operation" series, it means the 10 books with "Operation" in the title of the American editions. The first two Drake books are excluded, even though the London-based publisher Hodder and Stoughton issued *The Name of the Game Is Death* as *Operation Overkill* in 1973, and *One Endless Hour* as *Operation Endless Hour* in 1975. To complicate the matter, *Operation Flashpoint*, published by Fawcett in 1970, was originally called simply *Flashpoint*. Here, it's still part of the "Operation" series.]

Most Marlowe fans believe that none of the 10 "Operation" books, which were published from 1969 to 1976, rank among the writer's best work. In a 1977 article, a writer for *The Armchair Detective* noted that, in 1969, "Fawcett published *Operation Fireball* in which, God knows why, Marlowe hooked Drake up with the government. Drake becomes sort of a 'government agent,' in much the same way Alexander Mundy did on TV's *It Takes a Thief*, in exchange for 'safety' from prosecution." None of these books, *The Armchair Detective* article said, were nearly as good as *The Name of the Game Is Death* and *One Endless Hour*. "Marlowe should have left Drake a professional thief," the writer concluded.

This criticism of the "Operation" books rings true, with the possible exception of *Operation Deathmaker*, issued very late in the cycle. Still, they hold up reasonably well, braced by the strength of the Drake character and the oddity of his constant need to disguise himself and protect his fire-damaged and re-built facial features.

The covers of most of these books included a mug shot-like inset of a rough-featured man identified as DRAKE, "The Man With Nobody's Face."

With the creation of the "Operation" books, Marlowe's collaboration with Odell finally jelled. This is obvious from letters they exchanged while writing *Operation Fireball*. In *Fireball*, Drake resumes his relationship with Hazel at her ranch in Ely, Nevada, but then has to hide from the police. Drake is recruited for a job by an ex-partner, Slater. The goal is to get $4 million hidden in Cuba before Castro's takeover. Hazel provides front money and runs a shortwave radio for the operation, which also involves boat owner Chico Wilson, Slater and Karl Erikson, a cashiered naval officer.

The operation succeeds, but Slater and Wilson are killed. Before he dies, Slater reveals to Drake that Erikson is really a U.S. government agent who hired the group because the project was too risky to get official backing. Instead of collecting a full share of the $4 million, Drake is paid less than $2,000 in government per diem, and now he's dependent on Erikson to protect him from his criminal past. With this leverage, Erikson recruits him repeatedly for surreptitious government operations.

Marlowe's approach to these novels was to dope out a plot with Odell, and then have Odell write "set pieces"—rough-draft action-oriented chunks of the story—that Marlowe would then rewrite and blend into the overall fabric of the books. One set piece, for instance, was a scene in *Fireball* in which Drake, Erikson and Wilson enter the Guantanamo brig disguised as naval personnel, then break out into Cuba.

On Jan. 11, 1969, Odell wrote to Marlowe:

> This is the first 'set piece' which should contain enough data on the technical side, plus a few other observations which might form the basis for an adequate drop-in or conversion to an actual scene.

Tried to convey some character traits you might build on or use along the way—but held the participants down to a minimum.

Since you listed the "wanted" pieces in more or less chronological order, I'll work on them in turn so I will be keeping pace with you if you're working through the outline page by page.

I'll have other [sic] coming along, but I would like for you to give me some comments (guidance) as to whether or not the sort of thing I've concocted here is what you had in mind.

Marlowe and Odell were corresponding not only via letters, but by exchanging audio tapes, a practice Marlowe often employed. About two weeks after Odell wrote the above letter, Marlowe responded:

I rec'd your tape on the Gitmo brig scene, and since I can reply in a paragraph there seemed to be no point in turning the tape around.

I like it all as you have it with the exception of a couple of slight changes of focus. I don't think we can let them look lucky that Slater is not in the brig. They should have a plan—Drake's blowing out a wall, since the cell block is airtight if the building is not—and Drake and Erikson could be discussing the proper explosives when Wilson finds out from the Wave that Slater isn't there. This helps him pay his way in the story, too. Just about the rest of it goes as is, bad weather and all.

In the course of writing the book, Marlowe also called on Odell's expertise and background to rough out scenes involving the physical setup of a Cuban ambulance, installing a shortwave radio, setting up a jamming device on a cruiser, and slipping through American defenses into Cuba. *Fireball* came together quickly, and by late April, Marlowe met with Fawcett editors Knox Burger, Walter Fultz and Bruce Feld, and hammered out the final revisions they wanted in the story. He also gave them a verbal pitch on what he planned as the next entry in the series, *Flashpoint*.

The plot of *Flashpoint*, published in 1970, seems quite contemporary in today's world, which is beset by terrorist attacks, suicide bombings and Mideast tension. Drake snags a ride on a chartered plane full of gamblers headed for Las Vegas. He intends to deliver $75,000 that Hazel owes to a man there, but he loses the money when he's robbed by Middle Eastern terrorists who force the plane down onto a remote landing strip in Nevada. Karl Erikson shows up to investigate the terrorists, who are planning violent robberies in the U.S. to pay for overseas operations. Erikson enlists Drake to help because he can identify the bad guys. Drake agrees because he's determined to get Hazel's money back.

They trace the hijackers to New York City, where Drake discovers that the head of the operation is a Turkish diplomat at the U.N. Drake and Erikson break into the diplomat's safe, trying to find information, and find cash instead. Drake cops $200,000 of the loot for himself, in addition to Hazel's $75,000. Erikson makes official moves to stop the terrorists' efforts to steal a U.S. nuclear device, but in the end it takes Drake's clever plan and a flurry of gunshots to complete the mission.

Flashpoint makes use of Marlowe's background as a gambler, has plenty of action, and gives Drake a chance to go off on his own and have sex with a Turkish beauty named Talia. ("A tiny pool trapped in her navel reflected sunlight like a many-faceted diamond. The white bikini was almost transparent when wet, and it showed plainly her erect nipples and the dark triangle of her pubic hair.") These erotic diversions for Drake are always welcome for the reader of the "Operation" books, because—as the series continues—Drake settles into an almost man-and-wife relationship with Hazel, and their sexual romps become predictable and humdrum.

In 1971, *Flashpoint* won the Mystery Writers of America Edgar Allan Poe Award as Best Paperback Original of the year. Marlowe accepted the award, and Odell's contribution was not mentioned. Eighteen years later, however, in a short bio that accompanied an article he wrote for *Naval History* magazine, Odell would say that he "received the Edgar Award from the Mystery Writers of America," an obvious reference to *Flashpoint*.

By the time that award came along, Marlowe was already off on a new phase of his life, one that would take him away from Harbor Beach for extended periods of time. The change may have been triggered to some degree by the death of Marlowe's long-time literary agent, James Reach, ailing since at least early 1966. Reach suffered a heart attack on March 5, 1970, while dining at the Cattleman's Restaurant in New York and was dead on arrival at the Polyclinic Hospital. Marlowe went to New York for the funeral.

With the death of Reach, Marlowe lost a friend, a top agent, a savvy marketer, and an astute editor who always tried to smooth out the rough spots in his stories. Marlowe would market his own work to publishers for several years after this, building on the momentum created by Reach in launching the "Operation" series. The writer would also roam far from home in search of authentic background material.

On May 4, two months after Reach's death, Marlowe submitted a letter to the Town of Harbor Beach resigning his seat on the City Council, and several days later left for San Francisco for an extended stay. In a postcard from Denver postmarked May 8, he told Gempel he had "found a little night life here" and would probably reach the Bay Area early the following week "if green felt on tables at Reno doesn't slow me down too much." When he arrived, he at first rented a studio apartment, but by May 18 had moved into the Hotel Roosevelt at Jones and Eddy Street, luckily choosing it over a hotel that shortly was damaged severely by fire. Marlowe told Gempel: "Had a few drinks with a couple members of the local writing fraternity (whom I knew from New York) but otherwise I've been behaving myself. Have first meeting tomorrow with a guy who's been working on a script."

It's not clear who the "guy working on a script" was, but one of the writers Marlowe met in San Francisco was mystery novelist Joe Gores, a Notre Dame graduate and active private detective. In 1969, Gores had received an Edgar award for Best First Novel from the Mystery Writers of America for *A Time of Predators*, as well as an Edgar for Best Short Story, "Good-bye, Pops." Gores had met Marlowe at an MWA banquet in New York and had gotten on well with him. In San Francisco, their friendship flourished.

"He liked to take early-morning walks, so we'd meet about 6 a.m. and walk through Chinatown, then he'd go home and work," Gores said. Marlowe was good-natured, a straightforward man. "He beamed a lot," Gores said. The 55-year-old writer also sometimes seemed like a man out of another era. "Marlowe was up to my apartment one time and said something about 'the little woman' and my wife just about threw him out," Gores said. "That was my ex-wife. He had that sincerity and kind of an old-fashioned view of life. Though he never said anything about her, I think he missed his dead wife."

Gores recalled Marlowe with a novelist's eye for detail: "He was always courteous to women. He had red cheeks, like a drinker. He was a big guy, but he had these small, sort of precise hands."

Marlowe spent about eight months in San Francisco, apparently writing *Operation Breakthrough* and *Operation Drumfire*. It's also likely he was churning out four books of pornography that would be published in 1971 by Dansk Blue Books. Perhaps one reason he decided to spend time away from Harbor Beach was that he wanted more privacy to produce this large volume of porn, though even there he was producing sex stories that ranged from racy to raw, publishing them under pseudonyms. This period also proved sexually liberating for Marlowe, if we can believe a portion of a letter he wrote to his friend James Batson in 1977:

> There's a woman in Long Beach I've known ever since the year in San Francisco. She has a high-up job in the L.A. educational system and also inherited a bunch of money. Owns a couple of condominiums in Hawaii: that type of thing. A real swinger, far more than me. She opened me up sexually. I had been quite conservative before her advent.

Perhaps. But, as we shall see, Marlowe was expressing a strong interest in kinky sex at least three years before his stay in San Francisco. Gores said he wasn't aware that Marlowe was writing explicit sex books, but it wouldn't have surprised or shocked him. "A lot of extremely well-known writers were doing it, soft-core or hard-core," Gores said. "Some of them admit it, some of them don't."

One who admits it is legendary mystery writer Bill Pronzini, author of the Nameless Detective series, who met Marlowe in San Francisco on a Marlowe visit in 1969. In February 1970, Pronzini moved to Majorca for three years to live cheaply while he established himself as a writer. Pronzini also had another reason for living there:

Majorca was the home of the publisher of Liverpool Library Press, a sex-book operation based in France. The publisher liked to have a stable of his erotic-book writers around him, and Pronzini was one of those. To pay the bills and support his mainstream writing, Pronzini churned out some 25 erotic novels alone or in collaboration. Early on, he talked about this work to Marlowe, who he knew also wrote porn. "I was a little hesitant about it, a little embarrassed," Pronzini recalled, "and he said not to worry about it because it's… a good training ground for a young writer, and not to take it too seriously, which I didn't."

Marlowe's realistic approach and his life experience made him a good mentor. They also made him a good man to have along in a tough situation. Gores learned that when he introduced Marlowe to the street world Gores knew so well.

As a private eye, Gores was a "repo man," specializing in repossessing the cars of buyers who had fallen behind on their payments. In essence, he often had to legally "steal" cars from the deadbeat buyers by finding the vehicles, then starting them with picks, "hot-wire" setups, master keys, or "pop keys"—filed-down blank keys for a particular model that often would start a car if you inserted them and jiggled them around. During Marlowe's stay in San Francisco, Gores was still doing sporadic repo work, which piqued the interest of Marlowe and another writer who was in town.

"He (Marlowe) wanted to ride around with me on a couple of repos," Gores recalled. "And there was another writer who shall remain nameless who wanted to ride around with me. At the time Hunter's Point was a very scary place, with the (housing) projects and a lot of hostile blacks who were shooting out windows…The three of us went out there, it was like twelve midnight or one in the morning or something…and we spotted the car (to be repossessed). Dan and I got into the car in the front and the other guy got in the car in the back. I ran the pop keys on it.

"Suddenly, while I was doing that, a window went up on the third floor up there and a guy started yelling out the window, 'That's my car! I'm gettin' my gun!' And the guy in the back seat is yelling, 'We've got to go, we've got to go, he's got a gun!' I got the car started but I couldn't get the (emergency) brake off. And I said to Dan, while this other guy is screaming in the back seat, 'Would you look in the glove compartment and see if there's a manual in there that tells us how to get that fucking hand brake off?'

"So Dan is sitting there, calmly going through the manual, and the guy sticks a rifle out of the window and starts shooting. He's shooting holes in his own car that he's going to have to pay for. And this other guy is almost dying (from fear) in the back. And Dan says, 'Oh, Joe, when you put it into gear on this kind of car, the hand brake just goes off automatically.' So I did, and off we went. He (Marlowe) was cool as a cucumber."

CHAPTER 12:
Down Mexico Way

MARLOWE RETURNED TO MICHIGAN IN DECEMBER 1970, BUT HE'D developed an itch for change. "When I stay too long in one place, I find myself describing the same apartment bedroom three times," he later told a friend. Starting in July 1972, he began to winter in Mexico while spending spring and summer in Harbor Beach. He also sought out new living quarters in his home community. In May 1973, following the death of landlady Helen Hamilton, he finished moving his belongings from her house near the shore to an apartment over the *Harbor Beach Times* office at 123 N. First St.

The frost and snow of Michigan had begun to wear on him, and Mexico offered a temperate alternative. In September 1973, an article by Nussbaum in the *Boston Herald* described his living circumstances: "Today, Dan J. Marlowe lives in a white stucco house perched high on the side of Mirador Hill, looking down on the pink, multi-steepled parish church and the bull ring of San Miguel de Allende, Guanajuato, Mexico." In a letter the year before to Mel Cebulash, the Scholastic Magazines editor and novelist, Nussbaum described San Miguel as "a hilly village of about 20,000 that's a national monument. Very rustic in a Mexican-peon-of-the-1900's way. We've all seen parts of it in Mexican movies."

San Miguel, a historic town founded in 1542 by the Franciscan monk Fray Juan de San Miguel, was favored by wealthy Mexico City tourists and harbored a robust American and Canadian expatriate community, mostly retirees. As Nussbaum noted, it was declared a national historic monument in 1926 by the Mexican government, which decreed that development in its historic district would be restricted to preserve the town's character. Among its architectural gems were La Parroquia, the Church of St. Michael the Archangel, and the Temple of the Nuns.

After World War II, American ex-servicemen flooded to the town to study at its famed art school, the Escuela Universitaria de Bellas Artes. When it closed and a subsequent school couldn't get accreditation from the American Embassy, most of the veterans left. However, in the 1960s, a few years before Marlowe arrived, San Miguel began a period as a popular counterculture destination for the likes of such rebels as Ken Kesey (author of *One Flew Over the Cuckoo's Nest*) and the Merry Pranksters, the LSD-fueled psychic adventurers whose 1964 bus trip across America was chronicled in Tom Wolfe's *The Electric Kool-Aid Acid Test*. On Feb. 3, 1968, beat writer Neal Cassady died beside the railroad tracks between San Miguel and Celaya, possibly of exposure, possibly of a drug over-dose, after attending a wedding party in San Miguel.

Marlowe, a conservative now in his late 50s, wouldn't have been attracted by the counterculture aspects of the local history. The warm weather, the congenial surroundings and—above all—the inexpensive cost of living were the things that drew him to San Miguel. He rented a house with two living rooms—one glassed-in and overlooking the city below—two bedrooms, a kitchen, bath, what he described as "a small but handsome" garden, and a garage that was a tight fit for his car. "I've already scraped both doors on the passenger's side, and that's when I was sober," he wrote Pronzini. "Some night I'll come home pixilated from margaritas and Ron Collins and shove the house right down the hill into the bull ring."

A block and a half down the street was the restaurant Posada La Ermita, which Marlowe called "one of the nicest places in all Mexico." Owned by the Mexican comedian Cantinflas, it offered excellent food at prices lower than Marlowe had paid for meals in

Harbor Beach. The author also consumed a great deal of fresh fruit and bottled water in an effort to avoid diarrhea, which he referred to as "the Mexican two-step."

He quickly settled down to work and found the conditions to his liking.

"(O)ddly, it feels like the summers I used to spend in New Hampshire when I was first breaking in: isolation, quietude, peace," he told Pronzini. "I'm a connoisseur of sunrises, and Mexico's will stack up with any of them. I sit and eat cold melon and watch the sun's first rays catch the church spires below and then gradually lighten the plaza and the city. Oh, yes, the plaza: I promenaded it with the natives two nights in a row. Do you get the feeling I'm enjoying the place?"

A month and a half later, Marlowe was even more content.

"I like it better here every day," he wrote Pronzini. "Slow-paced, with time for everything. I'm reading five books a week. I haven't done that for fifteen years. Exceptional climate: cool, with no humidity. No industry, so no air pollution. And cheap: probably a third less expensive that it was in the states."

Marlowe jocularly said that the only drawback was that he was tempted to step up his drinking.

"I'm still learning the ropes," he wrote. "Mexican bars have one quaint custom: they never close as long as anyone's buying. For a guy like me who drinks 'em faster later in the evening, this can be hazardous. As a direct consequence I've witnessed a couple of sunrises I didn't get up to see."

Nussbaum, too, was hearing that Marlowe had found a beautiful home away from home. On Aug. 9, 1972, the bank robber wrote to Cebulash, "Dan has fallen in love with Mexico. He has an eight-dollar per week cook, maid, housekeeper combination who spoils him. That's a hundred pesos—the rate of exchange is very favorable."

Though Cebulash would never visit Marlowe in Mexico, his friendship would be quite important to the writer. Through Nussbaum's good offices, Cebulash had met Marlowe earlier in 1972 at the cocktail party Marlowe always threw during that period at the Mystery Writers of America convention in New York. Cebulash was favorably impressed by Marlowe.

"He was a real nice guy and introduced me to all those people at the cocktail party," Cebulash said. "He was a big deal in the Mystery Writers at that time… Every major writer was at his cocktail party and they sort of hung on what he had to say."

In preparing Cebulash to meet Marlowe, Nussbaum provided his own take on the writer. "Dan's a funny guy," Nussbaum wrote in an April 15, 1972, letter to Cebulash. "He writes such hard-boiled, unromantic stuff (he really excels in the action scenes, I think) and I don't think he has a hard bone in his body. He looks like someone's uncle, built along the lines of Archie Bunker on TV, and sounds like a New England native, which he is. If it hadn't been for his pushing and prodding—he writes once a week, sometimes more often—I'd have given up writing in disgust long before I learned to punctuate with fair consistency and otherwise became addicted."

In May, after the MWA party, Nussbaum told Cebulash that Marlowe's stories were far more hard-boiled than the material he, a real ex-criminal, typically produced. "I swear, the ideas he comes up with scare even me," Nussbaum wrote. "It's a good thing he's a writer, not a wronger."

By this time, the "Operation" books were selling briskly and Earl Drake had become a well-established adventure character. In *Operation Breakthrough*, published in 1971, Drake and Erikson crack a bank vault in Nassau, Bahamas, to steal Mafia records. Erikson is arrested and jailed by the local police. With the help of the black Nassau gambler, Candy Kane, and his tall, athletic Chinese girlfriend, Chen Yi, Drake helps Erikson escape from prison; all flee the island with the Mafia in pursuit.

Operation Drumfire, published in 1972, takes Drake, Hazel and Erikson to San Francisco to investigate a computer-betting syndicate. They find a violent militant group planning to kill U.S. and Mexican VIPs as a protest during a visit by Mexican bigwigs. Drake saves the dignitaries with the help of Candy Kane, but Kane is killed.

Nussbaum, as a technical advisor, helped to some degree with the book. He suggested that Drake, who typically carried a .38 Smith and Wesson Police Special revolver in a shoulder holster, replace this weapon with a 9-millimeter Smith and Wesson semi-automatic pistol carried in a cross-draw holster. This was done, no doubt, to modernize Drake's weaponry and make the character seem more "with it."

(It should be noted that, despite Marlowe's research and Nussbaum's advice on firearms—and Odell's, for that matter—errors about small arms pepper the novels. For instance, the gun-store clerk in *Operation Drumfire* implies that all hand-loaded cartridges have soft-nosed bullets, and that all commercial cartridges are copper-jacketed. In fact, hand loads and commercial cartridges each offer a mix of soft-nosed and copper-jacketed bullets. Also, in *The Vengeance Man*, the main character clicks off the safety of a .38 Smith and Wesson Police Special revolver, which has no safety.)

Operation Checkmate, also published in 1972 and set mostly in Taiwan, deals with Hazel's efforts to help her friend Chen Yi secure an inheritance. Chen Yi's large extended family is involved in events surrounding two political assassinations and corruption at the U.S. military command in Taiwan. People try to kill Chen Yi, but Hazel, Drake and Erikson save her. Erikson develops a romantic relationship with Chen Yi.

By 1973, Marlowe and Odell were dealing with a new editor at Fawcett Gold Medal, a clear-eyed but tentative man named Joseph Elder who later would open a literary agency and take up representation of the two writers. That year, they published *Operation Stranglehold* and *Operation Whiplash*.

In *Stranglehold*, Drake and Hazel again bail out Erikson, who has been jailed in Spain in a failed effort to free a presidential candidate's son who has been locked up on a marijuana charge. During a prisoner transfer, Drake and Hazel free the young man and Erikson, who has been injured, but are burdened by a young woman who the young man refuses to abandon.

In *Whiplash*, Hazel is lured back to Florida by a Mafia capo who secretly owned the money Hazel believed she had inherited from her second husband. The capo wants to kill both her and Drake, who is in line to inherit Hazel's money, but their cleverness and survival instincts prevail.

Operation Hammerlock, published in 1975, is the first Marlowe book set primarily in Mexico. While vacationing there, Drake and Hazel come upon a rape in progress and rescue a young woman who is both the wife of a sadistic police captain and the mistress of the local political boss. The police captain takes Hazel hostage, throws Drake in jail, and demands that Drake avenge the affront to the captain's honor by killing the political boss. Drake tries to stall the captain. Rather than killing the boss, Drake says, why not rob him of all his money? Drake pretends he wants to do this electronically with the aid of a young American-trained computer technician Drake met in jail.

Early in 1975, the year *Hammerlock* appeared, Marlowe's nephew Christopher stayed with the writer for six weeks while studying Spanish at the language school in San Miguel. He found his uncle a congenial host well-integrated into the American expatriate community. Marlowe hadn't lost contact with girlfriends in the United States. During the six weeks Christopher stayed in San Miguel, two women came to spend time with his uncle. "The women who visited him were very elegant, classy," Christopher recalled. "They were very self-assured and nice-looking."

When it came to finding companionship, Marlowe wasn't above pickups, but in Mexico that proved to be hit-and-miss. "The womanizing in San Miguel is an iffy thing," he wrote Pronzini. "Plenty of widows available, but in my age bracket, not yours. In the summer, loads of students, the girls eager to live 'Life.' Transients and drifters at all times, but never predictable. Usually *something*, though."

Because of the chanciness of that kind of pursuit, Marlowe had begun importing female company to Mexico early on. Doris Young, a Harbor Beach woman nearly 20 years younger than Marlowe, had visited him in Mexico during his first stint there. Young had begun dating Marlowe in 1971, when she was getting a divorce. Young, who has passed away, told the author in an interview in 2006 she visited Marlowe in San Miguel in 1973. She was under the impression he was living a monastic existence, devoting almost all his time to work rather than play.

"When I first got to Mexico, I was dressed in a bright yellow pantsuit," she recalled. "When the landlady (at Marlowe's home) opened the door, she was surprised. I think she thought he was gay before he showed up with me."

It's unlikely the landlady really thought so, but Marlowe was good at projecting a strait-laced image while juggling girlfriends. Marlowe's female company that year included not only Young but a hard-drinking woman from Kansas City. Marlowe noted this in his 1977 letter to Batson discussing women in his life.

> I met a woman the first time I was in San Miguel de Allende who turned into a companion. She's from Kansas City. Her father sold his construction business to Ashland Oil a couple of years ago. We traveled extensively in Mexico, and I've visited her several times in K.C. She's been to Harbor Beach twice. When I was drinking a lot she was an ideal companion: an absolute hollow leg. I could only stand her in short bursts, though. She was limited intellectually, not that I'm a giant, and after three days her conversation tended to be mostly about herself and her children, all of whom I met. One came to Mexico on his honeymoon and we traveled with them for a while.

Young said that Marlowe was a diligent researcher, and spent much of his time in Mexico backgrounding books to be set there. The two of them traveled deep into the country, including a trip to Mexico City, and she attended talks Marlowe gave in San Miguel. Young found the writer a charming man—"always a gentleman"—a hand-holder who sometimes wrote poetry. However, she believed Marlowe protected whatever lay at the center of his personality. Marlowe didn't like to have his photo taken, she said, and he didn't give gifts that carried much sentiment. As a Christmas present, he once gave her salt and pepper shakers.

"Everything was very noncommittal," Young said. "He was very guarded. His wife always told him he wasn't capable of real love. The first time I went out with him, he said he would never get married again."

Young interpreted this as Marlowe's inability to fill an emotional void: "I know he very much missed his wife and I don't think anyone would ever take her place."

In fact, Marlowe was terribly upset by his wife's death. However, his letter to Batson—either because of his true inclinations or his masculine bravado—exhibits a calculating approach to women that rules out real emotion. In it, Marlowe notes that he repeatedly betrayed his wife.

> …(T)here's a woman in North Carolina who used to be a friend of my wife. She was always very malleable material, and I

was making it with her even then, and continued through the period her husband remained alive…She liked a lot of the things I liked: the theatre, literature, etc. And I could impress my personality all over hers. When I was younger I conducted quite a few experiments.

Marlowe also tells Batson of another seduction he carried out during his marriage:

During my years in Washington there was a girl in the Swiss legation. This was much more of an undercover affair than most since I was still married. She was a lively number. I was still young then and thought she was what I wanted. Today I wouldn't look across the street [at her], even if she remained at the age she was then. Eventually she got into trouble with her bosses via some franc manipulation and was shipped home.

In the letter, Marlowe mentions one other relationship, further illuminating his attitude toward women.

There's a girl who was in my dancing class in high school days, back in Conn. I didn't hear anything about her for twenty years after I left town, eventually became curious, and tracked her down via the alumni association. For about ten years we would tear up a weekend every time I got to Conn., moteling it while she told her very jealous hubby that she was shopping in NY. That affair was purely physical: she had no brains at all, which she would be the first to admit. But it was good for a long time.

Marlowe noted that he was careful to keep all these women at a distance, even though he dated them over long periods of time:

I've always tended toward long-term relationships. It's the only kind which have ever worked for me. The above group all had one thing in common: they all wanted to get married. The married ones wanted to get divorces. They didn't want to marry me, particularly; they wanted to get married, period. I always had to put it up front in the relationships that there would be no marriage.

It's clear Marlowe's closest relationship in Mexico was with his typewriter, though still another girlfriend, Doris Henry, came to stay for three months during his years in San Miguel. He would spend mornings writing at his gated house on Mirador Hill, then drink and talk the afternoons away at the cantina on the square with other Americans. He sought out roguish types. "One of my drinking pals in San Miguel was Tom McGinty from Cleveland," Marlowe told Odell in a 1977 letter. "McGinty was a lawyer. His father had been tied up with the Moe Dalitz gang in Cleveland and I always thought McGinty had got into some kind of trouble back home. He lived well in Mexico. He was building a new home at the time I met him and I had a note from him perhaps a year ago that he was in it now. A clever, outgoing Irishman: he performed in all the plays put on by the Little Theater group, etc. A story all in himself, I always thought."

Marlowe's much younger nephew—then in his late 20s—mostly socialized with people of his own age, but Christopher Marlowe recalled two occasions when he accompanied his uncle on excursions that turned out to be quite interesting.

On one, Dan took Christopher on a visit to a nearby ranch owned by a man who trained fighting cocks. The rancher demonstrated how he taught the birds, equipping them with small knives strapped to their legs so they could slash their opponents.

On another occasion, in early February 1975, Dan Marlowe needed to make a quick trip to the border for typewriter repairs: A thin steel cable that operated the type-ball on his IBM Selectric had snapped. Christopher and one of his male friends, another student at the language school, rode along. A day's hard drive took the three men through the Sonoran Desert to Nuevo Laredo in Chihuahua, across from Laredo, Texas.

"We stopped at a gas station in a very desolate area," Christopher recalled. "Dan was outside fueling the car and me and my buddy went into the building to use the bathroom. Suddenly the lights went out and Dan yelled, 'Get the hell out of there!' He was sure it was robbery situation."

All three men piled into the car and roared off down the road. When they were safely out of range of the station, Dan

Marlowe started laughing about the fact that they hadn't paid. "He said we weren't about to pay in what looked like a robbery situation," Christopher said.

Marlowe's survival instincts were obviously still good.

Earl Drake's were also up to snuff in *Operation Deathmaker*, published early in 1975. After Hazel's niece is kidnapped in Los Angeles, and Hazel is badly injured by a car bomb meant to kill Drake, Drake pretends to follow the instructions of the kidnappers, but cleverly figures out who and where they are. Then he deals with them in his own way.

The story is one of the strongest of the "Operation" books, particularly because Drake is back on his own, helped by a friend of Hazel's who provides some sex interest. Drake's hard-nosed approach isn't compromised by interludes with Hazel and gimmicky government-intrigue subplots. Despite the book's potency, on March 30, 1975, the *New York Times* reviewer who used the pseudonym Newgate Callendar gave the book what Marlowe characterized as a "really miserable review." Marlowe told Odell that Callendar was "a well-known ripoff type" who liked very little of what he reviewed.

"I had thought we were safe from him because I had never known him to review a softcover original," Marlowe wrote. "This time he did a column of them. One got lukewarm approval (I had read it and thought it platitudinous), the rest zilch."

In fact, the column didn't offer a real review of *Deathmaker* at all. The piece was just a snide drive-by attack on current adventure and mystery paperbacks: "There they stand, in serried rank, and you can't tell them apart: Nick Carter or The Baroness or whatnot," wrote Newgate Callendar. "Each is written to order; each must have its combination of sadism and porno; each is written in elementary prose....take No. 11 in the Earl Drake series, *Operation Deathmaker* by Dan J. Marlowe (Fawcett, 95 cents). It tries to be hard-boiled stuff about murder and kidnapping, and it lovingly goes into detail about death as a way of life: 'The slug hit him right in the center of his fast-moving mouth. His teeth, or his palate, changed its direction, because it burst from the top of his skull. Part of his brain...' (On second thought, life as a way of death)."

The column was negative, yes, but, more important, it was dismissive of the kinds of hard-boiled novels Marlowe wrote. This one column can't be called a bellwether for changing tastes in commercial fiction, but it did coincide with a period in which editors and publishers were shopping around for new forms. Marlowe, always the businessman, would do his best to please them. So would Al Nussbaum. And Nussbaum would soon have considerably more freedom to do so. Things were looking up for the aging bank robber. His long writing apprenticeship in the most difficult of circumstances was approaching an end. He was leaving prison.

CHAPTER 13:
Crashing Out

BY 1976, AL NUSSBAUM HAD BEEN BEHIND BARS FOR NEARLY 14 years. He'd served his time in maximum-security federal prisons: first in Leavenworth, Kansas, and, later, in Marion, Illinois. For the most part, he had been well-behaved, taking classes, studying Transactional Analysis, and concentrating on his freelance writing. He'd gotten an Associate of Arts degree from a community college in Highland, Kansas, completed a course in the Leavenworth print shop to become an offset printer, taken part in correctional counseling and completed about 90 hours of college-level work.

These were tough lock-ups however, and staying alive wasn't always easy. "I saw three murders in prison and I was around the corner for seven more," Nussbaum later told a friend, the mystery writer Joe Gores. Always the strategist, the bank robber devised a stance for keeping violence at bay. Part of it had to do with showing he was disciplined and ready to fight. Gores recalled: "He always said that the way you survived in prison was you got your jeans pressed, you wore a big metal belt buckle shined up and anything that anyone said that you didn't like, you said, 'I know you are joking when you say that, because if you weren't joking, I'd have to do something about it, and you wouldn't like what I'd do.'"

Nussbaum, a stocky man who now weighed 190 pounds and stood 5-foot-7, was not imposing. He had tried to keep himself in good shape, though, both mentally and physically. Prior to sentencing, he told the officer preparing his pre-sentence report he was spending his leisure time playing chess and practicing gymnastics. While he stayed sharp, his survival strategy sometimes involved hiding just how sharp he was. At Leavenworth, he at times pretended he was mentally unbalanced, to give him an edge over truly dangerous inmates. Nussbaum was not a racist—he had befriended Curry, and worked with him in the Brooklyn robbery—but he made antagonizing comments to black inmates as part of his plan.

"Al—here's the kind of guy he was—he had this sardonic humor," recalled his friend Mel Cebulash. "He told me he was the librarian at Leavenworth, and that at that time a lot of the black prisoners were claiming they were political prisoners, and he told them, 'I'm not a political prisoner, I'm just a criminal.' All these black guys were beginning to separate themselves and form up into gangs. And he said he had to get these black guys thinking he was crazy. They were taking courses like Black Studies, and the librarian was supposed to get some textbooks and distribute them to the students. The black guys would come up to him and say, 'Did you get the textbook for Famous Black Americans?' He would say to them, 'Textbook? That's a pamphlet,' and he'd laugh this crazy laugh. He said when he'd do that, they'd think he was crazy and leave him alone."

By concentrating on his writing and avoiding conflicts, Nussbaum got along well in prison during his early years there. Shortly after arriving at Leavenworth in 1964, he was assigned to work as a clerk in the Education Department, and for the next six years, no disciplinary action was taken against him. Prison officials were still suspicious of his motives, however. On Dec. 29, 1970, according to a petition he filed for a writ of habeas corpus, he was "abruptly placed in solitary confinement; the following day he was told he was suspected of being part of a conspiracy to cause a disturbance within the prison."

It's not clear why officials believed that, but he'd apparently upset someone. After spending six days in solitary, he was put back in his cell and not allowed out. Five weeks later, he was returned to the general prison population, but assigned menial duties, which Nussbaum described as "traditionally reserved for new men or as punishment."

In filing the writ, Nussbaum asked a federal judge to declare that prison officials had abused their discretion in throwing him into the hole, not allowing him to work on his college correspondence courses during that period, and causing him to miss taking a college extension class. The judge turned him down.

Two years later, Nussbaum came under suspicion for receiving literature associated with radical groups, including the anti-government faction known as the Weathermen. This was ironic in view of his expressed view that he was not a "political prisoner." FBI records show that in April 1972, Associate Warden Clyde J. Malley of the Leavenworth prison asked the FBI to check into publications called the *I.L.S. Handbook* and the *Weathermen Anthology*, which Nussbaum had received.

"...Nussbaum has apparently received this literature through his contacts with the employees of the educational program as he has ingratiated himself with the staff of teachers in the penitentiary," noted a memo from the Special Agent in Charge of the Kansas City FBI office to the FBI director. Nussbaum's mail was still being censored because he was looked on as "an extremely dangerous and vicious individual," the memo said, probably referring to his crimes outside of prison, rather than to his conduct inside.

In response to the heads-up, the FBI's San Francisco office said it had never heard of the *Weathermen Anthology*, but that the *I.L.S. Handbook* was probably a publication of the International Liberation School actually called *Firearms and Self-defense, a Handbook for Radicals, Revolutionaries and Easy Riders*. The handbook contained information on ballistics, handguns, shotguns, rifles, gun safety, methods of buying a used gun, and methods for sighting, shooting and cleaning guns. The International Liberation School, with headquarters in Berkeley, California, had been founded in 1969 to train revolutionaries and support anti-establishment rallies. "Its principle members are well-known radicals who have publicly advocated violent overthrow of the United States Government," the San Francisco FBI said.

Though prison authorities suspected Nussbaum of radicalism, it's possible he was just gathering information to help with Marlowe's descriptions of anti-government militants in *Operation Drumfire*. Or Nussbaum might have intended to use the material in his own writing. By this point, his endeavors were going full blast. He described them in a letter to Cebulash on May 11, 1972:

> . ...I get along well with the people at Hitchcock's Mag [*Alfred Hitchcock's Mystery Magazine*]. They now have seven pieces of mine in their coffers. They've bought over two dozen of my stories and another dozen or so that I collaborated on with Dan. He and I, by the way, are supposed to be collaborating on an article for *The Writer*, but we haven't decided on a subject or format, yet. That *Am. Scholar* [*American Scholar*] article of mine has been reprinted a couple of more times in the last few weeks, too.
>
> I sent an outline and sample chapter to Atheneum and received a rejection in about a week. It's now at Simon and Schuster. Dan is circulating a complete book of mine, but there've been no nibbles. I have an editor at Bobbs-Merrill willing to "look" at a selection of short stories as soon as I can get them to him. I have a typist hard at work, making the published and unpublished look the same. Maybe I can slip a few losers past him.
>
> And did I tell you I've been reviewing books? I now have 10 major credits. My last review was carried by 5 papers, including the *Chicago Sun-Times*, *Minneapolis Tribune*, and *Baltimore Sun*. Several papers that haven't run the reviews I sent have offered to assign books to me. I'm turning into a one-man syndicate! This activity is a kick, but I'll be curious to see how this grand work will effect (sic) a book of mine if I ever get one published. Maybe I'll get a few reviews instead of a total blackout—HA!

Shortly after Nussbaum sent this letter, he was transferred— on June 2, 1972—to the federal penitentiary in Marion, Illinois. It was a move he had requested, possibly because of difficulties he'd had with authorities at Leavenworth, or possibly just to get a change of scene. Marlowe had urged Warden Charles E. Harris at Leavenworth to grant the request in a May 22, 1972, letter. "Since I am his only visitor, and since I feel I am aiding in his rehabilitation, I would like to add my plea to his," Marlowe wrote. "It would save me a day's driving time if he were that much closer."

On July 16, 1972, Nussbaum wrote again to Cebulash, talking generally about his situation at Marion. "Yes, I'm fairly settled in now—I've been here a month and half. But I wouldn't say this is a step toward 'out,' as you put it. The move was, I think, horizontal, neither up nor down. Living conditions are generally improved, though, and the food is of a better quality. This last could be an illusion since any change after 8 years in Leavenworth would probably be welcome."

Nussbaum continued to publish as he put his time in at Marion. From late 1972 to early 1976, his *Alfred Hitchcock's Mystery Magazine* credits included the short stories "The Unfriendly Neighbor," "Alma," "Fury," "An Easy Score," "Bypass," "Decisions," "Eddie and I," "Collision," "If You Want to See One," "Blue Gypsy," "A Left-Handed Profession," and "Where is Heinrich Herren?" And those were just the stories that carried his own name. During this period, the magazine also published the following stories he wrote under the pen name Alberto Avellano: "When the Captain Died," "Blue Devil," "Like Other Wild Animals," "Crime by Accident," "Open Sights," "Routine Investigation," and "Guest Spot." With Nussbaum writing as A.F. Oreshnik, the magazine ran "The Take-Over," "The Way Memory Works," "No Small Mistakes," "The Best Place," "Hunting Ground," "Home Ground," and "The Only Rule."

This success, and his behavior at Marion, were earning him high marks from his case manager there, V.W. Nylen. Nylen wrote in August 1975 that, "Reports indicate that Nussbaum is viewed as a model prisoner within the federal prison system. It is quite apparent from the reports received that Nussbaum is well thought of and considered to be one of the more congenial residents of this institution. In view of his excellent institutional adjustment and extensive participation in the academic program it would appear that Nussbaum's prognosis for success on parole at this time is favorable."

Despite this upbeat report, parole officials hadn't smiled on Nussbaum. He'd been turned down for parole in 1970 and 1973, and it appeared he wouldn't be able to try again until mid-1976. The courts had been forcing the parole boards to give specific reasons for denials, however. That resulted in a surprise hearing for Nussbaum. Once again, he was denied. He appealed, however, and the appeal hearing was set for January 1976. Parole officials didn't make it easy for him.

Though Nussbaum was locked up in southern Illinois and Marlowe was in Michigan, the hearing was scheduled to be held outside San Francisco. Nussbaum and Marlowe believed officials were trying to choose a spot so isolated that it would be hard for Marlowe to take part. If that was the goal, they succeeded. As much as he wanted to go, Marlowe had a conflict and couldn't appear.

Marlowe wasn't allowed to choose a stand-in, but Nussbaum could, and he selected Joe Gores. It was a reasonable choice. Gores, as a former private investigator, was familiar with the legal system, and he lived in San Francisco. He readily agreed to help. Marlowe and Nussbaum mailed him information about the case. Gores and his future wife Dory sat down and went through it. They then consulted with lawyer Jack Leavitt, an aspiring short-story writer. Leavitt said they needed to establish a legal record that Nussbaum had not had a fair hearing. This would pressure the board to grant him parole, so the board members wouldn't have to deal with the hassle of another appeal. Leavitt provided clear instructions.

"He said, you go in, you and Dory, and you say, 'We want to tape these proceedings,'" Gores recalled. "They will say, 'You can't do that.' Then Dory should say, 'I want to record these proceedings in shorthand. They will say, 'We can't allow you to do that.' Then I was to say, 'I am here to represent Mr. Nussbaum, but I'm not legally competent to do so.' That was to cover an appeal, later, after a turn-down."

Gores and Dory appeared for the hearing in San Mateo County. They were given 30 minutes to make their pitch before a panel of judges. FBI agents watched from the back of the room as Gores stood up. The writer contended Nussbaum was eligible for parole, but had been tripped up by illegal technicalities. Then Gores put some emotion into his argument.

"You judges are all thinking of a wild-eyed kid in his 20s coming out of a bank with a gun in one hand and money in the other," he said. "I'm thinking of a man who writes short stories and publishes them, who writes movie and television scripts and book reviews for hundreds of newspapers around this country. I've never met Mr. Nussbaum, but I've corresponded with him and I have read his material. If you ever want to talk about a man who has rehabilitated himself, Al Nussbaum is it. I don't know what you will do here today. I know Marlowe couldn't appear, so I am appearing in his stead. I want to tell you that whenever you have a parole hearing for Mr. Nussbaum, there will be somebody like me showing up to argue his case. We are not going to quit, because he is a man who deserves to be free."

Gores asked the judges to put themselves in Nussbaum's shoes. "Which of you distinguished gentlemen in your 50s and 60s would like to be judged on what you did as wild-eyed kids in their early 20s?" he asked. "You wouldn't like it." But Gores didn't seem to be getting through. Two of them were asleep. All right, the judges said, we'll be in touch. Gores and Dory packed their papers and left.

"We were depressed as hell," Gores recalled. "Then we went to the San Francisco Zoo, and that was a mistake, seeing all these animals in cages. We went to my home in Mill Valley. The phone was ringing as we walked in. A guy from Washington, D.C., was calling. He said in two or three months, Al will be put in a halfway house. We went wild."

* * *

For a long time, Nussbaum's plan for his transition from prison had been to go to Harbor Beach and live with Marlowe. Three years before Nussbaum was paroled, Marlowe had pledged his support in a letter to a caseworker at the prison in Marion:

> In May I was in Washington and I called upon the Federal Parole Board on Indiana Avenue and asked that it be made part of the record that if Al were granted parole, I would promise any life support that might be necessary until he could make it entirely on his own. I would appreciate it if your file showed the same.

Whether he needs a job, or financial support, or whatever, I will see that he gets it. If you require references as to my moral and financial stability, I will be happy to furnish them.

Al Nussbaum's writing ability has improved steadily in the past few years. There is a letter on file in Washington from Ernest Hutter, editor of the *Alfred Hitchcock's Mystery Magazine*, testifying to the same. Both Ernie Hutter and I feel that our eventual claim to literary fame may well be that we discovered Al Nussbaum.

As late as August 1975, Nussbaum was still planning to move from prison to Harbor Beach. In the next few months, though, he decided on Los Angeles instead. Apparently, his growing list of contacts in Southern California convinced him his job prospects were better there. At first, officials turned down his request, saying— among other things—that they had plenty of crime in L.A., and didn't need Nussbaum possibly adding to it. They relented however, and on April 26, 1976, a Greyhound bus dropped him in the City of Angels, in care of the Community Treatment Center at 1212 S. Alvarado St.

While living in a halfway house prior to his parole date, July 1, he established an office in Hollywood at 1585 Crossroads of the World, No. 103, and went to work. He also built on his relationships in the writing community. Both Gores and Cebulash came to visit him.

Gores and Dory first met Nussbaum in their motel room. He was friendly, but still edgy from prison. "It was awkward because we'd never met," Gores recalled. "Dory at that time still smoked, and she moves very quickly when she does things…Dory was sort of behind him and she reached quickly into her purse and took out her cigarettes. As she did, Al leaped about two feet in the air and whirled around and came down facing her in a crouch. Then he looked sheepish, relaxed and stood up."

Briefly, Nussbaum talked about the killings he'd seen in prison and noted, "You just get so sensitized." Afterwards, when Gores and Dory took Nussbaum to dinner at the Ship's Restaurant in Westwood, he ate with his left arm curled around his dinner plate, shooting his eyes from side to side.

Despite the tough life he'd led, or perhaps because of it, Nussbaum had a strong sense of humor, however, and he showed it on another night out, this time with Mel Cebulash and his wife Dolly. "We were in L.A. for a convention," Cebulash recalled. "We picked him up from that halfway house on Vermont and we took him up to Nick's Fish Market on Sunset in Beverly Hills. And he ordered Southern Comfort, which was the only whiskey drink that he liked. My wife was having a hard time deciding what she wanted. First she'd say, 'I want this,' then, 'I want that.'" Her indecisiveness amused Nussbaum, Cebulash recalled. "After the waiter left, he said to my wife, 'You'll never drive a getaway car for me.'"

CHAPTER 14:
The Dream Machine

ON MARCH 23, 1976, A FEW MONTHS BEFORE NUSSBAUM WAS
released from prison, Marlowe told a friend in a letter, "Gold Medal
has just cancelled flat my *Operation* series." Fawcett Gold Medal
editor Joseph Elder had informed Marlowe, "Basically this kind of
story is not working at all in today's market. The mystery/suspense
novel as a paperback category is failing left and right, and very few
of the category heroes are surviving." The decision came during the
pending CBS takeover of Fawcett, which didn't go into effect until
December 1976 but affected Fawcett for many months prior to that.
Though Marlowe and Odell held out hope until late that year that
Fawcett might reconsider, their long run with Earl Drake was over.
That year saw the publication of the last series entry, *Operation
Counterpunch*, which was set in San Antonio and Nevada.

Though Fawcett Gold Medal clearly believed the audience for
Earl Drake had dried up, a reviewer for the *Chicago Tribune* had a
much different opinion.

"Long-awaited," the reviewer said of *Counterpunch*. "In Marlowe's
12th adventure of 'The Man With Nobody's Face,' Drake's girlfriend,
Hazel, is the target of retribution by a psychotic Mexican multi-mil-
lionaire, Don Luis Morelos, from whom Drake had previously exacted

a million dollars' retribution of his own. 'Long-awaiteds' usually signal paperback publication of hardcover best sellers about which there is little to say except, 'Here it is, at last,' but Marlowe readers have learned to anticipate each new Earl Drake story with the same urgency."

Despite the enthusiasm of the *Tribune* reviewer, Odell and Marlowe had lost their outlet for the paperbacks that had served as the bedrock of their writing partnership for more than five years.

The previous year there had been rumblings that all was not well with the market for their books, though the two writers had been as industrious as ever. For much of 1975, Fawcett Gold Medal had delayed final acceptance of *Counterpunch* while requesting an outline for what would have been the next entry in the Drake series, a book called *Crossfire*, set in Colorado. When Marlowe returned from Mexico around the beginning of June 1975, he had polished off the outline for *Crossfire* after Fawcett pressured him to finish it.

"This seems to me as solid an outline as we've ever given Fawcett, but in the current state of the market I expect them to be more picky than usual," he told Odell in a letter dated June 6. "We'll see…I'm still getting reorganized because I dropped everything to jump on the outline after finding the letter waiting for me here asking what I was doing about it. I still can't get over their asking for this one when COUNTERPUNCH is still dangling."

Crossfire was never to be written, though Marlowe and Odell worked on the story until Gold Medal pulled the plug on the series the following year. As 1976 moved on, the writers continued to explore writing projects, together and separately.

By this time, Odell was making significant strides writing books on his own. An adventure novel, *The Leather Albatross*, had been published by Apollo Books under his name in 1972. He had also written *The Ultimate Code*, published that year by Charter Books in New York as part of the "Nick Carter" series. Written by a number of uncredited writers, the men's adventure books featured a secret agent named Nick Carter whose name also appeared on the book covers as the purported author. In the end, Odell would write two more "Nick Carter" books, *The Asian Mantrap*, published in 1978, and *The Nowhere Weapon*, published in 1979.

His collaboration with Marlowe, though, still showed the promise of producing higher-profile books than those he was doing on his own.

As the two continued to cast around for such a contract, they considered expanding their genre offerings—even kicking around the idea of doing westerns, possibly using plots cannibalized from Earl Drake books. They dumped that idea when a quick survey of leading paperback publishers showed editors had little interest in westerns.

The two writers also were still discussing the marketability of *The Puppet Master*. Marlowe wanted to update it to achieve more of a "ripped-from-today's-headlines" feel, but Odell argued that wouldn't be wise. The original plot, set in the mid-1960s, dealt with desperate efforts by high-ranking officials to expose the activities of the National Security Agency. By 1976, however, political positions had changed drastically and trying to recreate the story in the current Washington political climate might make it appear silly, Odell said.

"I appreciate what effort you're trying to make to find a workable solution for TPM, but I hesitate to encourage you to pursue the suggestion that we update the story to the present (or even the future) for the very reasons that we floundered with TPM," Odell wrote to Marlowe on Oct. 28, 1976. "I'm still of a mind to put TPM back where the conditions I reiterated above would pertain. We'd be working with factual situations and wouldn't be digging holes to fall in in an effort to concoct a plausible and supportable non-real incident…an incident that could be rendered ridiculous by a sudden turn of events that would negate a once-great idea."

As the writers went back and forth on what appeared to be a tired project, they were offered another chance to write the kind of high-dollar novel they had been pursuing for so long. Marlowe received the news in a letter from New York literary agent Joseph Elder. Elder, Marlowe's editor-in-chief at Fawcett, had become an agent—and had begun representing Marlowe—after being jettisoned as a result of editorial infighting during the CBS takeover.

In an Oct. 27 letter to Marlowe, Elder said an editor at New American Library had run across a news clipping he thought might springboard a lively thriller. Marlowe, possibly confused, was to later say he had told Elder about the clipping, rather than the other way around. Marlowe recalled it as a *New York Times* story about a West Coast private eye who was shot through his kitchen window one night:

"Everyone thought he was just a sleazy little divorce private eye," Marlowe wrote, "but it turned out he had a file of 250 tapes that incriminated a lot of very important people (this was in California) in shady and illegal deals…I proposed having the tapes be the object of a frantic search by people trying to keep the lid on and letting one of the searchers be the protagonist who is hired or coerced into doing his searching, and is led from one to another of those involved, which would be the development of the story."

Though he said the investigator was in California, Marlowe later dropped a letter to his friend James Batson enclosing a clipping about a murder in New York that he said "was the basis for my original proposal." The clip was actually from *Time* magazine, a short article headlined "Death of a Wireman." It dealt with the mysterious slaying on Jan. 20, 1977, of an electronic eavesdropper named Frank Chin, "found crumpled in a hallway near his West Side Manhattan workshop with six bullet holes in his head." Chin had supplied bugging and recording devices both to cops and criminals—including police in Connecticut and New Jersey (some with mob connections), Communist and Nationalist Chinese, foreign agents, CIA operatives, and possibly the White House plumbers of the Nixon era. Listening devices Chin had put into place in the New York quarters of prostitute Xaviera Hollander had provided content for her 1972 bestseller, *The Happy Hooker*.

Whatever the true-life basis of the idea about the eavesdropping operative, the suggestion wound up in the hands of Jim Bryans, editor-in-chief of Bernard Geis Associates, a book packager responsible for such lurid bestsellers as *Valley of the Dolls*. Bryans came to Elder looking for a writer to carry out the new project, Elder proposed hiring Marlowe, and Bryans and Geis agreed.

"Anyway, what NAL seems to be looking for is…a novel revolving around a sort of seedy private-eye who is murdered as a result of his connections with big money, with show biz, with Mafia or whatever," Elder wrote. "It should have a southern California background. Jim Bryans' idea is to have the detective killed at the outset of the novel, and then have an investigative reporter as a protagonist who delves into the life of the late detective and uncovers whatever it was he was involved in that led to his murder. Through the reporter's efforts, we get to know the private eye as if he were a living character. What you have here is really no more than an idea, a taking-off point, a concept and an ambience for a novel; the rest would be up to you. The story should be handled in a truly novelistic manner and should be fairly substantial in length, say 80-90,000 words, or even more if the plot you devise for it warrants it."

Elder said he believed that he could get at least $10,000 for Marlowe as an advance from Geis, and also a piece of whatever extra money Geis could squeeze out of NAL. "It sounds like the kind of novel you could handle very well," Elder told Marlowe, "and it provides you a good opportunity to move out of category mystery writing, which, as you know, I feel is a necessary move for you at this time."

The project sounded good to Marlowe and Odell, too. Odell was concerned about too-rigid guidance from the Geis crew, but believed the job was quite doable: "Between us, there's very little lacking in experience when measured against this particular task," he told Marlowe. Odell even believed that, should the NAL-Geis project prove successful, they might take *The Puppet Master* to Geis to give it one more chance at publication.

Marlowe, his agent and Bryans met in New York on Nov. 18 to discuss the direction the California thriller should take. The meeting went well, and Marlowe signed a two-book deal with Geis and NAL. ("I hope to convince them to make the second one the 'big' book I've had in the back of my mind for so long," Marlowe later told Odell, without spelling out what that "big" book idea might have been. The use of the vague term "big" is puzzling, since Marlowe would later say Geis also thought of the size and scope of the first novel as "big.") At the meeting, Bryans told Marlowe that the investigative reporter protagonist in the West Coast novel should somewhat resemble the wisecracking, laid-back journalist featured in Gregory McDonald's novel, *Fletch*, which had won the Best First Novel Award from the Mystery Writers of America two years previously.

In an effort to get a fix on this character, Marlowe acquired a copy of McDonald's successor book, *Confess, Fletch* (which Marlowe called "a hell of an awkward title, to my way of thinking"). In analyzing the story, he told Odell he found several interesting things: "The reporter possesses no special skills, for one thing, other than those developed from his newspaper background. He never faces a gun in the course of the story, and he throws a single punch, part of the same scene (sic). There is no overt violence other than that attendant upon the finding of the murder victim. Dialogue advances the story line to a degree almost unmatched in this type of story."

Marlowe told Odell the editor didn't want a suspense novel, as such. If what the editor wanted was a novel similar to *Fletch*, however, that did not bode well for the efforts of Marlowe and Odell, because McDonald exhibited a lazy humor nowhere evident in the books churned out by the *Operation* writing team.

Another complication was that Elder suggested not using Marlowe's name as the author. "Elder feels we should keep the name for suspense, since that's what it has always been connected with," Marlowe told Odell. "He recommends giving Geis an exclusive on a pseudonym which could continue to be used if the first book is successful, and pre-stating all of this in the contract. I can see some advantage to this: it would permit us to cannibalize from previous material wherever we thought it feasible, à la what we were considering doing with westerns."

Odell wrote back to Marlowe on Dec. 2, saying he was surprised at Elder's suggestion. "I would think that he'd jump at the chance for you to show the span of talent that hopefully this new venture will demonstrate," Odell said. "Wouldn't a book in a different genre provide the opportunity to increase an author's professional stature? I'm sure that you don't feel the limitations inferred by writing a major work under a pseudonym would suggest that your talents are restricted to suspense themes only."

Odell also said he couldn't figure why it would be a good deal to give Geis an exclusive on the pseudonym, since it would become Geis' property and he could use it on sequel books written by any other author.

Business considerations aside, the issue finally brought to the fore Odell's feelings about his long, pretty-much-uncredited writing relationship with Marlowe.

"If there is a real advantage to not using the Marlowe name in this case," Odell wrote, "I wonder if you were suggesting that my name might substitute. That would be generous of you, but in a sense appropriate, too, since we've done a dozen books together without any visible credit being passed along to me. I haven't objected to remaining the silent partner, and in a sense it has been good for me. I haven't been able to lean on anything we've produced together as a door-opener for individual efforts… so any success I've had has been strictly on my own. However, if you are thinking it might be time to allow some recognition to come my way, I'd be happy to provide the pseudonym."

In a letter Dec. 6, Marlowe expressed reservations, but said if Odell wanted to do it, that would work for him.

"As for not using my name on the project, I guess I didn't make it clear that Geis isn't thinking of this as a suspense novel," Marlowe wrote. "It's to be a 'big' novel, whatever that is. I agree with Elder that it makes more sense to reserve my name for out-and-out suspense, which is what it's known for. You're right that the pseudonym would become the exclusive property of Geis, and I ordinarily would balk, but right now I can't afford to balk. I would say let's use your name, as you suggested, except for the exclusivity feature. You may find yourself later unable to use your own name on something entirely different. If you think it's worth it, though, I'm entirely willing."

In another letter to Odell two days later, Marlowe expanded his explanation: "The Geis reputation is one reason I didn't hold out for my own name on the book. Quite the reverse, in fact. In the first place, I think it's bad business since this is to be a non-genre book and my name is almost totally associated with genre writing. Even more importantly, though, I can see a possibility, although I hope it never happens, that Geis will demand or insist upon something with which I wouldn't want to have my name connected. This is why the use of a pseudonym makes sense to me. Or the combination of reasons makes sense."

The issue of using the pseudonym, Geis' history of trying to dominate the novel-writing process, and his vagueness as to what the actual story should be, all complicated the process of getting the book approved and completed. Still, the writers forged ahead. Marlowe's assessment was, "There are a lot of negatives connected with this project, but I still think we can bring it off."

Early on, the working title of the book—an 80,000-word effort to be produced by the following June 1—was *Listening Walls*. Over time, the title would change to *The Dream Machine*. The plot had this basic story line: a little-known private investigator is killed and it turns out that he was an expert in wiretapping, other forms of electronic eavesdropping, and countermeasures against bugging. The investigation of his murder—and the surreptitious recordings he has made—threaten to reveal the shady dealings and sexual kinkiness of various high-profile people. Among them are an international financier, a businessman convicted of fraud, a horse trainer, a police captain, and various Hollywood and New York celebrities.

The main character is Clay Kittredge, an investigative reporter for *Events* magazine. His probe reveals that the private eye played a key role in a business called "the Dream Factory" or "the Dream Business," which enticed people into acting out their sexual fantasies, then captured their indiscretions on audio recordings and blackmailed them. Eventually, the blackmail operation was to play into a larger criminal operation, possibly an illegal arms sale, that would net millions of dollars for the perpetrators.

Even before the contract was approved and the first check issued in mid-January, Marlowe was churning out "set pieces" that could be dropped into the story, including one about a stud named Eddie Richards who sells his sexual favors to rich, unattractive women and caters to their most salacious dreams. Unfortunately, however, the process of getting Geis and Bryans to approve the outline for the book dragged on for more than six weeks. This made Odell jittery about meeting the June 1 deadline, though he remained hopeful about getting the go-ahead sign ("We shouldn't be sitting around waiting for shoes to drop," he wrote Marlowe. "But there should be Full Speed Ahead on the clock before long.").

Even when Geis finally signed the contract, agreeing to an initial payment of $1,000 against an overall advance of $10,000 to be handed over in increments, he dithered on approving a final outline. Word came through Marlowe's agent that Geis "loved" the initial scenes Marlowe had produced, but wanted more "scope." Meanwhile, Marlowe and Odell continued to refine the book's characters and story line. They also did research, such as obtaining an organizational chart for the Los Angeles Police Department. They even called on Nussbaum, now doing a writing gig in Los Angeles, to help them get detailed maps of the city and county.

Finally, in late February, Geis provided a critique of the outline that enabled Marlowe and Odell to proceed with more confidence. By March 18, Marlowe was moving ahead with the manuscript. In the first part of April, however, with Marlowe nearing the halfway point in completing *The Dream Machine*, Geis killed the project, apparently believing the manuscript lacked sufficient depth for what he termed a "big" novel. In its place, he asked Marlowe to come up with a concept for a supernatural thriller like those of Stephen King. (Though King's books were nothing like the ones Marlowe had written up to that point, Marlowe would say late in his life that he had met King at informal writers' gatherings and discussed writing with him.) The contract would go forward, and Geis would kick in an extra $500 to underwrite Marlowe's expenses in researching the new thriller.

Marlowe, ever the businessman, took the news with reasonable calm, or so his correspondence reflected. Odell was less restrained, and suspected that Marlowe wasn't as accepting as he appeared to be. "For some time I've been skeptical about the progress of the Geis deal....so why am I so angry?" he wrote to Marlowe. "I can't be any more ticked off than you...Ever since the first go-round with the comments in the initial expanded outline, I had the feeling that there was something peculiar going on...and the feeling persists."

In a later letter, Odell enlarged upon his feelings toward the decision, and toward Geis. "He's an arrogant man, impolite and pointedly patronizing," Odell said. "He's a bit dictatorial, it seems, and leaves no doubt as to who is in control and running the show. I wonder just how insecure he is behind his bluster."

Marlowe, too, despite his effort to move on, was wrestling with the quick change of direction. "I can't stir up many juices about his proposed project," Marlowe confessed. But nothing more attractive than the proposed supernatural thriller seemed to be on offer, so the writers moved forward. As Marlowe set to work, Odell described his efforts to place two earlier Marlowe-Odell joint projects being circulated under the titles *Nightmare* and *Doubled and Vulnerable*.

"I'm still beating on doors with *Nightmare* and *Doubled and Vulnerable*, despite the fact that suspense is apparently in low demand," Odell wrote. "I guess I'm the perennial optimist, and one of those manuscripts could arrive just at the time some editor needs a story and is in hopes that something better than the one he's about to be forced to publish comes along."

Before long, though, Marlowe and Odell turned to the project at hand—the one they actually were getting paid for. Marlowe read and synopsized several supernatural thrillers: *Audrey Rose* by Frank DeFelitta, *The Shining* and *Carrie* by Stephen King, *Samain* by Meg

Elizabeth Atkins, *The Omen* by David Seltzer, and *The Sentinel* by Jeffrey Konvitz.

This experience didn't get him excited about Geis' proposal. "Like you, I'm only lukewarm about the whole idea," Marlowe wrote to Odell on April 23. "My reading hasn't encouraged me much, with the exception of Stephen King's books. This guy has got it. As I think I said in my book report, the first three-quarters of THE SHINING impressed me as much as anything I'd read in years. It unraveled then, but I think he was trying to do too much. Or trying to top himself after CARRIE (I liked that one, too)." In a letter to Odell the next day, Marlowe enlarged on his thoughts about King: "From what I've read so far, Stephen King is head and shoulders above anyone else writing in the field. He could be a successful mainstream novelist if he never touched the supernatural. He creates believable, warm-blooded characters, while the majority of the others are dealing in cardboard."

Despite Marlowe's initial misgivings, when there was work on the table, he seized it. While attending the Edgar Awards festivities in New York City that year, he met with Geis and things went well.

"I sat down with Geis and verbalized a story with a supernatural tinge I felt I could live with," Marlowe wrote Odell on May 6. "I anticipated difficulty, but he loved it. He should have: I incorporated all the elements of current bestsellerdom, wealth, power, politics, kinky sex, a courtroom scene and horror. Onward and upward. Now I've got to get it down on paper from my skimpy notes."

Marlowe did so, and very quickly, producing an outline for a project referred to in memos at Bernard Geis Associates as "the Dan Marlowe novel of the Senator and the 14-year-old witch," but carrying the working title *Julie*. By the end of the month, one Geis editor critiquing the outline for *Julie* enthused, "We're on our way to greatness with this one." But this project, like *The Dream Machine*, would come to nothing. Too bad, because the book really would have had it all, including the fullest expression—at least in a commercial novel—of Marlowe's secret obsession: his spanking fetish.

CHAPTER 15:
Welcome to the Spank-a-Torium

IT'S HARD TO SAY WHAT MARLOWE AND GORDON GEMPEL WERE doing at the time. Gempel couldn't recall. Maybe they were having a couple of quick ones at Smalley's Bar and Grill, or eating at a restaurant in Detroit before catching a Tigers game, or at an out-of-town political affair. In any case a woman walked by, one with tight clothes, a good body and a certain attitude, and Gempel took note. With great originality, he commented:

"I sure love big tits."

"They're fine," Marlowe replied. "But I really like women with big round asses."

Marlowe wasn't shy about expressing this preference. He even informed his Long Beach, California, girlfriend that he liked "big blonde women with big butts." "[The woman] told me on the side that Dan liked to spank her before sex," Gempel told the author.

This won't come as a surprise to anyone who reads Marlowe. Sex, spanking, and nude female buttocks fill his novels. He was "researching" spanking shortly before his mind went blank, and he was fascinated by kinky sex. This is obvious from an exchange of letters in the spring of 1967 between Marlowe and a New York acquaintance who had access to erotic audiotapes.

On May 1, the New York man wrote to Marlowe that he'd met a woman author specializing in the psychology of sex behavior. This writer had obtained a grant from the Kinsey Foundation to provide material on sexual aberrations and deviations for its next report. She had "a bookshelf of hard- and soft-cover novels, all written by herself," the man said. Would Marlowe be interested in meeting her? "She also has given me a tape made by a certain 'Princess'—said to be the most famous dominatrix of all times, leader of a cult that flourished about 10 years ago. I thought it would be pretty good, and if you would like to hear it, let me know and I'll send it along, but I would like it back."

The man also had an audiotape from "a lady out west" that dealt not with domination but with sexual intercourse, containing "every conceivable variation of method and approach, all beautifully done, by herself and a friend."

Finally, the man had been keeping in touch with a "Canadian Amazon" who had sent him a tape. "I was somewhat disappointed, because it contained very little corporal punishment, but the sexual domination is incredible—her subject is made to perform the most demeaning acts one can imagine." The man didn't like the tape, however: "I was repelled by its extremism and do not care to keep it."

Marlowe's correspondent went on to ask: "Have you heard from your friend—the one who had the realistic movies? I certainly would be interested in seeing them."

Marlowe replied in a letter dated April 1:

> It was fine to hear from you again and to learn you had so many irons in the fire re the further development of our interest.
>
> Now to reply to your letter point-by-point.
>
> By all means give the woman writer on sex behavior and fetiches (sic) my name. As you know, I'm not bashful about my predilections, and that's all the more true with someone seriously interested in the subject. I'm enclosing a snapshot of my own Five Foot Shelf [Ed. Note: apparently Marlowe's published novels, as opposed to his porn books, though perhaps both.] that you might want to pass along to her. You can tell her that I'm perfectly prepared to level with her about my sex history if she's interested.

You might mention the taping aspect of communication (I have so damned little time for letter writing!) if she uses tape at all.

I would certainly also like to hear the "Princess" tape you mentioned, and I would certainly return it to you as per your specification.

The tape from the lady out west sounds intriguing, too. So damn few things of this sort are "beautifully done," as you mentioned, that it would be a welcome change to hear it.

I wouldn't be personally interested in the tape from the Canadian Amazon, but I know two people who would, and since from at least one of them I'm almost sure I could expect interesting material in return, material of a type in which you'd be interested, too, I'll ask you to send that one along as well in the interest of mutual back-scratching.

You have seen in the papers that civil war now threatens in Nigeria. Censorship has been temporarily placed on incoming and outgoing mail, and my friend is waiting out the storm. He is going on leave—to England and the Continent for six weeks—on August 15th, though, and he has promised if worse comes to worst to take the promised material—films, etc.—with him on vacation and mail them to me from there.

He seems confident however that I won't have to wait that long. He says that one of the London films is the genuine article, and I am very much looking forward to seeing it, after which I will send it right on to you, as I won't be required to return it until fall.

I don't need the enclosed snaps back. Pass them on to someone if they have no interest for you. I send you the colored one as the forerunner of some promised me in the same medium that are supposed to be more along the line of our own interest.

While Marlowe's inclinations prepared him well for the eroticism he explored in his novels, his readers also hankered for it, though possibly not so obsessively. The editors of the Fawcett Gold Medal books demanded a strong dose of sex, according to Odell. In a 1983 letter to James Batson, Odell admitted as much, though he may have been naïve about Marlowe's perceived indifference to the subject.

"Neither of us jumped at writing the sex scenes," Odell said. "In fact, all of them were an afterthought and included only because we knew the GM editor would only require them if the manuscript came in without any. They never had anything to do with the story—the Drake books contained sex scenes because that was the trend at the time."

Even so, Marlowe put gusto into his sex writing, and exploited sex in several ways. In addition to the erotic scenes he included in his novels, Marlowe also wrote pornographic books and soft-core porn for men's magazines. It seems to have been a reliable source of income.

"Dan did quite a few porno books," Batson said in an e-mail to the author. "We called them adult books. Those and the men's magazines were the major suppliers of money in those days. He used his earlier books (scenes from them) as starting points. Add in a little sex and pick up the check…I remember the first time he showed me some of his adult work. It came as a shock, but I understood it was just a way to make a living. He was good at it and seemed to enjoy it."

Making a living, of course, was a continuing struggle for Marlowe, as it was for many writers—especially paperback original writers—at that time. And pornography paid well. Mystery writer Bill Pronzini, who wrote erotic novels for a publisher in France early in his career, said he was getting $1,200 a book in the early 1970s. If Marlowe earned that much from each of the four porn novels he apparently turned out in 1971, he would have collected $4,800—more than half of his gross income from all the writing he did in 1968, which amounted to about $8,900. Such novels were fast jobs, too. Early on, Pronzini could knock one off in five days.

Batson said that Marlowe published the "sex stuff" under the name Jaime Sandaval. The author filled out papers so he could use that name legally, and even set up a separate bank account under that name so no one would know the identity of the writer. Later, Marlowe also used the Sandaval pen name for suspense stories published in *Alfred Hitchcock's Mystery Magazine*, *Ellery Queen's Mystery Magazine* and *Mike Shayne's Mystery Magazine*. It's not clear just how many soft-core porn articles (which he called "girly" articles) Marlowe wrote for magazines, but passages in his letters indicate this was a routine source of income. In a Dec. 6, 1969, letter to Nussbaum, he mentioned one such sale in passing. He also commented on the increasing raunchiness of the magazines, some of which were publishing material by or about "Iceberg Slim," a.k.a. Robert Beck, a Chicago pimp who wrote graphic autobiographical novels about street life. Marlowe told Nussbaum:

> Sandaval sold a short called THE JOYS OF FATHERHOOD to Candar Publishing Co. (*Wildcat, Charger,* etc.) Pretty far out stuff. Too rough for Volitant, my usual outlet. After reading the last couple of issues of *Adam* and *Knight*, though, with Iceberg Slim figuring prominently, it seems to me that nothing is barred in these magazines.

Volitant, Marlowe's "usual outlet," published such magazines as *Escape to Adventure, Man to Man, Action!* and *Sir!*, according to the book *Men's Adventure Magazines* by Max Allan Collins, George Hagenauer and Steven Heller (Taschen, 2004). Though tracking down individual Marlowe stories that appeared in these magazines is difficult, it appears some were simply adventure stories and others were sex-oriented. Marlowe was still writing for the men's magazines as late as Jan. 7, 1977, when he dropped a note to Odell in which he mentioned his latest sale:

> I sold a girly short story to CAVALIER for $250, and a 2000-word horseracing article to SPORTS ILLUSTRATED came back asking me to cut 1200 words, which I'll do over the weekend.

Some of these stories were merely "racy" or risqué: sex was dealt with frankly, but not in graphic detail. Others were explicit and raunchy, like the out-and-out porn books Marlowe produced. Marlowe's personal files at the Howard Gotlieb Archival Research Center at Boston University contain a selection of these stories, including a list the writer headed "Sandaval's sexy short stories." The list of 23 stories apparently contains Marlowe's original titles, some of which were retained and others changed when the stories appeared in magazines. Titles are: "Aunt Martha Cooperates," "The Bedroom Tape," "The Birthday Present," "Blind Date," "Blind

Man's Bluff," "A Coal Miner's Daughters," "A Coed's Secret Sex Desires," "Hell on Ice," "Honey in the Hay," "Honeymoon Dilemma," "Hotel Convention," "A Little Work Will Never Kill You…," "Master of the Parley," "A Matter of Style," "The Mercenary," "A Non-Virgin Goes to Sea," "The Paddling Syndrome," "Shake Hands on Your Marriage," "Sisters in Flesh," "Triangle on a Schooner," "The Wedding Present," "Wig Warm," and "Who'll Marry Millie." The files also refer to several other Marlowe stories, including one he called "The Man Who Kept His Cool the Most," which he noted was published in January 1969 in *Man to Man* as "She Who Got Spanked."

In the files, there are also several manuscripts of pornographic novels, including *Testament* by "Ward Malone," a coming-of-age novel filled with graphic sex, and *Give-and-Take* by "Weldon Mara," a sex novel about a woman with two "nubile daughters" who marries a much younger man—a story that may have been rewritten as *The Stepdaughters* (see below).

It's not known how many pornographic books Marlowe sold that were published, but a cluster of them appeared in 1971 under the Dansk Blue Books imprint. The basic research on Marlowe's possible authorship of these books was done by Victor Berch, former librarian for Special Collections and Rare Books at Brandeis University, who, under the pseudonym "Bart Choveric," published an article on *Mystery*File Online* titled "Was Dan J. Marlowe a Writer of Pornography?"

Berch, who turned up the leads on Marlowe while trolling through copyright records, linked him to several Dansk Blue Books published by Brandon House, North Hollywood, California, a purveyor of soft- and hard-core pornography. Registered to Jaime Sandaval were four books with author names that are anagrams of Dan Marlowe. "Rod Waleman" was listed as the author of *The Young Librarian* (February 1971), *The Stepdaughters* (March 1971), and *The Innocent Schoolteacher* (May 1971). "Major D. Lawn" was listed as the author of *The Orphan Girls* (March 1971). Berch also discovered two other Dansk Blue Books not registered to Jaime Sandaval, but whose author names are also anagrams of Dan Marlowe or Dan J. Marlowe. These are *Reluctant Wives* (February 1971) by "Mande Woljar," and *The Unwilling Mistress* (June 1971), by "Alma Werdon."

Interestingly, the publisher of *The Young Librarian* tried to capitalize on Marlowe's reputation without naming him, as an excerpt from the book's introduction, dated January 1971, shows:

> The Publishers of *Dansk Blue Books*, in an effort to seek the very best for their readers, contacted one of America's leading suspense writers early last summer and commissioned him to do a novel for this new series. Intrigued by the possibilities of this type of project, the author closed his palatial resort home in Michigan and moved into the near-ghetto, slum areas of New York and, later, San Francisco. Under the pseudonym of Rod Waleman, he became one of the hopeless and forgotten street people; he was one of them in clothes, in manner and in thought. For a man whose work has appeared on television and has been printed in almost every country and every language in the world, the Dansk Blue Books assignment was a revelation. Posing as a handicapped retired seaman with only a meager income, he moved into a shoddy hotel near the heart of the city. During the next three months, he was mugged at least three times, threatened with death by a member of a Black militant organization, a victim several times of extortion and petty robberies, a witness to several knifings, and—from his third floor hotel window—saw half a dozen gang rapes of drunken female bar patrons take place in the alley below his window.

Marlowe, who was still living in a more-or-less "palatial resort home" in Michigan—but not his own—in 1970, did move to San Francisco for a year starting in May, living at least initially in the Hotel Roosevelt at Jones and Eddy Street, where Earl Drake and his girlfriend Hazel stay in *Operation Drumfire*, published in 1972. In that book, Drake also is threatened with death by members of a Black militant organization. But did Marlowe ever live as "Rod Waleman," posing as a penurious handicapped retired seaman who witnessed a great deal of street violence? Unlikely. The author hasn't turned up any correspondence indicating that happened, or any accounts from people who knew Marlowe saying that it did. And *The Young Librarian* contains no details of scruffy street life of the kind we might expect from a writer who had made the sacrifice of living incognito in a bad part of town to infuse authenticity into his storytelling.

The Young Librarian, in fact, is simply a generic porn book that could have been written in a phone booth. It contains none of the technical detail, background description, or urgent narrative that Marlowe put into his suspense novels. The setting seems to be a small town or a medium-sized city, but there is so little description that that's just a guess. The book tells the story of Linda Brumiglia, an attractive 22-year-old librarian "with raven-black hair parted in the center." As the story progresses, Linda has sex with her 17-year-old niece Carole, her vibrator, the physical education instructor at the local high school ("Helen Dickinson"), the janitor in her apartment building and one of his Army buddies, and with her niece's boyfriend, Charlie, and three of his friends—Edmondo, Carl and Mousie. The four young men, as a group, repeatedly rape her in every way imaginable, and she feels degraded but (blush!) kind of likes it. No porn surprises here.

The only interesting thing in the book, for someone exploring parallels between Marlowe's conventional thrillers and his porn writing, is the incredible amount of space devoted to spanking scenes. The reader can wallow in three separate bottom-whacking sessions, taking up 22 pages of a 192-page book. Everybody spanks everybody. Linda and her sister Annette spank Annette's daughter Carole because she talked back to her mother, Carole and Charlie spank Linda in revenge for Carole's pain and humiliation, and Charlie and the members of his gang spank Linda in the midst of many other hijinks.

> Carole didn't reply. She aimed the hairbrush deliberately, snapping its flat surface against the whiter portions of Linda's rotating, crimsoning backside. Linda's resolution broke as the hot kiss of the brush built up and multiplied in her tender white cheeks.

> —From *The Young Librarian* by "Rod Waleman"

While the bottom-smacking sessions are far more drawn-out and sexually explicit than those in Marlowe's suspense novels, occasionally the reader of those novels finds a heavy dose of discipline, most notably in *Operation Breakthrough*, when Candy Kane becomes upset with his beautiful, 6-foot-4 Chinese girlfriend, Chen Yi (who, by the way is a fierce fighter, and genuinely in love with Kane):

> "GET THE CANE."
> For an instant, I thought she was going to refuse to obey. Then she went behind the kitchen door and took down from a hook a pliant looking cane about twenty-four inches long, the type I'd seen in movies involving British schools. In silence she handed it to Candy. He bent it double upon its own length, testing its flexibility, then gripped its knobby end. "Get your belly down on that table!" he commanded. "That smart mouth of yours will make your ass smart!"

Kane says he's going to give Chen Yi "ten of the best," and does, but when it appears he's going to administer more, she leaps up, grabs him, thrusts his whole body into the air, and appears ready to smash him on the floor, but then puts him down and leaves the room. This scene, complete with sound effects ("Swissssshhhhh-crack! Swissssshhhhh-CRACK!") takes up a page and a half of the book. But similar scenes in some of the suspense novels are perfunctory, and some are played for laughs. In *Strongarm*, Pete Karma, on the run from bad guys with his girlfriend Lynn and her 18-year-old cousin Augusta "Gussie" Bowen, wakes up in a darkened motel room and gets a rear view of Gussie, who he thinks is going after a locked bag of valuables in the closet.

> Although it was dark, from six feet away I could make out her figure bent over the bag. I opened the closet door wider to get it out of the way of my backswing, and delivered a smashing openhanded uppercut to the most prominent projection facing me from the closet. It lifted Gussie clear off the floor. As her strangled yelp assaulted my ears, my hand made an interesting discovery; between its salute and Gussie there hadn't been so much as a thread.

Occasionally, too, there's a scene that's simply weird. Probably the most far-out example is in *One Endless Hour*. Dick Dahl, an accomplice of Earl Drake who makes skin flicks when he's otherwise lying low, carries a video camera into a bank during a robbery in Washington, D.C., forces the women employees to get down on the floor and stick their bare behinds into the air, then videotapes them. Later, Dahl shows the video to Drake.

> Up went more dresses and slips as the first bare-bottomed duo dropped to the floor and stretched out. Another variety of underwear dropped and two more bare behinds popped into view, and then as the camera drew back slightly, three more…All plumped out attractively as their owners doubled up awkwardly and joined the first pair on the floor…"You'll notice that although there's two good-lookin' young heads in the crowd the best-lookin' ass belongs to that woman on the left, who must be forty-five if she's a nickel," Dahl said. "You'd be surprised how often it turns out that way."

Drake's response is to think about what turns him on sexually, and his thoughts lead to the big-bodied Hazel Andrews and, apparently, to his reaction to seeing bare rumps. As Dahl is disassembling the projector, he examines Drake's expression. ("Kind've got you, cousin?" he said shrewdly. "Don't get shook. It gets to most.")

Such scenes were central to the kind of writing Marlowe produced, part of his stock-in-trade. He had to write erotic scenes and it was in his interest to offer the reader something new. If other tough-guy writers spent their sex interludes focusing on breasts and legs, perhaps it was strategic for Marlowe to look to the rear to tickle the reader's fancy. Or maybe it was just his own kink and he couldn't contain it.

As he and Odell worked on what they hoped would be their breakout novel, getting a new wrinkle on the erotic was very much on Marlowe's mind. Writing to Batson on Dec. 3, 1976, he discussed the book he was planning to produce for publisher Bernard Geis:

> A number of sub-plots will be necessary. More characters than usual will be necessary. And since Geis is looking for some-

thing exploitable to promote, there will be more sex—and kinkier sex—than usual.

A plot summary he prepared in November 1976 referred to personal experience that would help him craft a female villain both titillating and evil:

> Years ago I knew a woman, a true intellectual, with bizarre sexual inclinations. She alternated between going away on weekends with two truck-driver types at a time to be sexually abused and degraded to initiating 14-year-old virgins into the rites of lesbianism.

Marlowe did include an erotic "set piece" adapted from one of his men's magazine stories (we don't know the name of the story, or of the magazine) in a draft of *The Dream Machine*, the novel—ultimately aborted—that he and Odell were preparing for Geis. In the set piece, a male prostitute named Eddie Richards performs sex with a wealthy, fortyish woman named Mrs. Cartwright as a birthday present to Mrs. Cartwright from her friend Elaine. At this point, Richards is interested only in sex-for-money, but as the story progresses, he will be drawn into a scheme to blackmail his women clients. After he goes to Mrs. Cartwright's apartment, overcomes her initial reluctance and has sex with her, Eddie asks her what her secret fantasy is so that he can fulfill it.

> "Well—" She hesitated. "I'm not sure I'd like it, because I've never tried it, but all my life I've dreamt—" Her voice picked up speed "—that I was doubled up over a pillow at the end of the bed and it was—it was being put into me from behind."

Odell, Marlowe's collaborator, thought this scene was just the ticket, as he explained in a letter to Marlowe on Jan. 4, 1977.

> As an insert. . .and one with sexual impact. . .this bit with Eddie Richards is something which I judge would be close to Geis' mood or tastes in literature. I'm sure he'll want a place found in the book for exactly this well-conceived episode.

In the end, of course, this book project was tossed, and Geis ordered up a supernatural thriller, which became the proposed book with the working title *Julie*. But the switch in stories didn't mean that Marlowe was going to dispense with offbeat sex. In fact, *Julie* is a story of sexual obsession, supernatural powers, and self destruction. Marlowe's outline for the book spells this out in great detail.

Raymond Desjardin, a married 39-year-old U.S. senator from Louisiana, comes under the spell of 14-year-old Julie Villefranche at a fundraising dinner in his home state. Julie is the sexual aggressor. They go riding alone on the plantation owned by Julie's mother, and Desjardin and Julie perform coitus in a "smoking consummation." When Julie and her mother visit Washington, D.C., Julie lures the senator out for a tete-a-tete and explosive sex, almost against his will.

> He curses himself later. What kind of fool is he to risk a potent political career for this admittedly inflammable piece of ass? Discovery would ruin him.

—From the outline for *Julie*

But he can't help himself. He turns to Julie's mother, Norma, for some explanation of Julie's personality. The mother says her daughter has always been a strange child, with inexplicable events happening around her. Julie, she says, is the student of an old Cajun crone—the grandmother of the Villefranche cook—who is considered a witch by the people of the swamps. Shortly after this conversation, the senator's wife disappears and her body turns up in a swamp; she's been the victim of a ritual murder.

Julie now proposes a startling strategy so she and Desjardin can be together. Marry my mother, she says, then we can be in the same house and have sex whenever we want. The senator sees how practical (!) this is, and does marry Norma Villefranche. For a while, things are quite satisfactory around the Desjardin household. The senator finds he likes having sex not only with the daughter, but also with the mother ("He enjoys her mature mind no less than her large, firm-fleshed body"). Unfortunately, the whole situation bursts into the open when a jealous Julie catches her mother and new stepfather en flagrante.

He comes home early one afternoon, finds Norma on the lower floor of the house, and by unspoken mutual consent they go upstairs to their bedroom. Ray is standing in the middle of the room while Norma kneels before him, giving him oral sex, when from the corner of her eye she sees movement inside her opened closet door. She springs to her feet and hauls a clawing, spitting Julie from the closet where she had been spying on them. Furious, Norma gives her daughter a tremendous bare-bottomed spanking in front of Ray, who cannot restrain his laughter.

—From the outline for *Julie*

Laughter, however, isn't the proper response to erotic stimuli in commercial novels. As we'll see, Marlowe re-thought the senator's reaction to the spanking in the month after he sent the outline to Geis. He also used this as an excuse to get some "research" material on spanking. On May 17, he wrote to Edcampden Sales, 24B, Crown St., Acton, England, to ask the merchant to send him, by air, the erotic film *Home Late From School*. Marlowe enclosed an American Express money order for $34 to cover the cost of the film and postage, but felt he might be sending too much, for he told the merchant, "Pse (please) issue credit for remainder, as I wish to order a subscription."

We know the nature of the film because he wrote his note to Edcampden on the back of a flyer advertising it. Edcampden declined his money order as payment and returned the flyer, found decades later among Marlowe's papers in Harbor Beach. The flyer describes the nature of the film in expansive terms:

HOME LATE FROM SCHOOL

A
"spanking"
new film

A dynamic Super 8mm. full colour film is now available— approx. 175 feet in length. Filmed to perfection, the story goes as follows:

"Despite repeated warnings, young Susan was always home late from school. One day her mother became very worried, and on her arrival, Susan was promptly marched into the living room, her knickers were taken down and her bare bottom was severely spanked!

The next day she was late again! and in desperation Susan's mother went out and bought a thin whippy cane. She burst into the bedroom and Susan Screamed in fright. She was truly caned— her bottom striped with the red lines of stinging pain left by her mother's cruel instrument."

These "schoolgirl discipline" films prove to be very rare all over the world, so if you are an ardent fan of this subject and like seeing justice being done to NAUGHTY SCHOOLGIRLS, send your order to us today while this popular film is still in stock!!!

Although Marlowe never received the film, he'd already made plans to develop the scene involving Julie, Norma and Raymond Desjardin. In a letter dated June 5, he responded to critical points raised by Geis and two of his employees about the outline. One Geis employee found fault with the scene in the bedroom, and Marlowe said he'd misunderstood; Julie's spanking was to inspire sexual arousal:

> I don't intend for Ray to be cynical about it. Rather, I was thinking in terms of a scene which should be one of domestic discipline but which because of the special relationships becomes one of sexual excitement, even to Norma.

The scene was never to be written. The morning after Marlowe wrote this letter, his mind blanked out his plans for *Julie*, along with all its other contents. He had been planning to visit his girlfriend in Long Beach, California, perhaps to do even more research into the eroticism of slapping rear amplitudes. But when his amnesia hit, it swept away his past and vaporized his memories of female backsides. The spank-a-torium closed down for good.

CHAPTER 16:
Blank Slate

No matter what anyone does, it just doesn't seem to help.

He sits there not moving, staring at the wall across the room. He refuses to talk and will not notice anyone unless they call his name. Maybe two or three times. Everyone is worried about him and hoping for some sign that a recovery will come soon. But there's nothing, nothing at all.

—From a letter by Marlowe's friend James Batson to Al Nussbaum, July 5, 1977.

MARLOWE'S CONDITION WAS A PUZZLE. THE DOCTORS COULDN'T find anything to explain his profound memory loss, but they kept passing him on to other doctors, hoping someone could come up with a satisfactory diagnosis.

After his girlfriend Doris Henry told authorities about the garbled phone call she had with him on the morning of June 6, 1977, after the police chief found him staring into space, after he was taken to Harbor Beach Community Hospital, everyone seemed at a loss. Dr. Oakes checked him out, but came up with a diagnosis that was merely descriptive and not very helpful: "Amnesia. Severe headaches. Cause for Amnesia not known. Severe headaches back of nose cause not known. Pan sinusitis. Brother stated (that patient had) same or similar occurrence when he was 25 years old."

This last bit is intriguing, indicating Marlowe had some sort of attack of amnesia—or possibly mental problems related to migraines—when he was much younger. Still, the details aren't clear. Oakes noted that Marlowe was currently exhibiting aphasia, a partial or total loss of the ability to communicate ideas in any form. Just why wasn't certain. Other medical records show Oakes speculating about possible diagnoses and symptoms: "non-psychotic organic brain syndrome," "circulatory disturbance of the brain," "brain hemorrhage" and "aphasia (due to probable hysteria), cause undetermined."

Marlowe's doctor was grasping at straws. After two days, Oakes shipped Marlowe off to St. Mary's Hospital in Saginaw, Michigan, where the writer was examined and treated by A. W. Farley, M.D.

Farley, like Oakes, found little wrong physically, and called in a psychiatric consultant. This was Dr. J. Cho, whose first language was not English, based on the syntax in the report of his psychiatric consultation of Marlowe:

This patient has a problem with memory loss, completely. At this time he doesn't remember anything. He doesn't even know his friend(s), apparently he was talking to them as a stranger...I talked to this patient about an hour. During this hour he seems to have no recollection in the past former week from now, however he is able (to) recall what happened since hospitalized here, about a week or so. Every answer that he gave me is that the nurse or doctor told him so, for instance what is the date today, he said the nurse told him is so and so, the doctor told him, etc. He seems to have completely loss (sic) his memory as I stated before, except for the last one week.

The only memory he is able to recall is President of the United States he is able to recall the current president's name of Carter, before him was Ford. He has a previous background of this Mr. Ford and then he is able to recall Nixon, what he was doing when he was president. He also announced that he was impeached and he had a problem with tape and before Nixon is L. Johnson, Johnson was a farmer and died of a heart attack and before Johnson, Kennedy was killed, before Kennedy he said Eisenhower was soldier and before him was Truman and before him Roosevelt. He has a pretty good memory for far back. He figured out at that time he was around 20, however he doesn't know what he was doing, where he was living.

Mental status examination revealed that he is cooperative, quiet, however, he was very gently talking. His conversation is relevant. There is no evidence of incoherence. He seems very frustrated not having recall of past. There is no evidence of thought disorder. There is no evidence of perceptual distortion and his thought content appears to be not disorganized. His recall of date, place and person, limited to a few, related to the past one week is good. His memory function the last one week is fine; however he has completely lost his memory for remote events except the president of the United States as I stated before.

His general intellectual function appears to be not impaired, for instance calculation... Abstract reasoning as interpretation was doing fine. Reality testing is not impaired. His affect in general appears somewhat flat...appears frustrated and seems to wander. Anxiety level throughout interview appeared to be (minimal). He states that he still has severe headache in the morning, it lasts a couple of hours. He states that he has some sort of pressure in his stomach and then the headache follows, but toward the afternoon he usually feels better, however, still headache is there. According to his friend he has been not drinking alcohol.

Dr. Cho said Marlowe did not appear to need any particular medication, and suggested that the writer be transferred to Saginaw General Hospital, where Cho said he could "work with him" long term, presumably on resolving problems related to his amnesia. Dr. Farley's final diagnosis, in combination with that of Dr. Cho, was "neurosis possible psychosis-depressive." Instead of being sent to Saginaw General Hospital, Marlowe was returned to Harbor Beach Community Hospital on June 22.

Over the next two weeks he refused to talk to people or couldn't talk. During this period, he was visited by James Batson, his friend from Ohio, who had come to Harbor Beach in the wake of Marlowe's amnesia attack and stayed in Marlowe's apartment. Batson played a tape recording of Al Nussbaum's voice. The author did not appear to pay much attention. He had retreated into silence. By early July, Gordon Gempel had been appointed his legal guardian. On July 6, Marlowe was transferred to Henry Ford Hospital in Detroit, where Batson saw him again.

Before the visit, Batson called a nurse who was in charge of Marlowe's care. She said Marlowe could recall everything in detail from age 25 back to childhood, but nothing since then. Batson volunteered to bring some of Marlowe's writings—*The Name of the Game Is Death*, as well as letters Marlowe had sent to Batson—to try to trigger memories.

"He did not recognize me when I entered his room," Batson said later. "I introduced myself. He was doing the *New York Times* crossword puzzle in ink. He had analyzed what the creator was thinking and explained the use of the words and meanings and their relationships in the puzzle."

Batson stayed an hour or two, gave Marlowe the paperback and the letters, and asked him to look them over. A handwritten note by Marlowe, found among the novelist's files, provides an account of this visit from Marlowe's perspective.

Yesterday scared me. I wanted to tell someone since I haven't seen Dr. Cho recently. I had a bad headache in the morning. When it gets really bad, I have to get into bed and try to hold myself together almost physically. I opened my eyes and my friend from Ohio was standing beside my bed. He had some things with him he wanted to talk about. My roommate had his family with him, so my friend and I went out to the lounge. I couldn't see very well because of the headache. He showed me books, other printed material, typewritten material. I could understand his individual words but I couldn't understand the point he was trying to make. Also, although I knew he was sitting beside me, his voice seemed to be coming down a long corridor. I began to shake and get very hot. He saw something was wrong and suggested I go back to bed. Later a nurse came in and asked me the daily questions about who I was, where I was, etc. For a second, I couldn't answer, but then it came to me. It took me most of the rest of the afternoon in bed reminding myself of those facts before the uneasiness began to subside.

When Batson returned to visit Marlowe, he could see the personal writings had not jogged any memories. Marlowe didn't realize he had written the novel, or the letters.

"The next day when I saw Dan, he told me that he had read the paperback and gave me his analysis of the story and the author," Batson said. "It wasn't a good review. He didn't connect his name to the author's because he thought of himself as an accountant, which is what he was at the age of 25. As far as the letters were concerned, he thought the author and I were good friends."

Marlowe spent about two months at Henry Ford Hospital. When meeting old friends, he didn't always understand who was who. However, he did re-establish contact with Gempel, George Scott, and some of his other friends. Early on, Batson was in contact with Nussbaum, who was now in Los Angeles working as a writer, and Marlowe himself reconnected with the former robber. Marlowe also got a 4 1/2-hour visit from his brother Don, by then a respected scientist employed by the U.S. Food and Drug Administration in Washington, D.C. Don filled him in on family matters while Dan struggled to remember.

"I had expected the meeting to be embarrassing, but it wasn't," the author said in a letter to Gempel.

The physicians continued to try to figure out how to treat Marlowe. Tests turned up physical as well as mental oddities. The diabetes he'd had for two years—for which he took insulin—seemed to have disappeared. For a while, he was placed on a psychiatric ward. He was plunged into play-acting scenarios—both in group therapy and one-on-one—to test his flexibility and resilience. These mock confrontations often bore no relation to real life and they frustrated and angered Marlowe. Later he would say he "blew fuses all over the place."

The physicians also injected Marlowe with sodium pentathol, popularly known as "truth serum," and asked him about his life. Marlowe was able to tell them things he couldn't recall otherwise. These recovered facts formed 50 percent of the background information about himself he later found usable. Interviews with his friends supplied the rest. However, this was an uneasy sort of knowledge. Marlowe's ability to trust the information continued to be unstable.

His recovery period was confusing and chaotic, but he gradually regained his ability to observe and analyze, as evidenced in an undated note to George Scott.

> This is different from the other wards. A lot of people with problems. Group activities to keep people busy. Much more freedom of movement. The other difference is that here we're supposed to wear our own clothes. The nurse said yesterday she would call Gordon Gempel and ask him about getting some down to me, so maybe she did it already. Two slacks, three shirts, three changes of underwear and socks. And a jacket. If the clothes haven't started by the time you receive this, please ask him to send $20 with them. I need a few things not provided by the hospital. Haircut, cleanser for dental plates, hair shampoo, etc.
>
> This is the fourth ward I've been on here. On each one they take your medical history all over again. Almost as if they don't trust each other but I suppose it's to prevent mistakes. Each time I tell them I was taking insulin for two years before coming here they rush in a lab man for more blood tests. Each time it's the same, no diabetes. Nobody here can understand it.

When Marlowe had been at Henry Ford for about a month, something happened that caused him great distress. On July 26, 1977, the People Page of the *Detroit News* ran an item headlined "Author Dan Marlowe is in Detroit Hospital." It said Marlowe was being treated in the psychiatric unit, and it quoted his agent, Joseph Elder, as saying the writer had complained about frequent, severe headaches when Elder had seen him in the spring. It also quoted Elder as saying, "A couple of weeks ago, a friend of his from Ohio called me and said Dan was in the hospital."

There were minor inaccuracies in the article, but Marlowe was far less concerned about them than he was about the implication that he was now a mental defective who couldn't be trusted to write salable fiction. On Aug. 12, 1977, he fired off a letter to an attorney named Joseph E. Crehan in Bloomfield Township, Michigan:

Dear Attorney Crehan:

I've been in Henry Ford Hospital in Detroit since July 6th with a speech and memory problem. On July 26th the DETROIT NEWS ran an item on Page 4-G (THE PEOPLE PAGE) in which the first paragraph stated: "One of America's most popular paperback mystery writers, Dan Marlowe, is in Detroit's Ford Hospital and being treated in the psychiatric unit." (See enclosure).

The gratuitous slap in the face damaged me materially with friends and business associates. I received telephone calls with offers of visits which I in no way wanted at that moment. Then came cards with similar offers. Now the mail is coming from both coasts, since the literary world is a very small world. Eventually I had to put a stop order on calls and visits to maintain some semblance of privacy.

The future looks no better. Having been branded crazy, and by extension, unreliable, I will find no publishers willing to deal with me as formerly. This included outline approval and half the contracted-for advance with the balance to be paid upon submission of the completed manuscript. Now publishers will demand to see the completed manuscript before they buy, and in the circumstances I can't say I blame them. There is a possibility I will never be able to sell again under my own name since any editor is entitled to ask himself "Did this nut sell the same thing somewhere else?" I've spent 21 years making my name worth something in the mystery-suspense-adventure genre. Now (if I can't sell under my own name) my earnings will depreciate 40%-50% if I submit under a pseudonym and lose the benefit of my hard-won reputation.

I called the NEWS the day it happened and asked to speak to the editor of THE PEOPLE PAGE. His name is McCormick, and he had the crust to tell me he hadn't seen the item before it appeared in print. When I asked him what the hell he was editing if not the page of which he was in charge, there was no answer. I wrote Mr. Peter Clark, the publisher, a letter stating my grievance and asking to hear from him or a representative. I've heard nothing from anyone.

My question is "Was I legally damaged?" I know damn well they wouldn't have run the item if I'd been an alcoholic in a sanitarium, yet they blithely run an article fifteen times more damaging.

The record is silent as to whether Crehan replied to Marlowe, but if the attorney did, he no doubt told Marlowe he was on shaky legal ground because Marlowe was a public figure—for whom damages are tough to collect—and because the article was substantially true. Marlowe appeared to blame Batson for the article, based on the quote from Elder that "a friend of his from Ohio" had called to say Marlowe was in the hospital. To this day, Batson says he never spoke to any reporter about Marlowe's condition, and was not responsible for the story. Even so, the story created a rift. When Batson went back to visit Marlowe after the story ran, he wasn't allowed to do so.

"The nurse told me that he didn't want to see me because of something in the newspaper," Batson says.

Batson continued to speak with and correspond with William Odell until Odell died in 2009, but he never again had substantial contact with Marlowe. Despite this, his interest in Marlowe and his desire to have Marlowe's life story told remained so strong that he supplied many valuable personal files as well as interview information for this book.

What should be obvious from the letter above, and even from Marlowe's quickly jotted notes, is that his ability to write clearly and eloquently was still strong despite his disconnected mental state. However, he and his psychotherapists believed that going back to writing fiction was not an option. In particular, this was the opinion of a "Dr. Nair," who appears to have been Marlowe's psychiatrist at the hospital. An undated letter from Marlowe to Gempel near the end of Marlowe's stay at Henry Ford, addresses this issue:

Dr. Nair stopped in to see me this afternoon. He said that it was now his opinion that the memory would not be recovered overnight, but would be a long term process. In view of this he said I could look forward to discharge in ten days or two weeks.

He also said he wanted to continue to see me on an out-patient basis. This would almost require me to live in the Detroit area, at least for the time being.

Group Therapy had been telling me already that I should look for other alternatives to writing to make a living, again for the time being, this because some of the staff seem to feel that the writing is one of the root causes of the problem. Since the article in THE DETROIT NEWS practically branded me as crazy, I doubt that I could get any publisher to work with me on the former basis, anyway. I feel I will have to take a 9-5 job and write part-time until I can re-establish myself.

Marlowe went on to say that he was planning to take job aptitude tests.

"I feel that I can handle almost any kind of office job that comes along, although it would probably have to be with a small concern rather than a large one where my age and the firm's pension plan might bar me…Physically I feel well except for the headaches, and these are not as bad."

Marlowe promptly went out and found a job as a bookkeeper for a struggling office furniture business in Detroit. By early September, he was adding up figures, tracking inventory, and assessing tax liability. Within three months, he'd gone from being a sought-after suspense novelist to being a numbers wonk struggling to make a living. He was back, almost, to where he had been in 1956. More than 20 years had been ripped from his life, but he was facing the situation head-on.

CHAPTER 17:
Letters From the Void

DAN MARLOWE HAD MANY FRIENDS AND ACQUAINTANCES, BOTH personally and in the literary world. Many of these friendships were kept up via correspondence, which, prior to the advent of e-mail, meant letters. Though his memory had fallen away from him, the letters didn't stop coming. Who were these correspondents? What experiences had he shared with them? Did he really want to take their assertions at face value?

Most were simply mystified by no longer hearing from him. But at least one, a woman in Chicago who wrote him on July 27, 1977, worried he had chosen to cut himself off from her. Though she tried to be jocular, she was obviously desperate:

> Hey, ol' Dan'l, I do believe I should be getting a letter from you rather than the other way around.
>
> Are you okay?
>
> Surely you haven't crossed me off your old-pen-pal list (after all these years?). Have I grown dull?
>
> Letters are so important to me—now more than ever. Hell, even junk mail! I read everything (but not without these glasses, for sure).

I'm pretty much house-bound, as I may've told you. Unless one of my circle takes me somewhere, I just don't go. Stuck here, dammit.

I hate bitchin'—it seems to turn your friends off—everybody's got their own problems—people seem to care up to a point then it's 'hey, lemme the hell alone, stay further away, you're not whole anymore baby, y'know?'

There, fercrissakes, I got it out—been wanting to spit that out for months. Man, what a rage that builds up inside—mostly self-directed but some for offshoot areas.

Jeez, pal, write me some long letters, how many books of yours haven't I rec'd the past yr. or 2?

Where ya been, whatcha been doin'—what's old, what's new, how are ya—ANYTHING, baby!

Oh, god—bear with me Dan—

Ever,

J

The writer did not include her name in the return address—5959 S. Kenneth Ave., Chicago 60629. Marlowe would have found it difficult to identify her. In 2009, research by the Chicago History Museum revealed the writer was most likely Marlowe's old friend Alexandra Jane Benchly, a Chicago novelist, short-story writer and newsletter editor who had been living at that address in July 1962, a year before Marlowe stayed with her while appearing on a show dealing with "The Writer and His Place in Contemporary Society" on WBBM-TV. (On Feb. 11, 1978, more than six months after the above letter was written, Marlowe did write to Gempel, possibly in response to a follow-up letter from Benchly: "Jayn Benchley's (sic) note didn't give me much of an idea what kind of response is expected from me, but I'll try a brief synopsis of events.")

Letters from other women were also showing up, and Marlowe wasn't sure how to respond. His girlfriend Doris Henry wrote from Pennsylvania, of course, but other females—status unknown—were also checking in. On July 10, a Mrs. Clifton Haywood Bradford wrote from Burlington, North Carolina, indicating that she and Marlowe had had a close relationship. She was worried about him, she said, because she had been in touch with still another of his girlfriends—the one in Long Beach, California—who was concerned because Marlowe hadn't shown up for a planned June 20 visit. Still another letter came from Helen Olmsted of Detroit, a writer (or aspiring writer, perhaps) who had been getting advice on fiction-writing from Marlowe. A letter dated July 13 arrived from a friend named Anne Perez-Guerra in Fort Lauderdale, Florida. Marlowe apparently had been using her Florida address for tax purposes. Why he did so is unclear.

"It's a good many weeks since I've heard from you—last letter April 23 when you were about to leave for the annual MWA affair in NY," Perez-Guerra wrote. "I'm not nagging. I'm concerned, and hope it is only because you are busy and not that you are ill." She went on to reference novels they had discussed, her own struggles with osteoarthritis, and dietary solutions that might ease her condition.

Sometime in August 1977, letter writers like this (though it's not clear specifically which letter writers) were getting a reply from Gempel meant to clear up the mystery of Marlowe's lack of response to them:

Dear Friend of Dan Marlowe,

Please excuse this photo copy method of correspondence. I would have preferred writing each of you personally, however Dan has so many friends with whom he corresponds I feel you would rather hear from me this way now rather than wait until I had time to write each of you personally.

Some of you already know that Dan has been in the hospital since early June and has been incapacitated to a degree. Part of Dan's problem is an affliction diagnosed as "Aphasia." He is feeling fine and making very good progress but at the present time is still in the hospital and he asked me to let you know why you haven't heard from him in the past couple of months. The prognosis is for complete recovery but the Doctors tell me that the recovery is sometimes slow and it could be several more weeks before Dan is released.

Of course Dan will be getting in touch with you when he is released from the hospital but in the meantime I will be handling his personal affairs and his mail. If you wish to contact me please feel free to write or phone me at any time.

The letter skated around the fact that Marlowe was suffering from amnesia, though a number of his friends in the immediate area knew that, and some had visited him during his hospitalization. That hospitalization ended in early September 1977, and Marlowe, who had landed a job as a bookkeeper at an office design and furniture company called Co-ordinated Interiors at 714 W. McNichols in Detroit, moved to a rooming house at 7440 Miller St., Dearborn, Michigan. He still had infirmities. His speech was hesitant, in contrast to his former rapid-fire delivery. He also was having mental difficulties, as he explained in a Sept. 13 letter referring to conversations with Gempel and George Scott.

> You and George said you thought I sounded the same. I don't know how I felt before, of course, but I encounter embarrassing shortcomings in myself almost every day. I can't seem to think quickly. I noticed it in the hospital but it is much more noticeable outside. I have read the outline which had been approved for me to write (Author's Note: apparently the outline for *Julie*), and I not only marvel that it was me who put it together but I feel badly that I couldn't do it now. I wouldn't know how to begin writing it.

Unsettling occurrences also emerged from Marlowe's past.

One night he took a phone call from a man in New York who wanted to know when he and Marlowe were going to complete "the five-book reprint sale." When Marlowe told him such a sale was news to him, the man insisted Marlowe had called him about the deal two months previously. He refused to give his name, and declined to say how he had gotten Marlowe's phone number. Finally, he hung up.

A man we will call Michael Newberry, who said he was a longtime friend of Marlowe, wrote from Chicago, quite concerned about three packages in Marlowe's apartment that were labeled with Newberry's name. Newberry—who said he had been injured while flying in World War II—asked Gempel to send him the packages via United Parcel Service, and said he would be "more than happy to pay packing and freight."

After Gempel agreed to send the packages, Newberry phoned Marlowe and told him the packages were apparently on the way. In a letter to Gempel, Marlowe remarked, "There must be platinum in there the way he worries about it." Later, the novelist wrote to Gempel, "I have a feeling (Newberry) is about 82 cents on the dollar. Is he a drinker? Once when he called me he sounded smashed." When Marlowe finally got together with the man, he wrote Gempel: "(Michael Newberry) turned out to be a strangely contradictory man. I'll tell you about him when I see you."

Newberry wasn't the only person concerned with items left in Marlowe's apartment, Gempel recalled in an interview in 2005. After discussing how James Batson had stayed in the apartment, Gempel described another incident. "Another fellow kept calling, English accent," Gempel said. "And he said there's a trunk that belongs to me up in Dan's apartment. He described exactly which closet it was in. Tied with ropes. I said to myself, when was he here? I never saw him. But anyway I got a hold of the lawyer (who was handling Marlowe's affairs after the amnesia attack), and he and Candy (Oeschger, Gempel's assistant) and I went over and opened it up and inside this trunk there was an article from the *Chicago Tribune*…about a young boy being killed by whipping. In the trunk there were whips and articles from 1935 in the Chicago newspaper. So this guy said, if I come and get it, can I have it? And I didn't want it and I asked the attorney and he said, why not? So this guy showed up, a little guy with arthritis and a little bitty car of some kind. And I took him to lunch or dinner at the local family bar and he thanked me and off he went with the trunk and I never heard from him again."

Marlowe, who now was focusing on making a living from his rusty business skills, settled into his job at Co-ordinated Interiors, which he quickly pegged as a shaky business. He continued to see Dr. Nair, the psychiatrist, but now began to get hints his condition might be linked to a physical cause. On Oct. 1, he wrote Gempel:

> I saw Dr. Nair again today. When I repeated to him that I didn't feel sharp mentally, he told me something I hadn't heard

before. He said that two of the many tests they gave me were inconclusive. Previously I had been told all the results were negative. He said that two tests, one of which he called a "cat scan," weren't negative but weren't positive either. He said that inconclusive tests like that sometimes indicated brain shrinkage or other damage in amounts not large enough to be picked up by the tests. It reminded me that in Saginaw someone said one of the tests there was inconclusive, too, but nobody ever mentioned it again.

This was an early hint that the cause of Marlowe's amnesia had been a stroke. Before long, Marlowe was routinely saying this was true. Whatever the source of his mental challenges, they continued as he wrestled with his bookkeeping work. "There is nothing in the requirements of the job I find difficult," he told Gempel on Nov. 12. "What I do find difficult is eliminating stupid mistakes which make things difficult for me: arithmetical transpositions, inaccurate copying, etc. It infuriates me that I create most of my own problems. A bookkeeper necessarily finds his own mistakes, and I give myself plenty of practice. It's both frustrating and time-consuming."

Still, Marlowe took a balanced view of his struggles.

"On the plus side," he told Gempel, "the nature of the job is such that many of the bookkeeper's errors are known only to himself. Keeping the office ticking is a breeze. One of the partners told me that I manage the cash flow—what there is of it—better than anyone they've had. The business is still no sure thing to make it."

Marlowe was having trouble making it financially, too. By the end of 1977, his total wages from Co-ordinated Interiors amounted to only $4,185. Meanwhile, Gempel had gone through Marlowe's accounts and found he had run up debts that would be difficult to pay off. He owed Peoples Bank of Port Huron more than $5,100 on two promissory notes and his MasterCard account, was several payments behind on his car loan with the State Bank of Port Hope, Michigan, and owed more than $6,500 on four promissory notes to the Huron County Bank. Furthermore, he owed more than $15,000 in principal and interest to three individuals from whom he had obtained loans the year before.

On March 22, 1976, he had borrowed $4,200 from Kenneth Gale Crawford of Washington, D.C. Four days later, he had borrowed $4,200 from Jeremiah V. Jenks, of Grosse Pointe, Michigan. And on May 25, 1976, he had borrowed $6,800 from Miranda de Toulouse-Lautrec (also known as Comtesse Charles-Constantin de Toulouse-Lautrec and Randi Redfield), who was represented by a lawyer in Madison, Connecticut. Later, Marlowe would tell Gempel he simply couldn't remember why he'd borrowed "all that money."

But a hint came in a letter to Gempel from Crawford on Sept. 20, 1977.

"On March 8, 1976, Marlowe wrote to me asking for the sum of $4,200, which he said would keep him going while he wrote a novel he had in mind," Crawford wrote. "He wanted to get away from the mystery novels he had been writing very successfully but abandoning this sure source of income at least temporarily would leave him without sufficient income until his new book was marketed." In a breezy follow-up note to Gempel on Oct. 25, 1977, Crawford indicated he wasn't too upset about the prospect that the debt would never be repaid. "Just to remind you about the letter to show IRS that I made a stab at collecting. It is the type of thing I'd forget, so I assume you will unless prodded. Tell Candy to write a note for you to sign, there's a good fellow."

Whatever Crawford's attitude, the fact remained that Marlowe owed upwards of $25,000 and had considerably less than that in assets, including cash, savings, equity in two lots of land in Highlands County, Florida, a part interest in a commercial lot in Harbor Beach, and some shares in Huron County Cable TV.

Gempel was surprised to find that this apparently successful writer was not garnering income from his past writings. While Marlowe had never lived high on the hog, he never seemed too strapped, either. Once when Gempel needed $5,000 right away, Marlowe had written him out a check on the spot, then was repaid by Gempel within a week.

The reasons for Marlowe's current financial distress became somewhat clearer after Odell got in touch with Gempel and explained Marlowe's earning struggles. Nussbaum also did some sleuthwork, and followed up with on-the-ground research while attending the Bouchercon World Mystery Convention in New York in October. In a letter to Marlowe on Oct. 17, 1977, the former bank robber explained what he had found out from Marlowe's agent, Joseph Elder, especially as it related to the *Julie* project. Nussbaum, used to sizing up personalities as a survival tactic in the criminal world, was blunt about his impression of Elder.

> I saw and talked to Joe Elder. He told me what I had already suspected: you are owed no monies. Anything that might have been paid to you would have been an advance against royalties and tied to the completion of the outlined book. The book was, however, your idea. Geis cannot pass it along to another writer without your okay. If he really is anxious for the book, and has no or few reservations about passing it along to another writer, you may be able to get a few dollars for letting him do it. But this is an outside chance at best.
>
> As for Elder himself, he didn't impress me very much except as a loser. I figure he's on a downhill slide. I'm surprised he was able to get you connected with Geis in the first place. Anyhow, that was how he struck me. He seemed very low key and not especially bright. I think an agent should come on a little stronger than that. But you were satisfied with him in the past, so don't let this off-the-cuff evaluation influence you too much.

This sizing-up of the agent, and of the money situation, was reinforced in late December, when Odell visited Marlowe in Detroit and got him away from his workplace for a discussion. Marlowe recounted the conversation to Gempel in a letter on Dec. 28, 1977:

> He did tell me quite a few things, at least one of which helps to explain the sudden dropoff in income. There was a change of publishers at Fawcett about 18 months ago, and the new one, a lady, decided to drop the various suspense series which had been Fawcett's staple and to go with gothics. In addition to buying the books, Fawcett had been marketing the overseas rights. When they stopped buying, they lost interest in the overseas market. Odell says I had just completed getting the copyrights transferred to my name—softcover books are copyrighted in the publisher's name, I don't know why—but hadn't had time to do anything about it. He's not sure anything could have been done, since the

suspense market turned soft, anyway. Odell has no very high opinion of Elder and said I didn't, either. We were using him to get a foot in the door in a new medium. He said Elder could have pushed to get another $500 Geis had promised, but chose not to. Geis had also promised to pay my expenses in New York last April, but Elder hadn't pushed to get that, either.

At this point, Marlowe apparently understood who Odell was and what his motives were. But, as time went on, Marlowe's shifting mental state would cause him to question Odell's true identity and to become suspicious of him. Despite the paper trail, stretching back years, that demonstrated the close relationship Marlowe had with Odell, Marlowe's core certainty about who his friends were had eroded sharply. This was also true on the few occasions that he returned to Harbor Beach, Gempel said.

"He didn't like to go to the local bar (Smalley's) because people would greet him and he didn't know who they were," Gempel said.

Even as he got reacquainted with his friends through hearing about them from others, Marlowe found it difficult to deal with some of them. The problem arose because his loss of memory was hard to grasp for many people, including Doris Henry, he noted in a letter to Gempel on Dec. 29, 1977.

> I'm surprised all the time by people who know my situation yet refuse to accept my limitations.
>
> I know I've told you that I've had a letter every ten days or two weeks from Doris Henry of Pennsylvania. She has been vehement from the beginning that the only place for me was Harbor Beach. I wrote her that you had been even more vehement about the same thing until realistically you admitted there was no employment there, important not only for the therapy but also as a beginning to pay the bills I'll be faced with. She's not prepared to accept that from the tone of the letters.
>
> Recently she's taken out after me because "You've never asked me to come and see you." With one or two exceptions, I've enjoyed—after the initial awkwardness—the people who came to see me, but with no knowledge of the basis for or the depth of a

relationship it seems to me it would be damned presumptuous on my part to ask anyone to come and see me.

She also asked me if any of her pre-stroke letters to me were in the apartment. Of course I didn't know. She seemed quite concerned about it. I was tempted to answer that anyone would play hell trying to find any particular letters in those files, but she would probably think I was trying to be facetious.

Later, Marlowe elaborated on his correspondence with Henry: "She said she had written me that we had been in Mexico, London, New York City and other places together, which pre-supposes 'a great and good friendship' to quote Romain Gary's ex-wife. Does she really want to try to resume with a man who doesn't remember things that she remembers and doesn't remember her? I doubt it." Still later, on Jan. 13, 1978, Marlowe continued the theme: "Thinking back, I may have stirred her up unintentionally by asking if she knew a Gertrude Bradford from North Carolina who writes to me, if D.H. and I were as close as you seem to think. The Bradford woman writes that we have known each other well since the 40's, and she keeps hinting at intrigues. Did I ask if you knew her? I meant to."

Marlowe did eventually spend time with Henry, in July 1978. She visited Harbor Beach while Marlowe was staying at the house of his friend George Scott, and sent Marlowe a photo of herself beforehand so he could recognize her. The encounter apparently went well, and they continued to be friends, but it's not clear whether they resumed their intimate relationship. Most likely, they did not. In fact, it appears that Marlowe's days of sexual adventuring ended with the onset of his amnesia, though he was to live for 10 more years.

Letters from people Marlowe had known helped him re-attach to his past. However, a different kind of letter pulled the trigger for the next chapter of his life. This letter, which arrived in the spring of 1978, came from Los Angeles. It carried the name of someone Marlowe didn't know. In fact, this was someone nobody knew.

CHAPTER 18:
The Editor Who Wasn't There

AL NUSSBAUM, WHO WAS MAKING A DECENT LIVING IN LOS ANGELES as a writer—peddling TV scripts, writing mystery stories and churning out short educational books—had been urging Marlowe to move to L.A. and join him ever since Marlowe had left the hospital. It was obvious that Nussbaum, grateful for the guidance that had allowed him to develop as a writer, wanted to repay the favor by helping Marlowe recover his writing ability. The former bank robber had done whatever he could to make the idea attractive. For instance, in mid-October 1977, he had written:

> I'll send you a few photos of my place out here as soon as I can get them taken and developed. Maybe seeing the place will give you a bit more enthusiasm about relocating. Maybe.
>
> Would you like to see the *L.A. Times* want ads? Purely for the sake of curiosity? Let me know and I'll send you the section from a Sunday paper.
>
> One more thing, about the pictures I'll be sending—if they don't convince you that you should be out here, wait until the snow starts to fall, then look at them again.

Nussbaum also wanted Marlowe to mine past writings for material to sell or re-sell. He and Marlowe went to Harbor Beach in March 1978 and Nussbaum leaped into the task of reviewing and organizing Marlowe's files. The ex-robber was a "dynamo," the writer later said. Nussbaum repacked a file near the bedroom door in Marlowe's apartment and another file in the basement, placed boxes of books upstairs, retrieved magazines with Marlowe stories from three or four different places, and figured out which books contained Marlowe or Nussbaum stories. Then he gave Marlowe a project, as Marlowe explained to Gempel:

> There are lots of foreign books in one of the trunks upstairs. He wants me to list these on future visits by country, publisher and title. Then he will write the overseas publishers and ask for the status of the current contracts and the chances for more sales. He feels that some easy money could be available in this area, no great amounts but all found, since no re-writing would be necessary.

Ultimately, Nussbaum's efforts didn't generate much money for Marlowe. But the former bank robber continued to lobby Marlowe to move to the West Coast. A boost for Nussbaum's arguments came from what appeared to be a fortuitous source on May 10, 1978, with a letter to Marlowe from Francis Arbeiter, editorial director of Bowmar Publishing Corp., headquartered in L.A.. The letter, which launched one of the oddest episodes in Marlowe's eventful life, began, "Dear Dan." It continued as follows:

> I seem to have been among the last to hear about your misfortune. I'm not writing to offer condolences, but to propose something that could benefit us both.
> Al Nussbaum tells me you are already 80% of your former self, and improving. He also showed me several of the letters you have sent him to illustrate that you have not lost any of your facility with the written word. That's enough for me.
> I have told you often enough how much I admire your fluent writing style, good grammar, and consistent punctuation.

Well, I will have a spot opening here in two or three months which can take advantage of all of it.

I would like you to edit a series of specially commissioned children's books which are strong on action, always your specialty. The position will pay $16,500 with the usual benefits package, and I hope you will give it your very serious consideration.

Don't let your present memory loss sway your thinking. You may not remember me, but I remember you. You have a lot of West Coast rooters. And I need you.

What do you think?

Your friend,

Francis Arbeiter

Marlowe—who did not remember Arbeiter—had notified Nussbaum of the letter, and the former bank robber shot back a reply dated May 26, 1978. Nussbaum's take on the offer was curious: After trying so hard to lure Marlowe to L.A., Nussbaum was surprisingly downbeat about Arbeiter and the golden opportunity he was offering:

Hi, Dan,

So our mutual friend at Bomar (sic) offered you a job. That's great, but not so surprising once I had time to think about it. And not because there is any charity in his heart. If he offers a job it's because he's damn certain he can use you. That's the way he is. He appears to be totally honest (he's never lied to me that I know of), but he is one of those people who is driven to succeed. He separates business from his social life. He would fire his own mother if she couldn't carry her weight, and he'd hire Charles Manson if he could write and was available at the right price. I first did business with him years ago from Leavenworth when he was with a New York publisher. I think you first met him at my urging when you went to one of the Mystery Writers banquets in New York. Anyhow, I'm sure he sees your accident as a golden opportunity for him to get a good man on the cheap.

Yes, I said on the cheap! The salary you mentioned isn't all that much. Really. I'm enclosing a letter I just received from another outfit offering me $8400.00 for writing the text for 12 picture books having a total of 24,600 words. That's just short of 35 cents a word! And the job can't take more than a month or two. What I'm saying is, the educational market is wide open.

If you come out here, and I sincerely hope you will because it's the perfect place to make a fresh start (I did!), I think I can promise you won't be sorry. There is enough work to keep you busy as much as you like. But more important, you don't have to saddle yourself with a full-time job to get by. There are enough short-term assignments available to allow you to pay your bills while using your best efforts for personal projects nearer to your heart.

But come out here and see for yourself. Try it at Bomar. See if you like it. You are certainly capable of editing anything they throw at you. And when you get ready to write again, there is no shortage of opportunity in that direction.

If you call our friend, you should know that he's a rather nervous and high-strung guy. I said he was driven and it's no exaggeration. He has no less than two ex-wives he's paying alimony to though he's only in his mid-thirties. And he likes to live well. As a result, he needs an income in the $40,000 range or better. He would prefer it to be better. I think he eventually sees himself as running one of the trade houses in New York and I wouldn't bet against him. His career has risen like a rocket in the ten years or so I've known him. He was a reader when I first came across him and now look where he is. Where he will be in ten more years is anyone's guess.

It's not clear how much contact Marlowe had with Arbeiter via phone or letter after this initial approach. There was enough to keep Marlowe's interest alive. Meanwhile, the L.A. situation was looking better than the Detroit scene because Marlowe's employer was on the skids. It appeared Marlowe's bookkeeping job was in jeopardy. Co-ordinated Interiors was hurting financially, and the two partners in the business were fighting, with Marlowe caught in the middle.

Marlowe had begun to worry that the partners' desperate efforts to survive, which apparently caused them to consider siphoning funds out of the business, might get him arrested. He wasn't about to let that happen, he told the partners in a letter June 22:

If this were an essay, it should probably be entitled "Save Thine Ass."

Regarding the proposed transfer of funds in connection with the Haywood Bank job, I have had legal advice, using no names. The advice given me is that if such a course were followed and at any time in the future Co-ordinated were taken over by another company or forced into a Section II or its equivalent and subjected to an audit, I as bookkeeper would be legally liable for what is called diminuation (sic) or bleeding of assets. The courts have held this to be so many times.

Accordingly, I cannot place myself in the position of making the necessary entries or drawing the necessary checks which would constitute my criminal negligence.

In view of the foregoing, should you find it desirable to replace me, I will certainly understand.

With pressure building on him in Detroit, and Los Angeles looking more attractive, Marlowe got a short note from Arbeiter in early July saying Marlowe's job interview with Bowmar had been moved from early September to early October. Marlowe told Gempel, "I'm thinking now of driving out, staying with Nussbaum, to check out the job. At the same time, I would list myself with Manpower [a business that placed temporary employees] for two or three days' work a week. Or if the editing job didn't work out for any reason I could always get a job doing what I'm doing here until something else in publishing opened up."

Marlowe followed through, quitting his Detroit job and traveling to L.A. He got there on Aug. 21, 1978, having covered 2,560 miles from Detroit, driving mostly at night because his Chrysler Cordoba's air-conditioner was on the fritz. The trip, he told Gempel in a letter, was "uneventful, but tiring." Nussbaum welcomed him to his Hollywood apartment, and Marlowe quickly set about the business of getting work. Always a practical man, his first concern was income. About a week after he moved to Los Angeles, Marlowe got together with the Bowmar editor, as he explained in an Aug. 29 letter to Gempel:

. . .I've finally met Arbeiter. . .The meeting seemed to go all right, but Arbeiter is a weird one. For one thing he is a bundle of nerves. I thought I detected a couple of hints during our luncheon conversation that his own job wasn't as secure as he might like. If I'm right, I hope he stays in the saddle until I get a foot in the door. But it's no big problem. The newspaper has a half page of ads daily of firms looking for bookkeepers.

While Marlowe had begun to question the Bowmar situation, he was going forward with his life. Only three weeks after he moved in with Nussbaum, he and Nussbaum found a new place to live and Marlowe was being welcomed into the local writing community. Nussbaum's Hollywood apartment had proved to be too small for two men, especially with the room taken up by the former bank robber's collection of more than 2,000 books.

By September 15, they had relocated 18 miles out into the San Fernando Valley, and had established themselves in Apartment 26 at 5911 Reseda Boulevard, Tarzana. The move, Marlowe told Gempel, not only provided more space but offered better air in the surrounding neighborhood, a boon for Nussbaum's sinus condition.

Shortly afterwards, Marlowe and Nussbaum went to a work-shop attended by a dozen or so writers. Marlowe hoped being around writers would get him back on track as a novelist, but he wasn't sure that would happen. For that reason, he was still hoping Bowmar would provide a stable foothold. But, as time went on, that seemed less and less likely. On Sept. 27, Marlowe wrote Gempel:

> The editorial job gets more iffy every time I see Arbeiter. He is damn near an emotional basket case. It would be nice if it still came through, but I'm not really concerned if it doesn't.

Marlowe pursued other income. On a visit to the local Social Security office, he learned he could apply for disabled status based on the physical and mental problems that had prevented him from returning to his profession. Furthermore, if disability were granted, he could start at once on Medicare, a big help with his medical bills. That was good, because his physical for Social Security showed his right side was definitely weaker than his left, both the leg and the arm, and that his reflexes were poor—symptoms consistent with the stroke that Marlowe believed had caused his amnesia. (Marlowe got his first Social Security check a little more than four months later, and his Medicare took effect on July 1, 1979.)

While Marlowe waited for a decision on disability, he took a temp job in the accounts payable section of a stereo speaker manufacturing operation. But he still held out hope for the Bowmar job. By Oct. 22, Marlowe was telling Gempel that Arbeiter was in the hospital, implying the hospitalization had to do with Arbeiter's nervous condition. "I'm not surprised," Marlowe said. "From what I've seen of him he is almost a classic example of a man shaking himself to pieces. I don't know whether it's job-connected or not, but for now at least everything is on hold."

Then the situation took another turn, as Marlowe explained in a Nov. 1 letter to Gempel:

> There has been a new development with the publishing company. Arbeiter is still in the hospital and seems unlikely to return to work immediately even when he gets out, but Arbeiter's boss called me into the office yesterday. I thought he wanted to satisfy himself that I was what they were looking for, rather than taking Arbeiter's word for it, and this may partly have been the case, but he also came up with a proposition.
>
> He suggested that I do a book or two for his company of the same type I would be editing. These would be children's books for 18-19 year olds but written at a limited vocabulary 12-year-old level, for slow readers. The stories would be semi-sophisticated but the writing would not. We kicked around a couple of ideas and I will shape one up and send it to him. If he approves it, I'll work on it in between the jobs the temporary employment agency finds for me. One thing that will make it easier is that he is interested in having sports backgrounds for these children's books.
>
> The principal reason I want to do it is because it's an almost painless step back into a writing environment where I eventually would like to be.

After this point, Francis Arbeiter vanished from Marlowe's letters, and from his life. But had he ever really been in Marlowe's life?

Nearly 30 years later, long after Marlowe's death, the truth about the editor was revealed: He most likely never existed.

Mel Cebulash, the educational publisher who had published Nussbaum's work while Nussbaum was still in prison, had been an executive at Bowmar during the time when Marlowe was supposedly being recruited by the publishing company. Cebulash had known Nussbaum for years at this point, and also had met Marlowe at a mystery writers' meeting in New York.

"The reference to Bowmar is incorrect," Cebulash told the author in 2006. "I don't know this Arbeiter, but I do know he wasn't at Bowmar... I'm puzzled by this story."

Cebulash, an accomplished writer of fiction and nonfiction, was the publisher at Bowmar in Los Angeles at that time, when it had only 15 employees. "Francis Arbeiter" could not have escaped his notice. What had happened? The scenario appeared obvious. Nussbaum, who had freelanced youth books for Cebulash, had asked Cebulash to offer Marlowe a job to convince him to move to L.A. Cebulash declined to do so, but let Nussbaum take some of the publisher's letterhead stationery, saying he didn't want to hear what Nussbaum was going to do with it. Using the letterhead, Nussbaum apparently wrote the "Arbeiter" letter.

After luring Marlowe to L.A., Nussbaum then continued the charade by finding someone to pretend to be "Arbeiter," who met with Marlowe. When "Arbeiter" disappeared because of a supposed nervous breakdown, Nussbaum handed off Marlowe to Cebulash, who—not knowing about the deception—contracted with Marlowe to write easy-reading books similar to those Nussbaum was producing.

"I think Al fashioned 'Arbeiter' from the stuff he was able to glean from me," Cebulash said.

However, Cebulash doesn't recall meeting with Marlowe at Bowmar, and it's odd that Marlowe did not mention Cebulash by name in his letter to Gempel. It's possible Nussbaum used still another person as a stand-in for "Arbeiter's boss" at Bowmar, rather than directing Marlowe to Cebulash there.

Nussbaum enjoyed such chicanery, and coming up with "Arbeiter" wouldn't have been a stretch for him. Using fake names was part of Nussbaum's operating style, as a criminal and a writer. He also was aware of the derivations of foreign names and liked to point out humorously that "Nussbaum" means "nut tree" in German. For what it's worth, "Arbeiter" in German means "worker."

Though Marlowe's connection with Bowmar had likely come via sleight-of-hand, it turned out to be productive for the novelist. He began writing easy-reading books, known as Fastback books, for Cebulash, and continued to do so after Cebulash moved from Los Angeles to Belmont, California, to work for another educational publisher. Among the titles Marlowe produced, many with sports backgrounds and others with mystery plots, were *The Hitter, Claire, Game Day, No Loose Ends, The Comeback, Small Town Beat, The Sixth Man, Turk, A Game for Fools, Foul Play, Winners and Losers, No Witnesses, Double the Glory, Ship of Doom, Janie,* and *The Devlin Affair.* Meanwhile, Nussbaum was turning out similar books, with titles such as *Snowbound* and *The Legend.*

Marlowe took to the work with enthusiasm, Cebulash said.

"He liked doing those books and he really did a great job on them," Cebulash recalled. "On a number of them, he would suggest the story. It was an honor to me. I might have been doing Dan a favor, but it was an honor to me to have him do the stuff."

Marlowe was getting about $400 to $600 for each of these books—miniature books running about 7,500 words each, about 30 pages long, Cebulash said.

"At $400, that was more than you would get doing a 7,500-word story for *Alfred Hitchcock's Mystery Magazine* or *Mike Shayne Mystery Magazine,* or whatever was around, and $400 was probably like $1,500 now," said Cebulash. "It was good pay for the time."

However, Marlowe did have reservations about writing for the slow-reading market, he confessed in a March 1979 letter to a young woman he had worked with at Co-ordinated Interiors. In describing his first efforts to her, he called them "bang-bang stories but written within a limited vocabulary straightjacket (sic) I found frustrating. It's more like doing a crossword puzzling (sic) than writing a book." With more enthusiasm, he boasted he was getting back into the spicy-writing market: "I've sold two short stories to men's magazines, male-chauvinist-pig-highly-exploitive-of-the-female-sex stories."

It's likely these two stories were "Mother Knows Best," for which *Cavalier* magazine paid $250 on Aug. 2, 1978, and "Undress

Rehearsal," accepted on Aug. 24 by *Cavalier*, again for $250. It appears Marlowe submitted the stories under the name "George Arnold," using the address 1939 N. Kenmore, Los Angeles, California. Someone at that address likely acted as a front for Marlowe, but it's clear he wrote the pieces himself. Among his files is a manuscript of "Undress Rehearsal" in Marlowe's handwriting and a typescript of "Mother Knows Best" carrying Marlowe's name and the Southern California address where he was living at the time.

Cebulash, who had long been close to Nussbaum, became a good friend of Marlowe, too. By this time, Marlowe had given up hard partying, but he still knew how to enjoy himself, Cebulash said.

"Dan would take a drink every now and then, but he didn't drink much at that time," Cebulash recalled. "He was recovering his memory. I used to go to the racetrack with him and he was a very good handicapper—Santa Anita and Hollywood Park racetracks, mostly Santa Anita. Dan would wait for a race he thought he had a winner in and, sure enough, he would have a winner in it. He seemed to make a living betting on horses. Dan didn't talk about his past as a gambler, but he retained his skills as a handicapper."

While Marlowe was still on shaky ground financially, things were improving. In July 1979, Gempel told him the cable TV stock he had bought in 1969 while living in Harbor Beach—12 shares of Huron CATV Inc.—would likely eventually bring him more than $14,000, enabling him to pay off many debts when the stock was redeemed.

Marlowe had more or less landed on his feet in California, but he still wasn't back where he had been.

"At that time he was trying to recreate books and work himself up to writing a long book, and Al was working with him," Cebulash said. "I got the sense that he didn't feel confident. And he didn't have a total recall of all of his characters, (which would have enabled him) to pick up on his Earl Drake character."

However, Marlowe would obtain support from a local writers' group he had begun to attend with Nussbaum. Its membership included a number of skilled and up-and-coming novelists, but it had an odd name. It was called Pink Tea.

CHAPTER 19:
Pink Tea

THOUGH MARLOWE COULDN'T RECALL HIS PAST LIFE AS A WRITER, he was welcomed back to the writing fraternity. His entrée was an ultra-insider's group for dedicated fiction writers: Pink Tea. Al Nussbaum, through his activity in the Mystery Writers of America chapter in L.A., was a member. So was Art Moore, a man of grim demeanor who wrote crime fiction and frontier tales (including *The Game of Death*), and Moore's ex-wife Marilyn Granbeck, a successful novelist (*Maura, The Fifth Jade of Heaven, Winds of Desire*). Moore had met Marlowe several years previously in Hollywood and had partied with him there, at MWA affairs in New York, and in London.

Even members of the group who didn't know Marlowe personally knew him by reputation—a good thing, since membership required some street cred.

"The Pink Tea was a private group, and its existence was something of a secret," said the late horror writer Richard Laymon (*Flesh, Funland, The Traveling Vampire Show*) in his 1998 book *A Writer's Tale*. "There was only one way to attend a meeting: you had to be invited by the person who would be hosting it. After the first meeting, you didn't necessarily get invited to another."

Laymon said Pink Tea was "an informal group of real pros, including the people who started the Los Angeles chapter of MWA and who were its early leaders." Pink Tea was an ironic name, like calling a fat man "Slim." Far from being tea-drinkers, the members were mostly two-fisted drinkers and smokers, hard-eyed when it came to writing and selling fiction. Twice each month, Pink Tea would meet at the house or apartment of a member and hold a party-cum-workshop. Participants would bang cocktails, suck cigarettes and pipes, flop all over the furniture and the floor and critique the offerings of members who wanted to read their stuff.

Two key members were Clayton "Matt" Matthews, and his wife Patricia. Matthews, described by Laymon as a "tough, wiry Texan" who was "gruff and a little scary," was a mystery-story writer and novelist who would later team with his wife in writing successful romantic and suspense novels such as *Midnight Whispers*, *Empire* and *The Scent of Fear*.

Patricia Matthews, who also wrote under several other names, including Pat Brisco, P.A. Brisco and Laura Wylie, was an accomplished gothic, romance and mystery writer. She recalled in an interview that Marlowe's efforts to blend with Pink Tea appeared to be uncomfortable for him.

"He felt awfully alienated," she said. "It was pretty weird. He said to me that people who said they knew him really well, he didn't remember at all." Even so, she recalled that Marlowe didn't let the situation get to him. "He wasn't a very excitable person on the surface," she said. "You didn't know what was going on underneath. He seemed to handle it pretty well. Dan said things seemed to be coming back, but he couldn't tell if they were coming back because people told him things (and current information might seem like an actual memory). He was afraid if he wrote something, it was something he'd already written before. So that kind of held him back. He was a very sweet man, I remember."

Gary Brandner, the bestselling horror writer most widely known for his werewolf-themed trilogy *The Howling*, was a member of Pink Tea who had met Marlowe at MWA events in New York but did not know him well. "I was just starting out, and, man, I was very thrilled," Brandner recalled. "He was 'big' Dan Marlowe and I was just a beginning mystery writer." Though Brandner wasn't close to Marlowe pre-amnesia, he knew him well enough to register a major difference in Marlowe after he moved to L.A.. "His personality had changed," Brandner said. "He was just very quiet. He had been very outgoing, very gregarious before. We all did whatever we could to get him functioning again."

No doubt, in some ways, Pink Tea's rowdiness was a tonic for Marlowe. Though some members of the group worried about his difficulties, others simply accepted him seamlessly into the hell-raising.

"On one memorable occasion at the Matthews' house, Dan Marlowe was sitting on a 'director's chair' that fell apart, throwing him backward to the floor," Laymon recalled in *A Writer's Tale*. "He was pretty old at the time, but that didn't stop us all from laughing our heads off. He wasn't hurt, and we were mostly a tad drunk. (Most of us were always mostly a tad drunk—or more so.)"

Laymon described still another incident in which Marlowe caused an explosion of risibility. Ironically, he got the laughs because of his understated manner, which, Laymon noted, resembled that of the earnest oddball on *The David Letterman Show* known as "Larry 'Bud' Melman." With his horn-rimmed eyeglasses and full, pink face, Melman really did bear a striking resemblance to Marlowe.

"On one occasion, the whole group (or at least all of the guys) went nuts, laughing hysterically, many of us in tears," Laymon wrote. "Dan Marlowe was reading a revenge story that he'd written for a biker magazine. To get back at a guy who had wronged him, this kid put horse laxative into a fellow's drink. There sat Dan, this soft-spoken, gentle, elder statesman of crime literature…reading to us about poop exploding into the fellow's pants, describing the stench of it, the texture, the agony of the man as he raced around the tavern, his pants around his ankles, slipping and sliding and falling down on the oozing brown lake…and we fell apart. It was a night I'll never forget."

Laymon, who was just getting a foothold in the writing business, greatly respected Marlowe, saying in *A Writer's Tale* that Marlowe was "one of the biggest names from the heyday of Fawcett Gold Medal, author of the Earl Drake series (*The Name of the Game Is Death* is one of the best hard-boiled novels I've ever read)."

Laymon believed that, despite his infirmities, Marlowe was making a great contribution to the group.

"Even though Dan suffered from amnesia, he wrote better stories than any of us," Laymon wrote. "And you always got the feeling, with Dan, that he was really listening to you, and that he cared."

By the time Marlowe joined Pink Tea, Nussbaum had been a member for some time. Though several members were—or would become—far more successful, Nussbaum had built a solid reputation, especially with his stories in *Alfred Hitchcock's Mystery Magazine* and *Ellery Queen's Mystery Magazine*.

Nussbaum also was working hard making pitches to TV, said novelist and scriptwriter Dudley Bromley. Bromley began working with Nussbaum shortly after Nussbaum left prison and did so for more than two years, until Bromley moved to Spokane, Washington. Bromley and Nussbaum co-authored a World War II book called *Crash Dive*, released under the pen name Lee Frederick, and wrote as many as 40 or 50 proposals for TV series, often science fiction or crime.

One proposed comedy series was called *Don't Get Mad*. Its protagonist was a character named Steven Even, who helped people get even with people who had done them wrong. Another proposal, called *The Guardian*, featured a character from another planet who did good deeds for people who needed help. Working alone, Bromley had written scripts for *Gunsmoke* and *Mannix*. Unfortunately, though, he and Nussbaum were never able to sell a script they pitched together. "Al never wrote any scripts that appeared on screen during the time that I knew him, but he may have had good success selling stories for TV series," Bromley said. "He was very good with plots." Other accounts say Nussbaum sold at least one TV script to *Switch*, a CBS crime series starring Robert Wagner and Eddie Albert. Nussbam's daughter, Alison Bukata, also said he sold a script to the TV series *Hart to Hart*, but believes the series was canceled before it could be shot.

Nussbaum's cleverness and his expansive personality won him friends and supporters, and he was politically active in the Southern California Chapter of the Mystery Writers of America. His criminal background gave him an authenticity no other writer there could match. In addition, Brandner said, Nussbaum was very open and very sharp, an intelligent man with a quick sense of humor.

"It was always amazing when we looked at his criminal record," Brandner said, "because he had an open, honest, sort of Elmer Fudd face." Brandner called Nussbaum "the most willing person to help anybody I ever met." When Brandner got his first screenplay assignment, Nussbaum drove all the way out to his place with a copy of the classic screenwriting book *Screenplay* by Syd Field.

Leo Whitaker, a Pink Tea member described by Laymon as a short-story writer and "sweet-tempered socialist," found Nussbaum "charming, fun, upbeat and calculating." Whitaker recalled how Nussbaum had won the chairmanship of the Southern Arizona Chapter of the MWA in an election that pitted him against John Ball, author of the novel *In the Heat of the Night*, which had been made into a highly successful movie starring Sidney Poitier and Rod Steiger. Ball had the bigger reputation, but his personal manner was stiff, and Nussbaum's was captivating, Whitaker said. "Al… was a charmer, and we all fell under his spell," Whitaker said. "Writers are such children."

For all of Nussbaum's winning personality traits, Whitaker confessed he grew queasy about Nussbaum's past. Whitaker recalled reading—on the last page of *The Gun That Made the Twenties Roar*, a 1969 history of the Thompson submachine gun by William J. Helmer—an account of Nussbaum holding up a bank with a Thompson. A thought popped into Whitaker's mind: *What if Nussbaum had encountered a security guard raising his revolver to fire?*

"No doubt in my mind Al would have sprayed him with bullets and as a result all sorts of additional people might have been killed and injured," Whitaker said. "Subsequently, I never regarded Al the same way again."

Whitaker's memory of the book was inaccurate. The pertinent passage in *The Gun That Made the Twenties Roar* actually reads: "Now and then the Tommygun still makes crime news, however. One of the more spectacular incidents occurred in 1961 when one Bobby Randall (sic) Wilcoxson robbed a Brooklyn bank with a 'chopper' in the true John Dillinger style, killing a guard and earning himself top billing on the FBI's 'Ten Most

Wanted' list. Wilcoxson's partner, Albert Nussbaum, had bought the gun from a part-time gun dealer who had acquired it from a gunsmith..." The book does not say Nussbaum carried a submachine gun into the bank, though it recounts how Nussbaum fixed up the gun Wilcoxson carried. That weapon had been discarded in a trash pile and was in bad condition, the book says, but Nussbaum cleaned it, replaced some parts and restored it to working order.

Nussbaum apparently never carried a Thompson into a bank, though he did rob banks carrying handguns. Still, Whitaker's uneasiness with Nussbaum's past, and with Nussbaum's outspoken references to his criminal career, was shared by others who knew and liked the former bank robber.

"Al was a strange personality," Mel Cebulash said. "He would tell you stories that were amazing about his bank robberies and he would laugh about them. And yet he seemed like a very gentle person. So there was that incongruity about this guy." A few years later, when Nussbaum was staying temporarily at his home, Cebulash came home one night and complained about a neighbor who had cut him off in traffic. Nussbaum told Cebulash to get an empty tin can, get a wick, and get two specific chemicals at the hardware store. "Light that up and put it on the hood of his car," Nussbaum said. "No-one will ever be able to get that out, not even the fire department, until it burns all through the hood and the block and comes out underneath the car." Cebulash, taken aback, replied, "Well, I'm not really that mad at the guy."

While some did look askance at Nussbaum, others were drawn to him. They were particularly impressed by his generosity to Marlowe. "What he did for Marlowe....magnificent," Brandner said.

The two men settled comfortably into the Tarzana apartment, a book-packed residence often fragrant with the odors of Nussbaum's cooking. "I have gained four pounds since I've been here," Marlowe told Gempel. "Al is too good a cook. I think I told you that his family was in the restaurant business for many years. I've told him to cut back on the groceries since I really don't want to gain."

Nussbaum was also a member of the Screenwriters' Guild, which meant he and Marlowe could get free tickets to movie previews, and they attended often. Though Marlowe in the past had not been a movie fan, he confessed that he enjoyed a number of the films, including Robert Altman's *A Wedding*, Woody Allen's *Interiors*, and the Italian film *Bread and Chocolate*. Marlowe, always the sports fan, also liked watching University of Michigan football games, which were taped and broadcast by one of the L.A. TV stations at 11:30 p.m. on Saturday night if the team had played that day. He also caught the Detroit Lions games on TV.

By late October 1978, Nussbaum and Marlowe had begun taking a one-night-a-week class in story analysis at a community college in Hollywood. "The class is aimed at teaching people how to do two-page synopses of books and plays in the manner that studios and producers want to see them," Marlowe told Gempel. "I'm hoping that having my nose rubbed in story creativity might help to get me started again. So far I've been able to keep up with the class assignments."

Marlowe began writing stories again, possibly reworking some of the material he had in his files, and reading them at Pink Tea gatherings. "His first tries were kind of like a beginner's short story, but he quickly began to get back some of the old Dan Marlowe feeling into his writing," Brandner said. "It quickly improved." By mid-December, Nussbaum believed Marlowe had made significant process. He said as much to Bromley, who had relocated to Spokane. "Dan is looking better every day," Nussbaum told Bromley. "He's put on a little weight and is writing again. I think what he's doing is more than good enough for publication."

In addition to making efforts at writing for adults, Marlowe was starting to embrace writing for the youth market. "I have made a start on a children's book after talking to the publisher," he wrote Gempel on Dec. 12. "It if works I'm hoping that it may lead to my getting back to something better. One of the hard things about children's books is that they have to be written with a very simplified vocabulary. It's a very slow process but I feel I'm making a little headway."

The quiet routine of writing and socializing was interrupted when Nussbaum's 69-year-old mother came to visit from Buffalo,

New York. The visit began pleasantly, but ended in tragedy, as Marlowe told Gempel in a letter on Dec. 31:

> If you're not in the mood for horror stories at this time of year, you had better stop reading here. I think I had written you that Al's mother was here for a visit. She had been here a week when she slipped on the walk and broke her ankle in three places. It was so bad it had to be operated on and pinned. She was then fitted with a hip-length cast. Therapy was hindered because of her age and because she was diabetic and had a heart condition. She couldn't use crutches—not enough strength—and she had a great deal of difficulty with a walker. Her doctor discharged her on the sixth day of hospitalization although neither Al nor I thought she was ready. The next day Al heard a crash from the bathroom and found her dead on the floor of a heart attack, probably from the exertion of using the walker. Al is in Buffalo now for the funeral. He will be back the day after tomorrow.

Despite the stress caused by this incident, and the uncertain financial prospects of writing, Marlowe and Nussbaum continued to get on well. Marlowe worked at home, while Nussbaum spent much time at the office he maintained at the Crossroads of the World building in Hollywood. Nussbaum's story "The Expert Victim" had appeared in the May 1978 issue of *Alfred Hitchcock's Mystery Magazine* under the pen name "A.F. Oreshnik," and late that year he was hard at work knocking out a series of easy-reading books for Fearon-Pitman Publishers, Inc., the operation Cebulash worked for in Belmont, California. In January 1979, Nussbaum told Bromley he was doing "another piece for *Oui* [magazine]...about my counterfeiter friend. He asked me to do it because he needs some good ink, and the editor jumped at the idea."

In March, Nussbaum was named Hollywood correspondent for *Take One*, a film magazine based in Montreal. The job gave him even greater access to free screenings, as well as other opportunities. A couple of months later he was hired by Fox to suggest a better title for the upcoming Robert Redford movie *Brubaker* and to write a few lines of copy that might be used in newspaper ads. The storyline was right down Nussbaum's alley, since Redford played an upright warden of an Arkansas prison farm taking on corrupt guards to protect prisoners who were being brutalized. Whether or not Fox used Nussbaum's title and ad copy, Nussbaum said in a letter to Bromley, he was to be paid $1,000. "Of course, if they don't use it, I'll probably never see any more of this kind of 'work,'" Nussbaum said. It's unknown what title Nussbaum suggested, or whether his ad copy was used. In the end, the movie was released as *Brubaker*.

This reminder of his own time in prison possibly reinforced Nussbaum's oft-stated desire never to go back. Even so, he was the first to admit that he was still drawn to crime, and couldn't resist casing banks whenever he went into them. Sometimes, too, he couldn't keep from dipping his toes back into the underworld and screwing with The Man.

On Aug. 6, 1979, agents of the federal Alcohol, Tobacco and Firearms agency who were watching a Lebanese resident alien they suspected of criminal activity saw Nussbaum meeting with the alien. According to Nussbaum's FBI file, federal agents concluded that the former bank robber had been listening in on ATF radio calls and decided to warn the man. Nussbaum had approached the alien, told him he was being followed and that his life was in danger. Nussbaum had gotten the man's phone number and told him he would fill him in later. The alien was confused. He called the Redondo Beach Police Department to complain about Nussbaum. When Nussbaum tried to meet with him again, driving Marlowe's car, the cops questioned Nussbaum briefly, then released him.

The FBI, thinking Nussbaum's antics might mean he had been involved in an apparently unrelated case, checked his fingerprints against prints collected in that case, but came up empty. It also took further action, as detailed in a memo to the FBI director dated 9/27/79:

"Los Angeles Division is alerting all squads handling any surveillance work to be alert for NUSSBAUM or the vehicle he is known to be operating intruding into any current surveillance situations. Additionally, a review will be made to determine if there are any cases where it appears a subject of a surveillance became tipped off and whether the tip can be attributable to NUSSBAUM."

The FBI told all federal, state and local cops in the area to be alert for Nussbaum listening to their radio calls and sabotaging their observation of criminal suspects. In the end, the feds got no more evidence on Nussbaum, and decided not to prosecute him in the Lebanese alien incident.

Far from being chastened by his close call—he was, after all, on parole and in danger of being sent back to prison—Nussbaum bragged to Leo Whitaker about this kind of activity. Nussbaum said he had a police radio installed in his car to listen to police transmissions and used it to play games with the FBI, though it's not clear what period of his life he was describing. He related one incident in dramatic detail. Nussbaum said he had come across two FBI agents having the following discussion over the air:

Agent One: "Now, you're absolutely sure the suspect is going to be at the Orange Grove Motel at one o'clock and go to Room 110? He'll pick up the key at the desk and when he walks through the room door we'll arrest him on the spot."

Agent Two: "Don't worry. It's all set up."

Agent One: "Now, I don't want this messed up. Room 110 booked for one o'clock in the Orange Grove Motel. He'll pick up the key at the desk."

Agent Two: "Guaranteed!"

Al pulled over to the curb. He got out and went to a pay phone.

Al: "Hello, Orange Grove Motel?"

Desk Clerk: "Yes?"

Al: "I've got a reservation for Room 110 for one o'clock. Please cancel it."

CHAPTER 20:
Guerilla Games

"I wasn't actually planning to use the knife myself. It gets late early with that kind of deal, and we needed him alive until he talked. It's rarely a problem. Everyone talks when the right button is pushed. There aren't nearly as many hard men around as the would-be hard men would like to think."

—From *Guerilla Games*

MARLOWE'S EFFORTS TO REGAIN HIS WRITING ABILITY STARTED SLOWLY. By early 1979, he was tinkering with writing easy-reading books, but the aftereffects of his stroke made even the typing process challenging. He practiced typing every day—often letters to friends—to try to regain strength in his right little finger and ring finger. He began to attract some interest from mystery editors, but the contacts were frustrating.

An editor of a magazine in England read a Marlowe story anthologized in a British short story collection and wrote to ask if he had any stories not published in England that might be suitable for her. She didn't pass along the title of the story she'd read, and neither Marlowe nor Nussbaum could remember it. Also, neither was familiar with her magazine or the types of stories she might use.

At a meeting of the Mystery Writers of America in Los Angeles, the editor of *Mike Shayne Mystery Magazine* asked if Marlowe had any unsold stories he might be able to use. Again, Marlowe didn't know. His manuscripts were all still at his apartment in Harbor Beach, and that collection was a mystery to him. "I must have had a filing system, but I don't know it now," he told Gempel, "and during the quick looks Al and I had at the files no system was immediately apparent."

Marlowe planned to get his files sorted out when he returned to Harbor Beach May 1 for the hearing that would be required to dissolve the guardianship arrangement with Gempel.

Meanwhile, tantalizing tidbits from his past pursued him. A check for $3.69 from the Columbia Broadcasting System arrived in the mail; he couldn't fathom why. It turned out the money was from a Japanese sale made in 1972 by Fawcett Gold Medal, which had been taken over by CBS in 1977. This reawakened suspicions—especially in Nussbaum—about the almost total cutoff of income from foreign sales after Marlowe's memory failed. These suspicions were sharpened when Doris Henry, on a trip to London, learned from the English publisher Coronet Hodder that two Marlowe books were still in print in England and that royalties had been paid as recently as December 1978.

"Al thinks there are two possibilities why no checks have come to me," Marlowe told Gempel. "It could be an honest mistake, occasioned by the fact that CBS took over Fawcett about two years ago. Or that fact combined by someone's knowledge of my circumstances could have tempted someone to siphon off whatever came in my name. Multiplied by the 13 European languages in which Fawcett was handling my books, it could amount to something. Al thinks the small Japanese check that got through to me could mean that whoever had been doing the siphoning was no longer there to keep a finger in the dike."

Marlowe wrote to Fawcett, asking for an accounting of royalties since the beginning of 1977.

Meanwhile, he was moving on with his life. In late April 1979, Marlowe and Nussbaum returned to Harbor Beach so Marlowe could attend the May 1 court hearing in Bad Axe, Michigan. The hearing went as expected: He was declared mentally competent and the guardianship was dissolved. That done, Marlowe and Nussbaum took care of other business. They loaded Marlowe's files into a trailer, continued on to Buffalo, New York, where Nussbaum packed up some of his own possessions, and swung down the East Coast to visit Marlowe's brother Don in Washington. Then they traveled to Florida to see what could be done about selling Marlowe's property there. Finally, they got back to Los Angeles on May 10. Two days later, Marlowe told Gempel, "I'm still bushed."

The two men settled back into domestic life: doing their writing, visiting friends, going to movies and tending to their two cats, Pretty Boy, an adult male, and Hilary, a kitten. Their lives appeared surprisingly sedate and free of female companionship, given that Marlowe, now 64, had been an enthusiastic womanizer before his amnesia attack and that Nussbaum was only 44, with a magnetic, upbeat personality.

In November 1979, they attended a wedding reception for Gary Brandner, who—Marlowe told Gempel—was "trying again for the fourth time in his mid-40s." Marlowe and Nussbaum brought small gifts for the bride and groom, and also brought a gift from Pretty Boy to the newlyweds' cat. "That present was the hit of the evening," Marlowe told Gempel. It was a sociable gesture, but a bit old-maidish. While it may be extreme to say it raised questions about the two men's sexuality, their living arrangement already had done that. When interviewed years later, Patricia Matthews volunteered, unasked, that there was "no indication that Al and Dan's relationship was homosexual"—an indication that the question was at least considered by the writing crowd.

The conclusion most observers reached was that Marlowe's physical difficulties and nervousness due to his loss of memory—and his concentration on regaining his writing skills—kept him from pursuing girlfriends. That was the assessment of Bob Ragan, who was manager of the Scene of the Crime bookstore in Sherman Oaks, California, when he met Marlowe in the early 1980s. "He really wasn't too big on socializing," said Ragan, who later became literary executor of Marlowe's estate. "By the time the day came around to the end, he was tired out. When he was younger, I guess, he went carousing, drinking, partying and all that. But by the time I knew him, he was pretty much a senior citizen."

Nussbaum had not sworn off women, but didn't make much headway with them. Dudley Bromley, who saw Nussbaum frequently during the two years he worked with him in the Crossroads of the World building, said Nussbaum tried professional companionship in an effort to reexplore his sexuality. "Shortly after I met him, there was a prostitute who worked in our office building, just down the hall," Bromley said. "She would see people, but she was pretty good about keeping it looking upright. It was pretty clear what was going on. She had regular customers. Al had an encounter with her. The way he explained it to me was 'I just wanted to make sure my handle still worked.' Outside of that, I really don't think he got out much."

Nussbaum, a short, thick, powerful-looking man with a bald head and a scar on his arm where he had cut a tattoo off, had a complicated personality, said Bromley, who remained friends with Nussbaum for years. Some of Nussbaum's traits were attractive, some unsettling.

"He had an absolutely wonderful sense of humor," Bromley said. "He had a great laugh, and he laughed a lot. And of course he was unbelievably smart. I play a lot of chess, and I never met anyone who could play chess like he did. I couldn't beat him…He also had a temper that was quite unpredictable. I finally learned to see it coming, because he would turn red. He wouldn't say anything until all of a sudden he would just explode. He'd rant and rave for a few minutes, then calm down."

Mel Cebulash said Nussbaum liked the opposite sex, had a crush on one of the female writers in the Mystery Writers of America chapter and may have dated her, but was very awkward around women. They, in turn, didn't quite know what to make of him. "They liked to stand around at cocktail parties and listen to his stories, but I think they were a little bit afraid of him, wary," Cebulash said.

Marlowe, on the other hand, was seen as non-threatening and pleasant. Even those who differed with him politically found him charming. "Dan was a dinner guest on two occasions at our home in Glendale, California," recalled Leo Whitaker. "He always arrived promptly with a fine bottle of California red wine. My wife Elizabeth and I enjoyed this dignified, quiet, soft-spoken Republican gentleman. Most of our friends, then as now, are left-liberals, Democratic Socialists and ex-Communists. Opposites, however, do attract."

Marlowe did continue to correspond with women, notably Doris Henry, with whom he regularly exchanged audio tapes—a method of communicating he liked. In December, Marlowe informed Gempel doctors had found a lump on one of Henry's breasts and had done a mastectomy. Marlowe sympathized: "She sounded cheerful enough about it on the tapes we exchange, but it has to be depressing for any woman." Marlowe also told Gempel a woman in Ventura, California, had sent him a packet of photocopied correspondence they had exchanged over the years. The letters revealed what each had been working on, but included few personal details that would have helped him reconstruct his past, Marlowe said.

Shortly after Christmas, Marlowe received a two-day visit from his brother Don and his wife, and the encounter caused his speech to regress, to become hesitant. "Al says that about the only time I have a speech problem now is when I'm thrust into a meeting with someone who knew me before," Marlowe told Gempel. "The speech still doesn't sound right to me, although I don't really know how I should expect it to sound. Al had some tapes I had made while he was in prison, and we've listened to them. He was surprised to find out how much more rapidly I spoke in those days, but he says that to anyone meeting me for the first time now my speech sounds normal, albeit a touch slow."

Marlowe was making progress with the aftereffects of his amnesia attack, but it wasn't straight-line progress. This became obvious as 1980 moved on and he tried to sort out whether someone at Fawcett Gold Medal had taken advantage of his loss of memory to highjack payments meant for him. On March 13, he told Gempel he had squeezed a check out of Fawcett that should have been sent to him in 1978. He also said, "I can almost prove now that the Fawcett rights and permissions director in 1976-77 (during the period of the CBS takeover of Fawcett, and my stroke) had short-stopped at least two overseas checks."

Marlowe now began to suspect his longtime co-author, William Odell, had collaborated with the Fawcett executive in diverting money. His suspicion appears to have been groundless. Odell, a forthright, generous man, had been diligent in trying to get Marlowe whatever money was owed him. But Marlowe was unsettled, uncertain. Though he had spoken to Odell and exchanged friendly letters with him, now he seemed to have forgotten who Odell was. "Did you ever meet him?" Marlowe asked Gempel. "He came to see me in Detroit when I was working for Co-ordinated Interiors. I thought it kind of strange afterward because he didn't have all that much to say." A couple of months later, Marlowe was renewing his questions about Odell, referring to him as "this man Odell who keeps writing to me."

Later in life, Marlowe would resume corresponding with Odell, apparently recalling him clearly, though not with full memory. Even so, his lapses concerning his former writing partner had ominous implications. It appeared that Marlowe's amnesia tended to come and go, or that he sometimes distrusted what he had learned about his past life.

Mind problems weren't impeding Marlowe's efforts to regain some of his status as a selling writer, however. As 1980 progressed, he was turning out easy-reading books and having reasonable success marketing adult fiction. His short story, "The Girl Who Sold Money," appeared in *Mike Shayne Mystery Magazine* on June 2, and the same magazine published his story, "Patterns," in August. A Japanese publisher who was re-issuing Marlowe's books agreed to pay him $250 for each title republished. Furthermore, Marlowe had begun mining his files for short stories published in the U.S., rewriting them to "de-Americanize" them, and selling them in Europe. He made a few sales, mostly for small amounts. When his German agent made two sales to *Penthouse Zurich*, each for $600, Marlowe exulted.

He was also attracting attention as an elder statesman of crime writing. A reporter and translator for a French magazine similar to *Ellery Queen's Mystery Magazine* interviewed him for two hours and captured his thoughts on audiotape. The editor of the Japanese version of *Ellery Queen's* magazine also requested an interview.

Furthermore, he—in effect—won a competition in October 1980 against a mixed lot of veteran and new writers. These authors were seeking to write one or more entries in the Phoenix Force series of men's adventure books planned as spin-offs of Don Pendleton's stunningly successful Executioner series. It happened like this:

In 1969, writer Don Pendleton had created Mack Bolan, a Vietnam War veteran and expert sniper known as The Executioner. After his family in Massachusetts was exploited and brutalized by members of the Mafia, Bolan swore vengeance against the Mob and set out on a campaign to disrupt Mafia operations and kill any bad guy who got in his way. The Executioner series was a huge hit. Pendleton churned out 38 novels featuring Bolan. His audience was clamoring for more. But after he suffered a heart attack, Pendleton didn't want to continue.

In 1980, Gold Eagle—an imprint of Harlequin Enterprises, well-known publisher of romance novels—bought the rights to the Bolan character and contracted with ghostwriters to churn out more books. Pendleton was still involved in character development and storylines. Mack Bolan now roamed the world, fighting terrorists of all types. Spin-off series were also created out of the Mack Bolan back story: Bolan supervised and sometimes worked with special-operations squads such as Phoenix Force and Able Team. These lethal specialists extended the reach of his anti-terrorist ambitions.

In 1980, when Gold Eagle was preparing to publish the Phoenix Force books, it approached nine writers, including Marlowe. Each was asked to submit 20 to 25 pages of the opening chapter of the Phoenix Force No. 1 book, with a storyline created by Pendleton. In addition, each writer did a character sketch of a Phoenix Force member. For this work, each writer was paid $300. Four finalists were to be chosen to write Phoenix Force books, receiving advances against royalties.

Andy Ettinger, then an editor at Harlequin, said Marlowe showed up better than some other veteran writers and was chosen as a finalist. "I do remember meeting Dan," Ettinger said in 2006. "He was one of the people who tried out and was successful. And I was surprised at some of the pros who couldn't really cut it…When we had readers go through the material, they didn't know who wrote it. And, surprisingly, some of the pros didn't make it and some of the new people did."

In addition to Marlowe, one of the finalists was William Fieldhouse, a young mystery and adventure writer then living in El Cajon, California, who went on to write many of the more than 50 Phoenix Force books. Marlowe struck up an acquaintance with Fieldhouse, possibly as a result of the Phoenix Force competition.

Work on the Phoenix Force series did not begin right away, and Marlowe's health began to decline. In addition to weakness from the stroke, he had developed severe arthritis in his arms, particularly his left. The pain at times made it impossible for him to comb his hair with his left hand. Sometimes he got an unexpected respite: the arthritis would ease dramatically for long periods, for no apparent reason. But other problems arose. In November 1980, after noticing a loss of vision, he was diagnosed with borderline glaucoma—pressure in the eyes that can lead to blindness—and began treating it with two different kinds of eye drops. The drops interfered with his sleep and made his vision fuzzy for an hour after he took them.

His maladies drained him, preventing him from putting in extended work days. "...I still can't get very much done of anything that needs doing in any one day," he told Gempel on Dec. 19, 1980. "I just have to keep nibbling at it. It adds up, eventually, but it's frustrating. If I could just put in six or eight solid hours at the typewriter, I could accomplish so much more."

He was still game for the work the Phoenix Force series would offer, however, and frustrated that it hadn't begun. In April, 1981, he wrote to Fieldhouse, "Sometimes, I wonder if this Harlequin project is ever really going to get off the ground." Suddenly, the call came. Marlowe wound up banging out his last full-length novel—55,000 words, 180 manuscript pages—at warp speed. A year later, Marlowe would tell New York literary agent Alex Jackinson, "Don Pendleton asked me to do a novel based on a spin-off of his Executioner series last summer. I did it, a quickie 6-week job, which they liked." Marlowe said he had done the book for Pendleton "when someone crapped out on delivering a book to him."

The book, *Guerilla Games*, was published in June 1982 as the second in the Phoenix Force series. It was credited to Don Pendleton and Gar Wilson (the pen name associated with all the Phoenix Force books). The copyright page carries the notation: "Special thanks and acknowledgement to Dan Marlowe for his contributions to this work." In the novel, Phoenix Force struggles to rescue a group of Americans who have fallen into the hands of Paraguayan terrorists. It's a high-octane story, a worthy throwback to Marlowe books of old.

Mark Howell, who edited the book, did not meet Marlowe, but was impressed by his work. "*Guerilla Games* was a painless book to edit because Marlowe's text, as I recall, was very professionally done and he largely understood what Pendleton was getting at with the Executioner series and its spinoffs," Howell said. Marlowe, Howell said, captured the driving philosophy of Mack Bolan and Don Pendleton ("Live Large, Stay Hard"). "I also recall that Dan's manuscript was unusually persuasive as a story of tension and violence. In some of the earlier ghosted books, we had to tighten the torque a bit, but Dan's style was quite sophisticated in its starkness, a fragile clarity."

Marlowe told Jackinson Gold Eagle had paid him a $4,200 advance against royalties for the book (eventually, his overall compensation for the novel amounted to at least $5,874). It was a big payday for Marlowe, but the writing had been stressful. His health now began to decline even more steeply. On Oct. 9, 1981, he suffered a heart attack.

"It was a classic awakened-in-the-middle-of-the-night type," Marlowe told Gempel on Oct. 27. "Two weeks at U.S.C. Hospital for tests and treatment. Now back at apartment. No prognosis as yet. I feel uncomfortable most hours of the day."

In November, another flare-up of the angina put him back in the hospital for five days of tests. The episode left Marlowe weak and unsteady, but medications kept the angina under control, at least until December, when another episode hospitalized him for nine more days. Marlowe would later say that particular attack "blew out the back wall of my heart." His doctors told him he probably would survive one more attack like that, but "two more and I'm gone." By March 1982, however, Marlowe was feeling better and taking steps to deal with his heart condition. He was walking 2 1/2 miles a day in 60 minutes without distress and taking treadmill tests twice a week at an outpatient cardiac lab. The healing of his heart was progressing well, his doctors told him.

Right about this time, Nussbaum apparently also got an offer from Don Pendleton to ghostwrite Pendleton books, though not Executioner books or spin-offs.

"About four years ago," Nussbaum wrote to Bromley on March 5, 1986, "I was supposed to ghost a series for Don 'The Executioner' Pendleton. The idea was, I'd write 'em, he'd put his name on 'em, and we'd split the loot. He could command about $50,000 for a book while my top offer had been less than ten. I turned down about ten lesser contracts and in full Croesus mode—as us computer owners might say—went happily off to Europe, spending much of the money I had yet to earn. When I got back we learned that Don's contract with the people publishing The Executioner wouldn't allow him to do anything that might put him in competition with himself. So that was out the window. I scrambled around, trying to pick up a few of the contracts I'd turned my nose up at and found that wiser souls had snapped them up. At the same time the federal money for education had dried up and I couldn't even sell a damned hi-lo book [an easy-reading book]. I had a couple of very lean years."

In the spring and summer of 1982, it appeared that Marlowe and Nussbaum needed each other more than ever, with Marlowe debilitated by a heart attack and Nussbaum hitting the skids financially. However, by June 1982, they were living separately. Marlowe had moved across the street to a one-room apartment at 5930 Reseda Boulevard.

Years later, their friends would speculate about what led Marlowe to move out. Mel Cebulash thought that Nussbaum may have been pushing Marlowe too hard with unrealistic expectations about how far Marlowe could go in regaining his status as a thriller writer.

"Dan thought that Al was directing him," Cebulash said. "Whatever Al had done to bring him back to his own, now that he's back on his own, he didn't need that much help, so there was this little edge of resentment. Al was really determined to get Dan back to the status Dan had been at, but Dan knew his limitations. He wasn't a young man, he couldn't be driven to go back to be his old self. He was lucky that he was able to piece it all together and that he was able to piece stories together and renew his life…Al had this elevated view of Dan, and he wanted him back on that level, and that may have been impossible...Al had expectations for Dan that were beyond where Dan thought he could go, or where he wanted to go, based on the fact that it would have taken so much hard work. Al was disappointed, too, in the turn in their relationship."

Bob Ragan felt that it was surprising that Marlowe—who Ragan pegged as a loner—was able to have a roommate for as long as he did, especially one like Nussbaum, whose personality was more expansive than that of Marlowe, especially in Marlowe's later years. "Al was kind of opinionated," Ragan said. "In a nice way, but it could be hard to live with, I would think." Ragan also noted that Nussbaum apparently never lost his taste for the fast shuffle, even when it came to Marlowe. Because of this, he had, on at least one occasion, angered Marlowe. This happened, Ragan said, in a left-handed attempt by Nussbaum to gain a claim on posterity.

Marlowe's biography and credits were included in a reference work called *20th Century Crime and Mystery Writers*, edited by John Reilly and first published by St. Martin's Press in 1980. When a new edition was to be printed, the editor sent a letter to Marlowe, asking him to update his credits. Nussbaum intercepted the letter and wrote back. Nussbaum listed Marlowe's novels and short stories, including some published under pen names Marlowe used. But he also added a number of stories written by Nussbaum under the pen name Albert Avellano. It's possible, Ragan said, that Nussbaum was acting more-or-less in good faith. Perhaps, the executor said, Nussbaum chose those stories because Marlowe had contributed to them in some way, by doing rewrite, providing ideas, or proofreading the manuscripts. Marlowe, however, interpreted Nussbaum's actions as self-serving.

"Dan was furious," said Ragan, "but eventually he said 'I've got to admire the guy in a way. He knew he'd never be profiled in a reference book and he wanted to get those stories credited to someone in a reference book.'"

Though all the factors described by Cebulash and Ragan might have played into Marlowe's decision to seek a separate residence, Marlowe himself—in letters written to his friend Gertrude Bradford three years after the split—explained the move as simply a clash of lifestyles. He wrote Bradford on May 31, 1985:

> Nussbaum and I no longer live together. We had reached a point where his literary activities were on the rise and mine of course if not decreasing were at least static. It required him to be away from the apartment quite often. This was complicated by the fact that he is a late-night person and I'm an early-morning person and this was troublesome to apartment living.

Marlowe enlarged on this explanation in another letter to Bradford two weeks later, on June 17, 1985:

> Our greatest problem was that he was a night person and I'm a day person. Towards the end we really weren't seeing that much of each other anyway, so I suggested it was time to rethink our situation, especially since our lives were going in opposite directions: I was drawing in on myself and he was expanding. But wherever he is (and he's back in New York right now) he always calls me once a week.

Despite the physical split, the two men remained close. Marlowe kept Nussbaum posted on his physical condition, discussed writing projects, and fended off the cops who came around to hassle the former bank robber. The two had differences, but they also had come through for each other when things were darkest. Their bond couldn't be broken. Marlowe's last letter, written three days before his death, would be to Nussbaum.

CHAPTER 21:
The Usual Suspects

AL NUSSBAUM WAS ALWAYS RETICENT ABOUT BOBBY WILCOXSON. Nussbaum talked about bank robberies, but never focused on his compadre. It was easy to see why. Wilcoxson was a savage little son-ovabitch. "Bobby was mean," a lawyer who once defended him said. "Bobby was the kind of guy who would murder your child for a Coke if he was thirsty." For someone like Nussbaum, moving back to the straight and narrow, it was best not to remind people that he'd part-nered with such a hardass. But the cops didn't forget. Every time they got interested in Nussbaum again, they linked him to Wilcoxson. How could they not? Recalling the exploits of the two men was like recalling the running title of the old "Thirty-Minute Theater" seg-ments that aired in the late 1960s: These Men Are Dangerous.

When Nussbaum got bounced in Redondo Beach in 1979 for tapping into federal agents' radio calls, an FBI teletype had noted, "His former crime partner was Bobby Randell Wilcoxson, who received a life sentence. The Wilcoxson-Nussbaum gang, before they were finally captured, had accumulated an arsenal of weapons, robbed eight banks of nearly a quarter of a million dollars, mur-dered a bank guard and wounded a police officer, terrorized the nation's capital with a series of bombings and bomb threats, violated the federal extortion statute, stole several cars, committed several burglaries, and had violated the White Slave Act and Federal and National Firearms Act."

Of course, authorities didn't have to worry about Nussbaum and Wilcoxson seeking each other out again in 1979. Wilcoxson was still behind bars. After being sentenced for the 1961 bank robbery, he spent time in the U.S. Penitentiary in Atlanta, Georgia, was transferred in July 1980 to the U.S. Penitentiary in Leavenworth, Kansas, (where Nussbaum had served time before being transferred to the lock-up in Marion, Illinois), and released on parole in early 1982.

At that point, Wilcoxson, 52, had been inside for about 20 years. As it turned out, that wasn't nearly long enough. His head had always been rough and cobbly on the outside, as if someone had stuck it into a sack and gotten busy with a baseball bat. The inside of his head, however, was looser and uglier. Before long, he would get involved in a scheme that would recall the classic 1944 film noir, *Double Indemnity*, in which an insurance salesman played by Fred MacMurray falls for Barbara Stanwyck and helps her kill her husband in a fake accident. Wilcoxson's real-life noir, though, would be a true comedy of horrors.

Way back when, someone had seen this coming. In 1964, the U.S Bureau of Prisons had done a classification study of Wilcoxson. The person doing the classification used bureaucracy-speak, but still got his point across with a vividness not often seen in such documents. Wilcoxson, who had not completed high school, "was slightly below average intellect," the classifier said, and had lost an eye in an accident and suffered severe head injuries in an auto crash. However, his physical distress was not nearly as bad as his psychological deficit, the writer said; he "had been diseased emotionally and socially all his life." The prisons employee, apparently a highly perceptive psychologist, then continued:

> In the interview, this subject was a very verbose, loquacious individual who describes (his) killing of (a) bank guard in a very cold-blooded, calculated tone of voice and seems to gloat over the fact that he shot first...He enjoys being interviewed and he told

me at great length the number of times he had been interviewed by psychiatrists on this case and how he out talked them. He claims he is a whole lot smarter than he ever realized before he got involved in this trouble.

... He states that he likes to read, especially the dictionary, and has been studying the dictionary for a year and one-half to improve his vocabulary...It is noted that he used several big words that did not fit in with what he was talking about and he evidently did not know the full meaning of the words...He is an amoral, callous, emotionally immature individual who handles the truth very recklessly and rationalizes his behavior so that it appears warranted, reasonable and justified, at least to him...he has a violent and uncontrollable temper...

...He is a shrewd, cunning, dangerous individual who should never be turned loose upon society.

If only the parole officials had listened, or had given more weight to the reports that Wilcoxson destroyed his cell, pelted guards with feces, urine and semen, was schizophrenic, hallucinated, had paranoid delusions, and had to gobble antipsychotic meds to keep his mind above water. Instead of using more caution, the parole gurus dumped him on the street after staff had damped down his schizo thoughts by pumping him full of Thorazine and Cogentin. Journeying to Chattanooga, Tennessee, he sought treatment at the Fortwood Pyschiatric Center. There he sucked more meds, or was supposed to. The therapists fed him the antipsychotic Stelazine to keep his thoughts from flying to Pluto. He didn't always take it.

Wilcoxson, who in his youth had worked as a field boss, house painter, service-station attendant and used-car salesman, was able to find some kind of employment, apparently doing menial work at a car dealership and sales at a photography shop. He also married another patient at Fortwood, a druggie. Domestic life didn't really suit him. Eventually, Bobby sent his wife off to visit her kids in New Mexico with a coffee thermos spiked with a horse dose of Elavil. There was enough of the antidepressant in there to bang her out permanently, which it did, bringing Bobby some inheritance income.

The marriage hadn't worked out, true, but Bobby had tried to be a good provider. Early in his marriage, Bobby had lined up a job that fit his real talents (hint: not the talents he had employed as a house painter, service-station attendant or used-car salesman). He made contact with an old friend: James Lewis, a blue jeans-wearing, burly man whose bushy white hair and beard made him look like Santa Claus. Well, Bad Santa. He was a convicted murderer and thief on federal parole. According to one of Wilcoxson's lawyers, Lewis had been Bobby's enforcer in the Atlanta prison. When Bobby had trouble with a prisoner, Lewis would throw him off the top of Cell Block One. End of trouble.

Lewis also was friends with Evelyn Mosher, a 35-year-old cokehead and former machine operator at the Du Pont nylon plant in Chattanooga. Evelyn was married to a man 20 years her senior, a respected chemical engineer at the plant named Bob Mosher. Lewis had met Evelyn in 1977. She had brought drugs to one of his fellow inmates in a Joliet, Illinois, prison. After his release, Lewis looked her up in 1978 at her home in Signal Mountain, an upscale suburb of Chattanooga. Hearing that Wilcoxson was heading for Chattanooga, Lewis told him he should give Mosher a call.

"But be sure you know before you get there that she may try to get you to do something to her old man," Lewis cautioned. "She's been trying to get me to kill him for years."

Wilcoxson was never one to miss a chance to brag.

"I don't know about that," he said. "But if she hires me she'll get the meanest sonovabitch she's ever met in her life."

He was as good as his word. Bob Mosher, 55, had survived for a long time with a wife who was trying to kill him. Now he was about to run out of luck. Evelyn had at one time given Lewis a 9-millimeter pistol and told him she'd buy him a new motorcycle. All he had to do, she said, was to go out to a certain marker on the Interstate and wait for Bob. Evelyn would send Bob out to him, and the rest would be simple, Evelyn told Lewis: "You walk up and blow his shit away." The ex-con had turned down the job because he liked Bob, but he hadn't done anything else to save the man.

Now Wilcoxson was on the case. He met with Evelyn, apparently even hanging out with her at Alcoholics Anonymous meetings. He took the contract on her husband. And—according to evidence in his 1985 murder trial—he brought in some help: one of his half-brothers, Cole "Green Eyes" Wilcoxson (sometimes known as Wilcox), a karate expert who at one time had run a martial arts studio in Altus, Oklahoma, teaching punches and kicks to the local cops. Though he was called "Green Eyes," he actually had hazel eyes. Maybe he wore green contacts. Or maybe the nickname was a reference to his liking for money, the way a child molester's liking for children causes cons to call him "Short Eyes."

Bobby, showing family pride, bragged about his half-brother to Lewis. He said Cole was a fifth-degree black belt, that people in Cleveland had offered him $5,000 just to "stand behind their back," that he was "145 pounds of rolling hell."

The deal was done. Evelyn would pay Bobby and Green Eyes $25,000 to kill her husband. Bob's life insurance would bring her $214,000 straight up, but she told Bobby to make the killing look like an accident. The insurance had a double indemnity provision, she said. That would pay her twice the face amount—in excess of $400,000—if her husband died accidentally. *Double Indemnity* was playing out. Bobby saw himself in the Fred MacMurray role, getting it on with Evelyn in the Barbara Stanwyck part.

Romance wasn't exactly in the air, however. Later—admittedly, after things went south—Evelyn would call him "a little sawed-off shrimp" and a "wrinkled old fart that kept trying to get me in bed… He turns my stomach."

Life isn't usually like the movies, and it wasn't in this case. On Oct. 23, 1982, about 10 months after Bobby left prison, Bob Mosher got a murderous visit. The following account is based on evidence in Bobby's murder trial—particularly surreptitious recordings of Bobby and Evelyn Mosher made by Chattanooga Police undercover detective Eddie Cooper. There are various interpretations of how things went down. Here's one of them.

Bobby and Green Eyes paid an evening call on Mosher, a nice guy who paid the bills, did most of the cooking for his family, worked around the house, and tried to keep his family together while his freaky wife snorted oblivion and schemed to turn his flesh and blood into hard currency. It was an easy autumn night, and the lights were on. Mosher was alone in the house in Signal Mountain,

Evelyn off at a Jimmy Buffett concert. Mosher had been drinking, no doubt to help forget his troubles. Bobby and Green Eyes slipped in and quietly checked out the scene. They found Mosher in the kitchen, up on a seven-foot ladder doing some remodeling work, with a plastic drop sheet to catch paint splatter. A pot of stew bubbled on the stove. The TV was on. Its sounds would mask unusual noises.

Perfect. Green Eyes moved in to hit Mosher, planning to knock him off the ladder. The weight of his falling body would break his neck. Neat. But then something shocking happened. Mosher, confronted by two menacing men, *stepped down off the ladder.* The assassins had never figured on a weird development like this. Gee. The accident thing was not going to look so plausible now.

Even so, there was work to be done. Green Eyes jumped in, punching and chopping Mosher about the head and shoulders. Mosher countered, striking back and grappling with him. Green Eyes hit and hit and hit, harder now. The blows were crushing flesh, knocking Mosher's face out of line. Blood flashed from his nose and lip, his forehead ballooned, red welts sprang up in his skin, gouges shaped by Green Eyes' hard knuckles. "You're killing me!" Mosher exclaimed.

Green Eyes hit him again. Mosher fell to the floor, unconscious, but still alive. His chest inflated and deflated with tortured breaths. *Still alive.* Mother fucker! How could they waste this sonovabitch? Well, at least they could use stuff that was at hand, part of the remodeling scenario. One of them grabbed the drop sheet, jerked it awkwardly over Mosher's head. The other snatched up a nearby push broom and thrust the plastic sheeting down Mosher's throat. The broom slid in hard, pressing against the plastic, ripping flesh and mucous membranes. Mosher's body trembled as the broom went in farther and farther, cutting off his air. He sighed terribly, his chest fluttering, collapsing. He went limp. At last. Christ, that had been some sweaty work. What a frickin' mess.

Bobby and Green Eyes hauled the body down a hallway and left it on a set of steps leading down into the garage, with the plastic sheet still sticking down Mosher's throat. The two master criminals went through the house, trying to make the invasion look like a burglary, strewing credit cards around one room, ransacking a closet and tossing prescription drugs on the floor outside it, dumping out a jewelry box. However, they overlooked $5 cash in Mosher's wallet. And then there was the little matter of the plastic sheet shoved down his throat. Kind of an unusual accident.

They walked outside.

"We can forget about double indemnity," Green Eyes said.

That's one version of how Mosher died. Even Bobby's defense lawyers couldn't agree on what had probably happened. One of them, Hiram "Hank" Hill, thought Bobby served as a lookout outside while Green Eyes did the dirty work. The other defense lawyer, Bates Bryan, thought Bobby may have done the job alone. "Bobby's ego was so great, I don't think Bobby would have any doubt he could do it himself," said Bryan. Bobby also would not have wanted to split the fee: the prospect of killing folks for money always got his motor going. "Bobby was the only person I ever represented who I thought was evil," said Bryan.

Nothing in Dan Marlowe's fiction quite compares with the bizarre Mosher murder, except for the scene in *One Endless Hour* in which filmmaking bank robber Dick Dahl is found choked to death. Dahl, in the presence of other hostages, has died at the hands of the criminally insane daughter of the assistant bank manager. Dahl had been trying to film her—possibly as he raped her—in the basement where she was caged up for her own protection.

> I couldn't remember if there was anything incriminating on his film aside from what he'd been shooting here. With Dahl one never knew. I grabbed up the smashed camera, jerked out the film cartridge, jammed it into my pocket, and threw the camera down. "Don't leave us here with her!" Shirley Mace screamed at me as I started for the door. "She'll kill us all!"

> —From *One Endless Hour*

The Marlowe story and the Mosher murder were both warped beyond belief. In phrases worthy of fiction, one prosecutor would say of Evelyn, "She's prostituted everyone she's touched. She's destroyed everyone around her. Not because of the drugs, but because of what she is." Three years after the Mosher killing, when

Lewis finally copped to the police about what had happened and investigators got their recorders cooking, Bobby would be overheard admitting, "It's a fluked-up deal." He and Green Eyes hadn't even gotten paid for wasting Mosher, except for "expenses coming in."

Bobby said Evelyn shouldn't be treating Green Eyes so lightly: "She's fucking with someone who can put her goddamn ass in the grave in a hurry." But Evelyn hadn't made the big score she had expected. She'd learned she never had a chance at double indemnity. For that, her husband would have had to die at his workplace. This misunderstanding was clearly her screwup, but she also was not impressed by Bobby's performance. She would be recorded saying of him, "He's incompetent. He thinks he's smart, know-it-all. He's a nothing. A nothing."

Both she and Bobby would be convicted, but not Green Eyes. He was gone: "in the wind," as cops say. Some people thought he was in Louisiana, but no one knew where. Efforts to push the case against him didn't get very far, assuming there was a case. Courtroom-quality proof that he'd taken part in the murder was lacking. Neither Bobby nor Evelyn had actually testified against him. Even if they had, that would have been the uncorroborated testimony of co-conspirators—not enough to convict in Tennessee. "There was never any usable evidence against him," Bryan said.

All the crucial investigative action in the Mosher case was still far in the future as 1982 wandered on. There was no immediate break in the murder, but that didn't mean the echoes of the past were silent. About six weeks after that killing, investigators elsewhere began to suspect the other main player in "the Wilcoxson-Nussbaum gang" was also at work. Oddly, the scheme they were probing also carried overtones of *One Endless Hour*. This case dealt with a bank takedown similar to the main one in *Hour*, in which robbers snatch the families of two bank officials, then force the officials to remove money from their bank.

Friday, Dec. 3, 1982, was a foggy, drizzly morning in Peoria, Illinois. At about 9:30 a.m., Charles Maibach, president of the Prospect National Bank at 3429 Prospect Road, had been at work for 45 minutes. His phone rang.

"You got an emergency," a male voice said. "Call home."

Maibach heard a click in his ear. The caller was gone. Upset, the banker dialed his home number. He expected his wife Annette to pick up. She didn't.

"I'm your emergency, 'cause I'm at your house," a man said. It was the same man Maibach had heard moments before. Probably white. Age? Hard to tell; 30s, 40s, 50s? No distinctive accent: he sounded Midwestern. "I have your wife," the man said. "Here are your instructions. Don't call the police, don't do anything foolish, the money is all insured. Take all the money you have at the bank and bring it to the telephone pay station on War Memorial Drive across from Leonardo's Pizza. You have five minutes to do this. Don't do anything foolish. We're watching you now."

The phone clicked again. Maibach was frightened, but still able to think clearly. He walked over to the desk of the bank's executive vice-president and told him to call a police lieutenant he knew. The cop said Maibach should follow the instructions, and that's what he did. He didn't have much time, but the phone booth was only a mile from the bank. As calmly as he could, he went to the vault, selected a white sack inscribed Prospect National Bank and stuffed it with all the cash he could readily find, mostly large bills, hundreds and fifties: $31,500. He included $500 in marked bills.

He jumped into his 1981 Chrysler LeBaron. He made it to the phone station on War Memorial. Three minutes later, the phone rang. This was a different caller, probably Caucasian. "Everything is going just right," the new man said. His voice was steady, more reassuring. "Get back in your car, drive west on War Memorial to Knoxville, turn south on Knoxville. There's a phone booth at Knoxville and Nebraska, across from the Shell Station. I'll call you there."

Back in the car, Maibach's stomach churned as the drizzle smeared his windshield. Outside, the winter morning was mild, temperature edging 60 degrees, but Maibach shivered. He hit the brakes next to the phone booth and jumped out. He could hear the phone ringing as he stepped swiftly to the booth, and the sound quickened his heart. He didn't want to miss. He grabbed the receiver.

"You're doing just great, Chuck," the caller said. This was the second guy. Was that triumph in his voice, even a bit of playfulness?

"Get back in your car, go south on Knoxville. In the next block there's a Wendy's. Pull into the parking lot to the right-hand corner where there's a trash container in an enclosure. It's blue." Enclosure. A sophisticated term, bureaucratic. Was this robber well-read, or had he been some kind of a petty official? "Put the money bag behind this container."

"What should I do after that?" Maibach asked.

"Go home and make whatever calls you need to make."

The line went dead. Maibach didn't hesitate. He was back in the car quickly, moving down the street to his destination a block away. At the Wendy's Old-Fashioned Hamburgers restaurant, he turned in, glanced around the parking lot. The traffic seemed unremarkable. He slipped from the car, glanced around quickly, tossed the cash bag behind the trash bin, and left.

In minutes, he was at his home at 4129 W. Hollyridge Circle. His wife was there, surprised to see him. No, no one had called her, no one had been in the house. Everything was just as it had been when he'd left for work. No one had used the home phone.

The police descended. They had descended earlier, actually, but apparently muffed the surveillance on the drop site: The bag had been snatched and whoever did it got away clean. What investigators discovered was intriguing. Someone had cut the Maibachs' phone line outside and attached a needle-point connector. Whoever had spliced into the line had been able to intercept the call from Maibach at the bank. A white male in his mid-30s, wearing a hard hat and a slick yellow parka to fend off the rain, had been seen by a neighbor running down the driveway of the house at about 8:30 a.m., jumping into a late-model, bluish-gray, small Chevrolet. A cop thought he'd seen a car like that later near the bank, but he hadn't gotten a license number. Nobody had.

Now, *this* looked like the perfect crime. Except that evening, several people came into the Peoria Police Department and laid the whole thing out—supposedly. Two days before, on Wednesday evening, they had been in the Averyville Tavern on North Adams Street in Peoria. They'd spoken with two men seated at the bar, one of them quite drunk. The drunk and his companion had said they were going to "hit the bank in Peoria" on Friday and "get all the money from the bank" without ever having to enter it. They had a foolproof plan that would make the matter "as easy as taking candy from a baby," and they expected to score $250,000.

Using the witness descriptions, checking probation records, and pulling photos, investigators wound up watching the house of Peoria resident Carl DeTienne, a.k.a. Carl Davis and several other names, 50 years old, 160 pounds, blue eyes, gray hair, FBI No. 370-003B. DeTienne had done a long stretch in prison for the attempted robbery of the First State Bank of Beecher City, Illinois, on Sept. 25, 1968, a crime in which two other men also were convicted. On Monday night, two days after the Peoria bank job, surveillance led to a car stop in which DeTienne's wife Mary and Harry L. Morgan Sr., her passenger, were picked up on alcohol charges.

Morgan told police he had been staying at the DeTienne home and knew about the bank extortion, but didn't take part and didn't know where the $31,500 was. He passed a couple of polygraphs. Morgan said the job had been carried out by two men. One was DeTienne. The other, Morgan said, was a man named "Al," who had stayed at the DeTienne home for two weeks planning the heist.

He knew little about Al, Morgan said, except that he was a former FBI Top Ten who had been paroled to a large city in California. According to an FBI report, "…(He) further stated Al was extremely intelligent and a person who would drink nothing stronger than milk." Shown a photo, Morgan identified "Al" as Albert Frederick Nussbaum, a bank robber paroled to Los Angeles in 1976. The report continued: "Additional investigation reflects Albert Frederick Nussbaum is a self-employed writer who travels between the Los Angeles, California, and the New York City, New York, areas."

At this point, the net seemed to be closing in on Nussbaum, who the cops suspected had run into lean times in the writing business and had gone back to his tried-and-true profession. It seemed obvious. The bank extortion, in addition to echoing aspects of *One Endless Hour*, a book Nussbaum had helped Marlowe write, involved the kind of clever electronic ploy—tapping into the bank official's home phone line—that Nussbaum loved and was perfectly capable of carrying out.

The cops arrested and booked DeTienne. But then, nothing. Armed with search warrants, investigators went through DeTienne's home in Peoria, as well as his cabin in Goofy Ridge, Illinois, an isolated hamlet about 30 miles south of Peoria that harbored rough types with criminal pasts who played free-and-easy with game laws. The investigators—police as well as FBI agents—found no evidence relating to the bank extortion. They wired up at least one person close to the suspects (or gave him a telephone recorder—the record isn't clear). The plan was to try to get them to make damaging admissions. It didn't happen. Further interrogations didn't help, either. DeTienne, a veteran at this game, didn't tell investigators anything useful.

Neither, apparently, did Nussbaum, assuming investigators actually talked to him. The file is unclear. They did check airline records and car rental records, but found nothing. Jack Leuck, who was the FBI case agent assigned to the extortion, recalls that DeTienne was the type of person—suspected of involvement in prostitution and gambling, in addition to bank jobs—who sounded like a strong suspect, but the case couldn't be made. Leuck doesn't even recall, for sure, that Nussbaum was approached for an interview, though he thinks that would have been done as a matter of course.

Furthermore, the Speedway, Indiana, Police Department reported that a bank extortion following the same pattern had occurred in its jurisdiction on Feb. 5, 1973, when Nussbaum was still in prison. The only person anybody had actually seen who seemed to be linked to the Peoria extortion—the man in the yellow rain parka running down the Maibach driveway—had been in his 30s, much younger than either DeTienne or Nussbaum. A little more than a year later, according to an FBI memo, the local assistant U.S. attorney decided "all logical investigation has been conducted, but insufficient evidence has been developed to pursue Federal prosecution." The case was closed, with the proviso that it could be reopened if more evidence emerged. Apparently it never was.

Could Nussbaum have partnered in the Peoria extortion or in other bank robberies? He always denied that he'd gotten back into the game, said Mel Cebulash. Nussbaum told Cebulash that bank robbers sometimes asked him to review their robbery plans and offered to pay him to do it, but that he always turned them down.

"He just didn't want to go to prison anymore," Cebulash said.

He still had his tough edge, though, according to an article by mystery novelist Lawrence Block in the Holiday 2010 issue of *Mystery Scene* magazine. In the early 1980s, Block said, Nussbaum reported "with a mixture of disgust and incredulity," that someone had tried to mug him.

"The clown sticks a gun in my face," Nussbaum said. "I said, 'Get out of my way, you moron. I just got out of the joint.'"

Nussbaum pushed past the assailant, Block said, leaving him to find a more cooperative victim.

Was Nussbaum still brazen enough to pull off the Peoria scheme? Dudley Bromley thought so. Told about the job, Bromley said, "That sounds like Al. I wouldn't be surprised if it was him." Nussbaum never seemed to be bringing in much money from writing, Bromley said, and he loved crime—it had been like a drug for him. "I used to wonder," Bromley said, "*How does he survive? He must be doing something.*"

The cops could never bring themselves to believe that Nussbaum had gone straight, either. They would continue to monitor his whereabouts, speculate about his activities, wonder whether he had been involved in this crime or that. And when he dropped out of sight from time to time, they would pressure his old friend, Dan Marlowe.

Marlowe really didn't mind. He was used to doing the two-step. What he did mind was not selling as much fiction as he would have liked. Even so, he kept trying.

CHAPTER 22:
Last Call

VERY LATE IN LIFE, WILLIAM ODELL WOULD RECALL HIS OLD FICTION partner Dan Marlowe this way: "He lived all by himself and all he ever did was write. He had no activities besides that. He was quite a loner. He had some relatives but he wasn't very close to them. Writing was just about the only thing he ever did."

This was not exactly true. Marlowe enjoyed crossword puzzles, sports, politics, occasional but intense female company. The bottle, when it wasn't hitting him too hard. The theater, on rare occasions. Books, always books. And Marlowe actually had many friends, but never one as good as the empty page.

Starting in his mid-60s, and continuing to the end of his life, Marlowe's chief regret was that he wasn't able to spend endless hours at the typewriter, the way he once had. He'd loved those eight-to-10 hour sessions. Still, like a punchy old prizefighter who can't stop climbing back into the ring, he was drawn to the battle again and again. The sound of the IBM Selectric rattling out the words, the lines popping up on the heavy white bond, the rhythms of the sentences rippling through his mind and onto the paper: These were his keenest joys.

As 1982 blended into 1983, Marlowe was still doing what he had been doing ever since he hit L.A.: churning out short stories, attempting to get full-length fiction projects started again, trying to market the stuff he'd sold long before. In 1982, he wrote to Alex Jackinson, head of The Alex Jackinson Literary Agency in New York and author of *The Barnum-Cinderella World of Publishing*. Would Jackinson represent his work? He would. Jackinson made diligent attempts over two years to place Marlowe's books and short stories. He had no success. Even so, he got along well with the writer, even after Marlowe found another agent.

In April 1982, Marlowe told Jackinson the rights to the Earl Drake series had reverted to him. Thereafter, Marlowe tried to resell the Earl Drake books and some of his other novels, sometimes under different titles. In 1982, he submitted *Four for the Money* and *Route of the Red Gold* to Harlequin Books, suggesting the novels would work for its Raven House imprint. They didn't. Marlowe was told by Wallace Exman, managing editor of Raven House, that it wasn't publishing reprint books. In 1983, Marlowe submitted the manuscript of *The Vengeance Man*, apparently under its original title, *Nobody Laughs at Me*, to St. Martin's Press in New York. It was turned down. The next year, he submitted 60 pages of *Never Live Twice* under the title *Never Look Back* to Warner Books, but was again rejected. He also submitted the manuscript of another of his out-of-print novels to Holloway House in Los Angeles, not knowing that the publisher only issued African-American fiction. Obviously, that resulted in another turn-down.

In 1984, Marlowe signed with Los Angeles agent Jim Heacock and his wife Rosalie at the Heacock Literary Agency. The Heacocks put a lot of energy—and their L.A. connections—into their efforts to place Marlowe's work. On Nov. 1, 1984, Marlowe wrote to Jackinson, "My Earl Drake series is being read at HBO for possible option/sale. It looks as though they might take it on. As part of the deal, they are also looking at the two unpublished novels, the horseracing book and the amnesia book, for print/film deals. I'm less sanguine about anything happening with that. I sell a short story about every other month. I have one coming out in the next issue of *Espionage*. Also, in the next issue of *Saint*, if there is a next issue."

The "horseracing book" possibly was an unpublished novel called *The Sisters*, which contained plenty of heavy-duty sex. The manuscript, found among Marlowe's files, carries the pen name "Ward Malone," one Marlowe used for pornographic writing. It's not clear what the unpublished "amnesia book" might have been. Marlowe at one point had written a proposal for a nonfiction book about his experiences with amnesia, but he apparently did not complete a manuscript. His only known novel in which amnesia plays a major role is *Never Live Twice*, which had been published.

Nothing, apparently, came of the HBO negotiations, and Marlowe's efforts to reprise his success with *Guerilla Games* also were shortstopped in 1984. Marlowe asked Gold Eagle Books if they would consider him for another entry in the Phoenix Force series. The publisher's director, Mark Howell, told him the whole series had been handed over to writer William Fieldhouse, subject to Fieldhouse's being able to boot out six of the books each year, and assuming sales stayed strong.

Marlowe had corresponded at times with Odell, but did not keep up the relationship, as Odell told James Batson in a letter on Sept. 30, 1984:

> About Dan...that's something I can't understand. I've been mulling it over for some time...even when we were close partners... he always was a tad distant, especially when it came to sharing credit for work done. I think he would rather not admit that I had anything to do with our writing success...and since he's lost his memory, he's been reluctant to accept the fact that we were side-by-side for so long. I've written and remembered him on special occasions, but I haven't gotten a response for nine months. I've taken the attitude that he'd just as soon I remain out of his life, so I've done that. I care about him, but it's apparent he would just as soon I not bother him.

Marlowe's suspicions about Odell, arising from his muddled, damaged memory, may have led to his reticence. Marlowe had a lot on his mind, too. In addition to struggling to get his fiction sold, Marlowe had to side-step investigators probing Nussbaum's doings. Nussbaum was in and out of L.A., probably just dealing with literary projects and visiting friends and family. The cops suspected otherwise, however, and they didn't mind leaning on Marlowe when Nussbaum wasn't available.

In December 1984, Nussbaum went to Buffalo, New York, to stay with his sister Doris, who needed help because her husband was recovering from difficult surgery. A month later, he told Marlowe he was "settling in," finding it nice that someone else was doing all the cooking and laundry. Back in L.A., the local cops were getting antsy. Someone from the Riverside County Sheriff's Department had periodically run checks on Nussbaum. On Jan. 27, 1985, Marlowe wrote to Nussbaum this appeared to be happening again:

> You had a phone call here last week from a really persistent type. You know, you turn off three or four questions and that's usually it. This guy had a dozen or fifteen. I gave him the usual routine of "back east." He seemed to know better. A couple of times, I thought it was Riverside but I'm still not sure (when I say he seemed to know better, I mean he seemed to know that I knew where you were). If it was Riverside, he was sober for a change. It probably wasn't him, since he would try for better answers by knocking on the door.

Though investigators were obviously worried that Nussbaum might be engaged in nefarious activities, he was, in fact concentrating on his writing. On Feb. 4, Marlowe wrote a friend, "...Al keeps flitting in and out of town. He made a sale recently to *Espionage* and is working on a novelette for them which is pre-sold. If anything is ever really pre-sold: editors keep changing their minds. He has a book he really wants to write and I think it's a pretty good idea. But he has the same old problem of not wanting to settle down to it." (Later in the year, Nussbaum would tell Marlowe that mystery writer Joe Gores had urged him to write his autobiography, which Gores thought should be called *Armed and Dangerous.* "Jeez!" Nussbaum said. "I have absolutely no interest in anything like that." However, Nussbaum's daughter Alison Bukata turned up evidence that Nussbaum had been vigorously floating the possibility himself until at least the late 1970s.)

The law, including the U.S. Marshal's office, continued to keep tabs on Nussbaum. On March 3, Marlowe told him:

> Half an hour after we hung up yesterday the same U.S. Marshal that was here before showed up at the door. I thought it might be

trouble because he had another guy with him. They both were wearing tan suits that looked like uniforms but weren't. Dark tan. The second man never showed any identification and never opened his mouth. The one I'd seen before danced the same waltz. "They" wanted to talk to me downtown. I gave them back the same jive: too old, too ill, couldn't be removed from medication. The only change was that he said, "We know you are forwarding mail to Nussbaum." I said, "You're telling me you are interfering with the U.S. Mail? Anyway, if mail is being forwarded to him, it's not from me." He said, "We're not interfering with the mail," and I dropped it. I say it was the same guy but upon thinking it over, I'm not positive. He was big and seemed to me to look the same, but I really didn't recognize the face or the name. Junius A. Rivera. He didn't look like a chicano, either. Anyway, they went off with no more satisfaction than the first time. The bastards hang on, don't they?

These were only minor distractions for Marlowe and Nussbaum. More troubling for Marlowe was that, because of his various ailments, his physician was urging him to consider moving into a nursing home. Marlowe hated the idea. He didn't want to lose his freedom, and he didn't want other people making decisions for him. In the end, he vetoed the suggestion and appeared to continue to get along reasonably well

On other fronts, things were beginning to pick up. With Nussbaum out of town regularly, Marlowe was depending even more on the Pink Tea get-togethers for companionship, as well as for career encouragement. In April, one of these meetings stunned him. He was sitting listening to writer Carol Law talk about the First International Crime Congress in London. She wasn't saying anything particular about it, just recalling it, and Marlowe was nodding along. Suddenly, Marlowe remembered how, during the Congress, he and Doris Henry had gone to dinner with Carol and her husband Warner, and had taken in a show afterward. A mundane memory, surely, except Carol Law hadn't said anything about it. No one had. Something big stirred inside Marlowe. His pulse picked up. It was crazy, but it was happening. He'd just had an independent memory, his first since 1977.

This was a secret thrill, though. Marlowe didn't trust it, not yet. Quietly, over the next few weeks, he plumbed his mind, searching for other memories. It wasn't a full house, not at all. There had been no bursting of the dam, no total recall. No. Each memory needed a trigger. Someone would mention a personal incident from the past. He would think it over, then realize he did in fact remember it. The process was gradual and partial. Even so, there came a time when he couldn't contain himself. "News, news, news! My memory is returning," he wrote to friends.

He didn't do that right away. His first letter was measured. Written on May 19, it was directed to a family practice physician in North Ridge, California, Dr. Myron Greengold:

> I'm beginning to get at least some of my memory back. I didn't believe it when it began about three weeks ago…It seems to be triggered by conversations about the past. I had never lost anything I had learned (as nearly as I could tell), and I had always remembered places (with some limitations), but I hadn't recalled my own personal connections to people and places prior to 1977. Twice now in three weeks conversations (about Boston and Mexico) have me recalling situations in both places in which I took part myself. It never happened before…The reason I know it's for real is because I went to my file and read letters written to me in 1977 by people who had known me well, and who (later) were complete strangers to me. I can now identify with the themes they are writing about and some incidents they bring up.
>
> Not everything. I imagine it will always be an imperfect process. You're the first I've told, because I can foresee problems in the future very similar to when the lights went out after the stroke. If I made a general announcement it's very unlikely that I would remember everyone who had had contacts with me in the past (especially since in the present I have days now of galloping senility). And if I had to admit to individuals—or groups—after making such an announcement that I didn't recall them in my renewed state of memory that would be a wet fish in the face of those who might have been a good deal closer to me than some I do remember.

> So I'll play it by ear for a while, but I certainly wanted you to
> know. You were so encouraging when I first saw you, long after I
> had given up hope, myself, that memory could return.

Although he told himself to move cautiously, the phenomenon was a psychological kick in the pants, and he couldn't
restrain his excitement. "Believe me, there is no way to tell you
the way I feel presently while experiencing this lifting of the
veil," he told one friend. To another, he said, "I went down near
San Diego to visit Clayton Matthews, who has known me longest
among the West Coast writers, and we had a two-day do-you-
remember session that was pure joy." He wrote to novelist Joe
Gores, recalling incidents from the time they spent together in
San Francisco: "I remember going with you to the gym near
Union Square where you used to work out. I remember you
coming down to the hotel mornings and we'd go out for breakfast. One of your recent short stories contained an incident
which I'm sure I recognized." To Mel Cebulash and his wife
Dolly, Marlowe wrote, "Isn't it something that after eight years I
can now consider myself un-freaked out?"

It wasn't clear why the blank slate of Marlowe's mind had
begun to refill. As quickly as his memory had disappeared, it was
back—not as sharp as it had been, however, since he was eight years
older and subject to the vagaries of memory associated with aging.
And even his recovered memories seemed to be fragile, here today
and sometimes gone tomorrow. This return of the past apparently
didn't dramatically improve his writing or production, either. His
physical problems weighed him down too much. "I have a plot for a
book I'd like to do, but since my typewriter time is now limited to
2-3-hours daily, a book is really a commitment," he told a friend.
Still, the rush of joy eased his way forward.

Other good things were happening, too. On Aug. 31, Marlowe
told Jackinson, "Heacock sold one of my oldies, substantially revised
and updated. The buyer is a new outfit here in L.A.: S.O.S.
Publications, Paul Bradley, publisher." S.O.S., Marlowe said, was
issuing 6-by-9-inch hardcover books, selling them for $6.95 on
supermarket racks. This was encouraging, and Marlowe began
pouring energy into other ideas.

He had been working with Josh Pachter, a writer based in West Germany who had published dozens of stories in major mystery magazines and edited six story anthologies. Marlowe and Pachter put together a proposal to jointly edit an anthology of 16-20 tales to be called *The Crime Story I Most Wish I Had Written*. The stories would be selected and introduced by "the cream of contemporary crime writers." Unfortunately, the proposal was rejected by St. Martin's Press and other publishers. On Jan. 13, 1986, Pachter wrote to Marlowe that there had been "no takers for the anthology idea."

At some point in 1986, it's not clear just when, Marlowe and Heacock appeared on *The Mort Cooper Show*, a Los Angeles talk show hosted by Morton Cooper, Ph.D., a voice and speech pathologist who had authored several books, including *Change Your Voice, Change Your Life*. Cooper, who was called "The Voice Coach to the Stars," typically focused his weekly cable TV show on voice and speech, so it was an odd venue for Marlowe and Heacock. Even so, it produced a video record of how Marlowe appeared and spoke late in life.

He's lean—obviously much lighter than he was in middle age—and his Boston accent comes through, along with his humor and matter-of-fact personality. Marlowe says he started writing late, gleaning some of his material from his seven years as a professional gambler.

"If I'd known what was involved, I might never have started," he says, "...It's more a process of learning what to leave out than what to include. You leave out all the purple adjectives and adverbs. You leave out all the extraneous information that you so carefully gathered as background, because it stops the flow of the story. You have to lean it down ..."

Cooper asks him for titles of books he'd written.

"The one that did the most for me was one called *The Name of the Game Is Death*, which became the beginning of a 12-book series and which Jim has just sold to an audio company to put it on tapes," Marlowe says.

"You could become a wealthy guy doing this, did you ever think about that?" Cooper asks.

"I thought about it...but it never happened," Marlowe says. "My ambition these days is to write stories that an editor is going to accept…These days I sell about 85 percent of what I write. A lot of it is to order. Jim hustles the business and I write."

As Marlowe indicated, Heacock had been able to drum up some work, and was seeking more. As 1986 wore on, the agent was trying to land Marlowe an action series called *Barracuda Reef.* On June 23, Marlowe wrote to Cebulash, saying, "Heacock has come up with a work-for-hire project that looks interesting." A book packager in New York named Cloverdale had concluded a contract with Ballentine Books for an action-adventure series, set mostly in the Caribbean. The deal would have paid $7,500 each for two books, with the packager furnishing the characters, background and plot. "I talked to Art Moore about doing it with me," Marlowe wrote. "We may take a hack at it."

In the same letter, Marlowe cited a nod of respect from Stephen King, who by now was hugely popular. "Stephen King mentioned me among a list of golden oldies," Marlowe said, adding jocularly, "Where was he when I could have used him?"

It's not clear who the other "golden oldies" were, but this apparently was a repeat of a reference Marlowe had included in a letter to Cebulash the month before.

"I was really surprised that King listed me in such company," Marlowe wrote. "Maybe he felt he was paying off an imagined small debt. He goes back farther than people think. Back in the days when I was on the road and only getting into New York a couple of times a year, there was a party whenever I did. A bunch of us would hole up in a hotel suite (f)urnished liberally with bottles and buckets of ice and kick the gong around until collapse intervened.

"I don't recall who first brought King around…In those days King was trying to write mysteries. In fact he eventually published a few. He and I had harder heads than the rest of the gang and about five in the morning we would still be arguing about character construction, viewpoint, motivation and the rest of the technicalities that can drive a writer crazy. Then we would pack it in and crawl down the corridor to our own rooms. He surely found a genre that paid off for him, didn't he?"

In July, Odell, who hadn't been in contact with Marlowe for 2 1/2 years, made one more attempt to reach him, sending him a packet of 2,000 letters Marlowe had written to him during their

collaboration. To Odell's surprise, Marlowe wrote back, expressing thanks but indicating that his memory still hadn't fully
healed:

> Thanks for sending me the correspondence. I hope it will be
> helpful. I have talked so much to the California writers who knew
> me before that when something comes up about the past I occa-
> sionally wonder whether I'm remembering something or whether
> it's something that was told to me in the more recent past. It's
> impossible to be sure…I do feel at times like THE WONDERFUL
> ONE-HOSS SHAY. Did you have to learn that poem in school?
> …I hope everything is fine with you.

Though Marlowe's attitude remained hopeful, his health was
eroding. He served on jury duty in Van Nuys, but the experience
wasn't good. On July 23, he wrote Cebulash:

> I've been grounded, I trust temporarily.
> Hindsight says I should have seen it coming. For about
> three months I've had a dry cough which occasionally turns into
> a real paroxysm that leaves me wrung out. I blamed it on the little
> bit of exercise I try to do to keep the angina in check. It got worse
> during my courtroom time in Van Nuys, but I figured I was aller-
> gic to something in the building: rugs, whatever. I mentioned it
> when I went in for my quarterly medical checkup last week and
> they sent me to the X-ray lab. Turns out there is a fair-sized spot
> on my left lung.
> It turns out also that just about everything they had me doing
> to help with the angina is not the thing to do for a lung condition.
> So they're working up a new program and a new diet: the sugar
> free/salt free diet I've been on for the past four years is also not the
> best thing for a lung condition. So there'll be some tradeoffs which
> they'll let me know in ten days. Meantime they said: sit. Avoid
> exercise. Avoid smog. Hah! What bothers me most is that sitting
> will evaporate the little bit of muscle tone I've retained to this point.
> When I mentioned that they said they'd work out something.
> I say I should have seen it coming because I've been experi-
> encing an increasing inability to concentrate which brings on

increasing bouts of irritability. At least I know why now. It's no plus to feel weaker but it is a plus to know why. I think.

So the boys at the clinic will come up with a miracle drug which will take care of all this bullshit and I'll be calling you to say I'm bubbling with ideas again. Till then it's waltz time.

There was enough left of the old spanking enthusiast in Marlowe to add a humorous postscript: "Dirty story of the week: I was walking through the local mall with two teen-aged girls (15-16) in front of me. One says to the other: 'That guy gets more ass than a toilet seat!' Out of the mouths of babes these days…"

As July changed to August, Marlowe's reserve of strength was fading. On Aug. 11, he wrote to Gertrude Bradford:

I believe I had mentioned to you previously an increasing sense of tiredness. I had been blaming it on the angina, but an annual X-ray showed a spot on the left lung. There will be no operation because of the angina. Instead, they are plotting several forms of chemotherapy to see which my constitution can stand with the fewest side effects. It will probably begin in about ten days. I don't feel badly. It's strange to sit in a chair, reading, and fall asleep, then get a good night's sleep on top of it. It really is a feeling of lassitude.

Eight days later, Marlowe wrote his last letter. This one went to his old friend in New York with whom he'd shared so many writing adventures, and through which he'd vicariously lived the criminal life. To Nussbaum, Marlowe wrote:

I sold the car. I got $700 for it which I thought wasn't bad considering it wasn't running. I'm going to let the mail box lapse when it runs out, I think the middle of next month. I can't get up there. I go in twice a week for cytotoxic treatment, combinations of chemicals which they add to and subtract from to find a combination that has the least side effects. Which include vertigo, nausea, and damn-near hallucinations. When you talk to me now about any details, make sure I'm tracking right before you believe me. I feel spaced out most of the time. Right now I'm supposed to do nothing but sit until the chemical program is completed, in two months, perhaps. Then they'll come up with some kind of an exercise program intended to keep my leg muscles from deteriorating. For now all I can do is circle the wagons.

I'm not in any pain but I'm not good (f)or anything, either.

Four days later, after Marlowe failed to answer his phone, friends called the police. At 9:30 a.m. on Aug. 23, he was found in his chair, a book nearby. The Los Angeles coroner did no autopsy, but the cause of death was listed as "arteriosclerotic cardiovascular disease." Apparently, Marlowe had been done in by one final heart attack. He was 72.

He was flown back East for burial. He'd arranged for that long before. While his family members prepared for the funeral, one received a letter from a Marlowe friend in Los Angeles. It contained the following eulogy. No one now knows who wrote it. No doubt, though, Marlowe would have enjoyed the reference to "a novel that could have been his best." The comment seems to have had no basis in fact.

A REMEMBRANCE OF DAN MARLOWE, 1914-1986

Few well-known writers seem to stand taller than the books they have written. Dan was the rare exception. If his Drake series gained a wide audience for its hard-boiled plots and writing twists of character, Dan as a person was always a gentle man, often brilliant, always supportive. Perhaps Art Moore once said it as well as anyone: "Dan is a very classy guy." But if he had class, it was most of all as a friend.

We will miss him. And perhaps, in human contacts, we can also emulate him. While Dan would never instruct, in his quiet manner he gave us a great deal. He once said that good advice was worth a cup of coffee anytime. Yet, like himself, it was beyond any value.

Writing to his last days, and composing a novel that could have been his best, our Dan Marlowe died comfortably in his reading chair, one leg crossed, a book beside him, on about August 22, 1986.

CHAPTER 23:
Postscript

Dan marlowe, who always seemed to be living on the road, went home at last to his wife. On Aug. 30, 1986, he was lowered into a grave in St. Michael's Cemetery in Stratford, Connecticut, next to Evelyn, buried there 30 years before. He had loved her and betrayed her and, in the end, had chosen to be with her forever. After a life of carousing with rowdies, drinkers, gamblers, writers, politicians and crooks, Marlowe was seen off by family members who knew only the outlines of his complex life. In attendance were his brother Don, his half-sister Mary Jones, and his half-brother Richard.

It's not clear whether Nussbaum heard about Marlowe's death before the funeral. He did discuss Marlowe's passing with Gary Brandner, and told Brandner that dying with a book close at hand was exactly the way Marlowe would have chosen to go. Nussbaum also made a passing reference to his friend's death in a letter to Dudley Bromley on Sept. 18, 1986: "Maybe I'm just getting more picky as I age. By the way, speaking of age, Dan Marlowe died at the end of August. He was 72. But that no longer seems very old to me. Relativity."

At the time, Nussbaum was only 52.

After moving to the home of his sister Doris in Buffalo, New York, in December 1984, Nussbaum stayed. He had developed diabetes, and that may have played a role in his decision. Though he sometimes talked about returning to Los Angeles, which he called "Happy Valley," he never did. Two things apparently kept him in Buffalo. One was money, or the lack of it. It appears he just wasn't earning enough to continue living on his own in L.A. The other was family. In addition to Doris, his sister Phyllis and his ex-wife Lolly lived in the area, as did his now-grown daughter, Alison Bukata. He occasionally took Alison to dinner and a movie or a play. She had his intelligence and charm: She was completing law school, and would become a lawyer specializing in bankruptcy.

The shape of Nussbaum's continuing literary efforts can be seen in letters he sent to Bromley, who still wrote fiction even after becoming a software systems engineer. Nussbaum worked on novels of his own, and continued to spin out easy-reading books, mystery and science fiction. But he chafed at the small amount of money he was making.

He also asserted he had experienced a failed collaboration with acclaimed mystery writer Clark Howard. As Nussbaum explained it to Bromley, Nussbaum was to rewrite one of Howard's unpublished novels. That was to become the first of a series, with Nussbaum and Howard splitting the work and money going forward. But just as Nussbaum was finishing the rewrite in March 1986, Howard sold the paperback rights to his newest book, a Texas saga, for $300,000. The windfall set Howard off in a new writing direction and doomed the collaboration, so Nussbaum said. Howard, however, said recently he never collaborated with Nussbaum or any other author. Furthermore, he said that he and Nussbaum were only casual acquaintances within the Mystery Writers of America, their only substantial contact coming when Nussbaum served as a member of a short-story Edgar committee that Howard chaired.

One way or another, Nussbaum was trying to secure some real money out of writing, either through his sole efforts or through collaboration. Nussbaum and Bromley tried to come up with a novel they could do together, centering on a math professor who stumbles across an alien spaceship, but those efforts ran out of steam. Nussbaum also kept trying to get producers interested in *The Guardian*, the children's show he had written with Bromley about a helpful space alien. Those efforts also went nowhere. Nussbaum's last significant published pieces appear to have been three stories that came out in 1988.

The stories, issued under the pen name Carl Martin, appeared in *Ellery Queen's Mystery Magazine*: "Fatherly Love," in July, "A Slightly Less Dangerous Insanity," in September, and "Don't Play with Strangers," in December.

Nussbaum gradually lost touch with his circle of writing friends in Los Angeles, except for Mel Cebulash, Marilyn Granbeck and Brandner.

On March 31, 1994, he wrote to Cebulash and his wife:

> This has been the worst winter since I came out here from L.A. And it doesn't seem to be over yet. We've had snow the last couple of days and the forecasts aren't very promising. After California, I never did get used to cold weather. The cold goes right through me no matter what I wear. Brrrrr!
>
> But I'll take snow over the quakes they get in L.A. I was never in a big one but I lived through a few minor tremblers. Scary! Nothing ever made my hair stand up like a quake. There's nothing quite like waking up in the middle of the night with your bed covered with books that have fallen from their shelves. I was even shot at a few times, but the quakes shook me up more.
>
> Hope all's well with you people. I hear from La Granbeck about once a week, but almost no-one else. The old crowd has scattered to the winds or gone and died on me. When I first came east I couldn't wait until I'd be able (to) afford getting back to L.A. Now every day gives me less reason for returning. You guys are the last of the people I was close to, except for Gary Brandner.

Less than two years later, on Jan. 7, 1996, Nussbaum died in Buffalo at 61. His diabetes had been worsened by kidney disease, and that malady finished him off. Cebulash sent Nussbaum's sister Doris $500 so that a proper marker could be placed on his grave. Nussbaum had not been forgotten by the writing community. In the summer 1996 issue of *Armchair Detective*, Clark Howard wrote a eulogy for Nussbaum.

"Crime writers come from all walks of life and many varied backgrounds," Howard wrote. "Al was certainly one of our more unique colleagues, not only in the life—or rather, lives, he led, but also in the help, both personal and professional, he gave to other mystery writers…Those of us who knew Al will remember and miss him."

Howard noted Nussbaum's efforts to help Marlowe regain his writing skills, and said Nussbaum had similarly aided Chris Steinbrunner, co-editor of *The Encyclopedia of Mystery and Detection*. After Steinbrunner became seriously ill, Howard said, Nussbaum moved in with him to do the shopping, cooking and other chores he could no longer do for himself.

Nussbaum's old partner, Bobby "One-Eye" Wilcoxson, would be remembered far less fondly. Wilcoxson, who had been sentenced to death for the murder of Bob Mosher, kept fighting his case legally, and his lawyer got the death sentence overturned. Wilcoxson was due to be resentenced when he died in prison on Dec. 9, 2006, at 77. After being diagnosed with non-small cell lung cancer in February 2000, he had refused follow-up treatment and medication. As of this writing, Evelyn Mosher, the woman who hired Wilcoxson to kill her husband, is still serving a life sentence.

Dan Marlowe's most prolific collaborator, William Odell, died on May 2, 2009, in Montrose, Colorado, at 93. His obituary on Legacy.com is primarily devoted to his Air Force career, though it does note that he "authored books, including about his time in the Night Flyers."

As the years passed after Marlowe's death, Marlowe faded into the background of hard-boiled history. The reasons were various. One was that none of his books ever appeared in an American hard-back edition (some were printed in hardback in England, however). Another was that his name was easily confused with his mystery-writing contemporary, Stephen Marlowe (*Homicide Is My Game*, *Jeopardy Is My Job*, *The Man with No Shadow*), whose true name was Milton Lesser. Still another is that when people think of "Marlowe" and "mystery" in the same sentence, their typical reference point is Philip Marlowe, Raymond Chandler's iconic private detective.

Additionally, few outside the mystery writing community knew much about him. Instead of living in a high-publicity market like New York or Los Angeles, Marlowe spent his most productive years far from the public eye in tiny Harbor Beach. Michigan readers were familiar with him through stories in the Detroit newspapers, but few others were.

Marlowe also was neglected by the Internet, when that communications medium flourished after his death. Information about
him was always sketchy. This was underlined in 1999 by a correspondent to Rara-Avis, a Website mailing list devoted to the study
of hard-boiled and noir fiction. "Does anybody know what happened to Dan J. Marlowe?" the correspondent wrote. "I seem to
recall hearing he lost his memory at some point, stopped writing
and, when he read his own novels he couldn't remember them, but
thought they weren't bad."

Despite his obscurity, Marlowe's books fought their way to the
surface. In the 1980s, the Black Lizard publisher imprint, based in
Berkeley, California, re-printed a number of crime classics, including Marlowe's *The Name of the Game Is Death, The Vengeance Man,
Never Live Twice* and *Strongarm*. In 2007, Stark House Press re-
issued *The Vengeance Man* as one entry in a three-book volume
called *A Trio of Gold Medals*.

Marlowe never completely left the public eye, however, and
late 2011 and early 2012 saw a hint of a Marlowe revival. Ed
Brubaker, creator of the celebrated graphic novel series *Criminal*,
became intrigued by Marlowe's personal tragedies—particularly
the death of his wife and his amnesia—and ran an essay about him
in his comic *Fatale*. Rosalie Heacock, now Rosalie Grace Heacock
Thompson (Her husband Jim passed away in 1994), was still working hard as Marlowe's agent, and she coordinated contracts and
agreements for the reissue of many of Marlowe's books. Stark House
Press contracted to reissue softcover versions of *The Name of the
Game Is Death* and *One Endless Hour*. The author's estate issued
Name, Hour, and *The Vengeance Man* (now called *Vengeance Man*)
as e-books. F+W Media contracted to publish many more of
Marlowe's novels as e-books. International interest was also begin-
ning to reawaken: An Italian publisher concluded a deal to reissue
Name.

"The Wrong Marlowe," my essay on the author's years in L.A.,
received much favorable attention when published by the *Los
Angeles Review of Books* under the direction of the site's able noir
editor, Boris Dralyuk.

Over the years, writers and film makers expressed interest in
making movies of some of Marlowe's books. Los Angeles novelist

Hugh Gross, director of the film *After the Wizard*, wrote scripts for *The Name of the Game Is Death* and *Four for the Money*, and still holds the movie rights to those books. Several times, he says, it appeared both would be made into movies, but financing or distribution efforts fell through. Gross also holds first refusal rights on *One Endless Hour*, and character rights to Earl Drake. *Never Live Twice* was optioned in 1995 by Niki Marvin, producer of the 1994 film *The Shawshank Redemption*, based on a 1982 Stephen King novella. But, again, financing fell through and the option was not renewed.

Stephen King, who praised Marlowe's books while Marlowe was still alive, has continued to do so since his death. The dedication of King's 2005 novel *The Colorado Kid*, published by Hard Case Crime, reads: "With admiration, for DAN J. MARLOWE, author of *The Name of the Game Is Death*: Hardest of the hardboiled."

On *CBS Sunday Morning* on Oct. 9, 2005, King talked about how he loved pulp fiction writers, and particularly Marlowe.

"He wrote a book called *The Name of the Game Is Death* and the main character in the book was a killer, a stone killer," King said. "The last line of the book made a huge impression on me."

It's easy to see why the ending of the book affected King. It's brutal, heavy with menace, powerful in its personal drive. The protagonist, burned beyond recognition, languishes in prison, waiting for the authorities to let down their guard. The murder of his friend, the savage retribution he's taken, his personal disfigurement—none of these has quenched his fire. He's not beaten. Far from it. His attitude could be that of the ghost of Marlowe, which has languished in semi-obscurity all these years. Eventually, given the right opportunity, the character says, he will rise again:

> If I can get back to the sack buried beside Bunny's cabin, plastic surgery will take care of what I look like. With a gun, I'll get back to it.
>
> That's all I need—a gun.
>
> I'm not staying here.
>
> I'll be leaving one of these days, and the day I do they'll never forget it.

PHOTO GALLERY

In 1965, Marlowe was at the top of his game. *Detroit Free Press* photo.

Dan married Evelyn Chmura in 1946. Left to right, Evelyn's sister Helen, Dan, Evelyn, Dan's brother Don. Family photo.

Evelyn Chmura, 1945. The portrait Dan would carry with him for the rest of his life. Family photo.

Gordon Gempel, 2007. Gempel was Marlowe's best friend in Harbor Beach for years, but harbored suspicions about the writer.

The house at 123 N. First St. in Harbor Beach where Marlowe was stricken with amnesia.

Smalley's Bar and Grill in Harbor Beach, Marlowe's favorite hang-out.

Bobby "One-Eye" Wilcoxson is brought to federal court in Brooklyn, N.Y. on Nov. 15, 1962, to face charges of bank robbery and murder. Men in hats are federal marshals. *New York Daily News* photo.

FBI "Wanted" poster photos of Bobby Wilcoxson, taken in 1959.

Al Nussbaum is captured in Buffalo, N.Y., on Nov. 4, 1962. Photo from the Buffalo State Butler Library Archives *Courier-Express* Collection.

U.S. Marshal Alvin Grossman points to a waiting car as he escorts bank robber Al Nussbaum from Erie County Jail in Buffalo, N.Y., on Nov. 20, 1962. *Buffalo News* file photo.

The Writer, the Robber —and the FBI, Too

Fin Press
Detroit
Sunday
Nov 28, 1965

Dan J. Marlowe: He's still in touch with "his" bankrobber.

Marlowe's career was linked forever to Nussbaum's in an article that appeared in the *Detroit Free Press* on Nov. 28, 1965. Image used with permission of the *Detroit Free Press*.

William Odell, dashing aviator and author, would be Marlowe's writing partner, seldom with acknowledgement, for more than 12 years. Family photo.

Marlowe at work. *Detroit Free Press* photo.

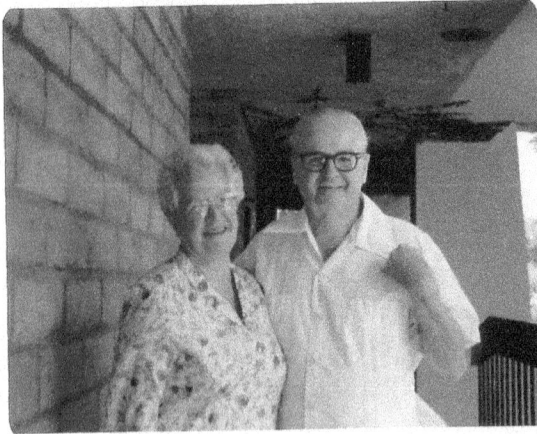

With Don in Los Angeles
Jenney '81

Marlowe with his sister-in-law Corinne in Los Angeles in 1981. Family photo.

THE WORLD'S LEADING MYSTERY MAGAZINE

ELLERY QUEEN'S

SEPTEMBER 1992
$2.25 U.S.
$2.95 CAN.

MYSTERY MAGAZINE

NEW STORIES by Carl Martin & Antonia Fraser

PLUS
11 others

Carl Martin

Al Nussbaum, under his pen name "Carl Martin," was featured on this cover of *Ellery Queen's Mystery Magazine* in 1992, dressed as an old-time pool player. Copyright © 2012 by Penny Publications LLC/Dell Magazines. Reprinted with permission of the publisher.

In 2012, this article about Marlowe's life and career ran in the graphic novel *Fatale*. Image used courtesy of Ed Brubaker and Sean Phillips.

THE "OPERATION" COVERS

The covers for the "*Operation*" series are mostly not very attractive, but they have a claim on hard-boiled history for two reasons: the mug-shot gimmick and the designer of the first two covers.

As has been noted, most of them feature a mug-shot-like inset of "DRAKE, The Man With Nobody's Face." Unfortunately, the man in the inset is a stock Italian gangster-type, and the action illustrations that complete the covers are stiff and uninspired, especially compared to the striking covers of the original issues of *The Name of the Game Is Death* and of *One Endless Hour*, which presented a God's-eye view of three armed bank robbers casting sinister shadows as they rushed to a getaway car.

However, the main character inset links the books to other genre novels that employed it as a graphic gimmick. It was used, for instance, for the covers of hard-boiled series such as Richard Prather's novels featuring detective Shell Scott and Donald Hamilton's books recounting the adventures of tough guy Matt Helm. For the "*Operation*" books, the mug shot was adopted after the series got rolling, and after the covers of the first two books, *Operation Fireball* and *Flashpoint*, had been done by the celebrated cover artist Robert McGinnis. (McGinnis also designed the covers for the Marlowe books *Death Deep Down* and *Route of the Red Gold*.)

Operation Fireball didn't include the mug-shot gimmick when it was published in 1969, but it was incorporated into the cover when the book was re-issued in 1972. Similarly, when *Flashpoint* was first published in 1970, it had a non-mug shot cover, but the re-issue that same year, *Operation Flashpoint*, did include the gimmick. The mug shot continued to be used for the Drake series through *Operation Hammerlock*, published in 1974.

Dan J. Marlowe Bibliography

Doorway to Death (1959)
Killer With a Key (1959)
Doom Service (1960)
The Fatal Frails (1960)
Shake a Crooked Town (1960)
Backfire (1961)
The Name of the Game Is Death (1962)
[published in UK as *Operation Overkill*, 1973]
Strongarm (1963)
Never Live Twice (1964)
Death Deep Down (1965)
Four for the Money (1966)
The Vengeance Man (1966)
The Raven is a Blood-Red Bird [w/ William Odell] (1967)
Route of the Red Gold (1967)
One Endless Hour (1969)
[published in UK as *Operation Endless Hour*, 1975]
Operation Fireball (1969)
Flashpoint (1970)
[published in UK as *Operation Flashpoint*, 1972]
Operation Breakthrough (1971)
Operation Drumfire (1972)
Operation Checkmate (1972)
Operation Stranglehold (1973)
Operation Whiplash (1973)
Operation Hammerlock (1974)
Operation Deathmaker (1975)
Operation Counterpunch (1976)
As Gar Wilson:
Guerilla Games (1982)

TIMELINE

1914, July 10: Daniel James Marlowe born in Lowell, Massachusetts.

1934: Marlowe gets accounting certificate from Bentley School of Accounting and Finance in Boston, Massachusetts.

1934 to 1941: Marlowe spends seven years as a professional gambler, playing poker and betting on horse races.

1945: Marlowe marries Evelyn Chmura.

1956, Aug. 4: Marlowe's wife dies of acute hemorrhagic pancreatitis in Silver Spring, Maryland, at 35.

1959: Marlowe publishes first novels, both featuring Johnny Killain: *Doorway to Death* and *Killer With a Key*.

1961, Dec. 15: Al Nussbaum, Bobby "One-Eye" Wilcoxson and Peter Columbus Curry rob the Lafayette Bank in Brooklyn, New York. Wilcoxson shoots and kills bank guard Henry Kraus.

1962, February: Fawcett Gold Medal publishes Marlowe's most famous novel, *The Name of the Game Is Death*.

1962, July: While he is living in Harbor Beach, Michigan, Marlowe gets a call from bank robber Al Nussbaum, who is pretending to be a fan named "Carl Fischer."

1962, Nov. 4: Nussbaum is arrested in Buffalo, New York, after a 20-minute chase through downtown streets. For seven months, he's been on the FBI's Ten Most Wanted list.

1962, Nov. 10. Wilcoxson and companion Jacqueline Rose are arrested in Baltimore, Maryland.

1964, Jan. 24: Marlowe is first introduced to the man with whom he will collaborate on many novels: Col. William C. Odell.

1964, Feb. 7: Nussbaum sentenced to 20 years in prison; Wilcoxson and Curry sentenced to life.

1976, July 1: Nussbaum paroled.

1977, June 6: Marlowe stricken with amnesia at his apartment in Harbor Beach.

1978, Aug. 22: Marlowe moves to Los Angeles to live with

Nussbaum.

1982: *Guerilla Games* is published. Also this year, Marlowe moves to a separate apartment, ending his living arrangement with Nussbaum.

1982, Oct. 23: Wilcoxson, possibly with the help of his half-brother "Green Eyes," carries out the contract murder of Robert Mosher, a chemical engineer for the DuPont Company, at Mosher's home in Signal Mountain, Tennessee.

1982, Dec. 3. Bank robbers extort $31,500 from the Prospect National Bank in Peoria, Illinois. Nussbaum is among the suspects, but is never arrested or charged.

1986, about Aug. 22: Marlowe dies in Los Angeles at 72.

1996, Jan. 7: Nussbaum dies at 61 in Buffalo, New York.

2006, Dec. 9. Wilcoxson dies at 77, succumbing to cancer.

2009, May 2: William Odell dies at 93 in Montrose, Colorado.

2012, March: Article *Dan J. Marlowe: Echoes of a Hard-Boiled Past*, appears in graphic novel *Fatale No. 3*, by Ed Brubaker and Sean Phillips. Also, the article "The Wrong Marlowe" about Marlowe's time in L.A., is published by the *Los Angeles Review of Books*.

HOW THIS BOOK CAME TO BE

The beginnings of this book go back to 2007, when my first novel, *Pay Here*, was about to be published by Point Blank Press. Seeking to publicize it, I found the Web site Noir Originals, run by the talented Scottish thriller writer Allan Guthrie. To help authors draw attention to their work, Allan offered to publish the first chapter of any upcoming noir novel. In payment, he asked that the author supply him with an article on a noir theme.

I immediately thought of doing a piece on Dan J. Marlowe, whose writing I had long admired. Marlowe was a mystery. The Internet offered little about him. Someone recalled meeting him on a plane; someone else mentioned he had served as mayor pro tem of Harbor Beach, Michigan; at some point he had been stricken with amnesia. That was all.

I doubted I could pierce the obscurity. He had died more than 20 years earlier. It would be hard to find people who recalled him, I believed. And he had lived so long in such a small town. If he had been reclusive, the prospects of learning much about him would be grim. But, as a long-time reporter, I knew how to proceed. My first call was to the Harbor Beach Historical Society. There I reached local historian Carol Messner. Local historians always exist, and are always invaluable.

Messner came up with information about Marlowe's service on the Harbor Beach City Council. She also told me Marlowe's best friend in Harbor Beach, insurance-agency owner Gordon Gempel, was still alive. This, of course, was an enormous break. The break got even larger when I called Gempel. He told me that he had boxes of material about Marlowe: legal documents, medical records, personal correspondence. Incredible! How had he gotten the documents? Gempel told me he had accumulated them after he became Marlowe's legal guardian when Marlowe was stricken with amnesia. Gempel had held onto them for years thinking he would eventually write a book called *Dan and Me*. Come to Harbor Beach, Gempel said. I'll show you the documents and tell you racy secrets about Marlowe.

Several days later, I jumped on a plane in Phoenix, rented a car in Detroit, and was on my way. When I arrived in Harbor Beach, Gempel invited me to his home, cracked open a couple of beers to oil our conversation, and told me about some of the odder aspects of Marlowe's local sojourn. He also allowed me to cart boxes of Marlowe material back to my bed-and-breakfast to examine them. The next day he and his assistant Candy Oeschger, who also had known Marlowe, invited me to copy documents at the insurance agency office, talked in more detail about Marlowe, and introduced me to Doris Young, one of Marlowe's former girlfriends. She came down to the insurance office and I interviewed her.

Gempel showed me where Marlowe had lived, took me to Smalley's Bar and Grill, where Marlowe drank and shot pool, and told me of still more local people who had dealt with Marlowe.

In going through Marlowe's papers, I noticed references to William Odell, who had co-authored at least one novel with Marlowe. After I returned to Arizona, I called Odell, then in his late 80s and living in Colorado. He told me he had co-authored not one, but many books with Marlowe. This surprised me. Was Odell exaggerating? Not at all, I found, when I followed up on Odell's suggestion to get in contact with James Batson, who had been a friend to both Marlowe and Odell.

Batson had collected a huge amount of material from Marlowe and Odell, primarily correspondence and partial manuscripts of work published and unpublished. For many years, he had served as an informal Boswell to both writers. Without his generosity and guidance, this book would have had much less reach and depth. He kindly shared his information with me, and I was off and running.

More material, including ancestral research and family photos, came from Dan Marlowe's nephew Don in suburban Washington, D.C. I was able to supplement the material from Gempel, Batson and Don Marlowe with material from the Dan J. Marlowe Collection at the Howard Gotlieb Archival Research Center at Boston University.

Marlowe's Los Angeles-based literary executor, Robert Ragan, was also quite helpful, as was the author's agent, Rosalie Grace Heacock Thompson, who—with her late husband Jim—had represented Marlowe when he was alive. Rosalie still represented Marlowe's estate.

My three great sources of information were Gempel's papers, the material Batson had assembled and preserved, and the Dan J. Marlowe Collection at Boston University.

But other people provided key information and help.

Alison Bukata, Al Nussbaum's daughter, was very generous in sharing with me not only memories of her father but research she had already done on him, including a copy of his FBI file. She also did research in the Marlowe archive at Boston University, which was invaluable. I supplemented Alison's information about Nussbaum and his partner, Bobby Wilcoxson, with other interviews, prison records, and court records. The court records included extensive testimony from the Brooklyn bank robbery trial, from Wilcoxson's trial for the murder of Bob Mosher, and from the separate trial of his co-conspirator, Evelyn Mosher.

Editor and author Mel Cebulash, who now is retired and living in Scottsdale, Arizona, with his wife, Dolly, also supplied key correspondence, and was especially helpful because he knew both Marlowe and Nussbaum well, and was able to share with me his insights about them. I'm also indebted to writer Dudley Bromley, who provided me with letters from Nussbaum, and vital information about Nussbaum's L.A. years.

Also key were mystery writers Bill Pronzini and Joe Gores, who shared their memories of Marlowe. I supplemented Pronzini's recollections with his correspondence with Marlowe, preserved in the Pronzini Collection in the state archives in Sacramento, California.

Other people also supported my effort. Jim Winterhalter, a longtime resident of Harbor Beach, kindly researched the many columns Marlowe wrote for the *Harbor Beach Times*, and sent copies to me, asking only that I pay the postage. Several former members of the Pink Tea writers' group in Los Angeles wrote to me or granted me telephone interviews. Author Francis M. Nevins gave me copies of letters from Marlowe, including one describing

Marlowe's encounters with author Cornell Woolrich. Reporter Brian Lazenby put in several hours copying news articles in the files of the *Chattanooga Times Free Press* on the Evelyn Faye Mosher and Bobby Wilcoxson murder trials in Tennessee so that he could send them to me. Reporter Brian Haas at *The Nashville Tennessean* provided valuable court research on the Evelyn Mosher trial.

To all those people, and to everyone else who made this biography possible: Thank you so much.

Long before all the research was done, I did that article for Noir Originals, calling it *Mystery Man*. That article attracted a long-overdue reawakening of interest in Marlowe's work. It was the seed that grew into the book you have just finished. I thank Allan Guthrie, especially, for giving me that original platform.

I also thank Patrick Millikin, noir expert extraordinaire, and Ed Foster, a redoubtable copy editor, for editing this book.

Sadly, Gordon Gempel did not live to see the results of his help. Gempel died of heart failure and asthma at 77 on April 22, 2006, in Saginaw, Michigan. I hope that, wherever he is, he will be pleased that there now is a book that incorporates the story he wanted to tell: *Dan and Me.*

ACKNOWLEDGEMENTS

Documents and letters provided to the author by James Batson are used courtesy of James Batson.

The author was allowed to research documents, unpublished manuscripts and other personal papers in the Dan J. Marlowe Collection at Boston University by the Howard Gotlieb Archival Research Center there.

Content of letters written by Dan Marlowe's literary agent, James Reach, has been used courtesy of his daughter, Carol Reach.

Content of letters written by William Odell and photo of Odell are used courtesy of William Odell's daughter Carolyn Jensen and Pamela Odell, his daughter-in-law.

Content of letters, articles and fiction written by Al Nussbaum has been used courtesy of his daughter, Alison Bukata.

Photo of Dan J. Marlowe's wife and other family photos are used courtesy of the heirs of Dan J. Marlowe and the estate of Marlowe.

Excerpts from correspondence between Dan Marlowe, Al Nussbaum and Mel Cebulash are used courtesy of Mel Cebulash.

Charles Kelly, formerly a reporter for *The Arizona Republic*, was co-winner of the Arizona Journalist of the Year Award in 1992. In his career as a reporter, he found missing heirs, helped get a wrongly convicted tugboat captain out of a Mexican prison, and investigated the 1976 murder of *Republic* reporter Don Bolles. Kelly is the author of the novels *Pay Here*, published by Point Blank Press, and *Grace Humiston and the Vanishing*, a finalist in the 2012 Amazon Breakthrough Novel Award contest. He also wrote the short story *"The Eighth Deadly Sin,"* published in the collection *Phoenix Noir* issued by Akashic Books. His Web site is http://hardboiledjournalist.com/

www.ingramcontent.com/pod-product-compliance
Lightning Source LLC
Chambersburg PA
CBHW031242090426
42742CB00007B/275